Critical Essays on
Edward Schillebeeckx's Theology

Critical Essays on Edward Schillebeeckx's Theology

*From Theological Radicalism
to Philosophical Non-Realism*

Corneliu C. Simuț

WIPF & STOCK · Eugene, Oregon

CRITICAL ESSAYS ON EDWARD SCHILLEBEECKX'S THEOLOGY
From Theological Radicalism to Philosophical Non-Realism

Copyright © 2010 Corneliu C. Simuț. All rights reserved. Except for brief quotations in critical publications or reviews, no part of this book may be reproduced in any manner without prior written permission from the publisher. Write: Permissions, Wipf and Stock Publishers, 199 W. 8th Ave., Suite 3, Eugene, OR 97401.

Wipf & Stock
An Imprint of Wipf and Stock Publishers
199 W. 8th Ave., Suite 3
Eugene, OR 97401

ISBN 13: 978-1-60899-389-5

To
Jeffrey M. Fehn,
Mark T. Smith,
Craig A. Stern,
and
all the friends at R. Templeton Smith Foundation

Contents

Foreword / ix

Introduction: A Word of Clarification / xiii

1. Re-Branding Christian Theology through Secularization / 1
2. Re-Defining the Concept of God / 29
3. Re-Kindling the Natural Awareness of Man / 57
4. Re-Shaping Christology from Jesus to Christ / 84
5. Re-Assessing the Doctrine of Resurrection / 113
6. Re-Imagining Religious Belonging in Ecclesiology / 139
7. Re-Tracing the Boundaries between the Church and the World / 166
8. Re-Inventing the World / 193

   A Concluding Synthesis: Edward Schillebeeckx's Theological Radicalism as Philosophical Non-Realism / 220

Bibliography / 247

Index / 261

Foreword

The Dominican scholar Edward Schillebeeckx (1914–2009) is one of the most influential theologians of modern times, and not only within the Catholic tradition to which he belongs. As is usually the case with seminal thinkers, his ideas have generated a good deal of debate. Schillebeeckx's more than 400 published works (representing several decades of research, reflection, and teaching) have elicited a wide variety of responses and indeed within the Catholic Church serious questions were asked about his orthodoxy. The present volume—written by a Romanian Evangelical scholar—is an important contribution to the Schillebeeckx debate, not least because of the range of issues which the writer addresses.

Readers should take note of Corneliu Simuț's stated intentions in writing this volume. He makes it clear that he does not intend to present an analysis of the full range of philosophical, cultural, and ecclesiastical contexts which form the background to Schillebeeckx's work; nor does he set out to engage with his entire corpus. Simuț also leaves us in no doubt right from the start that he is very critical of Schillebeeckx—even while admiring his impressive academic record—and he expresses an awareness that some readers will be very critical, even dismissive, of his appraisal of the distinguished Belgian theologian. However, just as Schillebeeckx himself has never been afraid of criticism and controversy, Corneliu Simuț will not be afraid of critical responses to his own work. Debate is of the very essence of theological enquiry, and what this author does is to challenge people to think about the implications of Schillebeeckx's theology and about their own stance regarding different aspects of the historic Christian faith. This work—a collection of essays—is written with a pastoral concern about what Simuț believes to be the false paths inherent in Schillebeeckx's understanding of the Christian faith and it will stimulate the reader—even one who does not agree with the general assessments—into thinking further about his or her understanding of God and his dealings with the world.

Foreword

A major concern of Schillebeeckx has always been the presentation of the Christian Gospel in terms which modern people can understand. Of course, he is not alone in this and it would be something of a truism to say that we cannot communicate anything to anybody unless they actually understand us! However, the questions always remain: at what point does a restatement of the Christian message in modern terms become in effect a different message altogether? What, in any case, are "modern terms"? Simuț warns us in particular not to think of the Western world as "the modern world," and he points out that many people still find the traditional categories intelligible; the fact that they do so does not mean that they are locked in some kind of medieval time-warp.

Another significant emphasis in Schillebeeckx's work has been the role of experience in theology and Christian theology has often operated with the framework of the famous quadrilateral: Scripture, tradition, reason, and experience. Simuț finds Schillebeeckx misleading in the way he appears to give human experience and human existence a place reminiscent of the anthropocentric theology which became so dominant in the nineteenth century. In particular Schillebeeckx is weak in his assessment of the seriousness of sin, at least as regards its roots—humanity's rebellion against a holy God—even if he devotes considerable attention to the effects of sin in the history of human suffering. To what extent should our own experience shape our understanding of God and of ourselves? Simuț challenges us to consider whether Schillebeeckx's answers to such questions are really adequate in the light of the teaching of Scripture and of the Christian tradition. The name of Friedrich Schleiermacher does not appear in Simuț's book, but readers will probably find that this study of Schillebeeckx raises questions frequently associated with his great German predecessor.

The debate over Schillebeeckx's understanding of Jesus Christ and of salvation through Christ, will probably never end. This is hardly surprising given the centrality of these issues in any interpretation of the Christian faith. Although never expressly repudiating Nicaea and Chalcedon, Schillebeeckx's thought suggests that they are more of a liability than an asset. Simuț's analysis takes our minds back to the whole question of the relationship between "the Jesus of history" and "the Christ of faith"—mercifully he does not go over all this old ground again!—and, in spite of the awesome scholarly contribution of Schillebeeckx to New Testament exegesis, we are still left wondering if his reconstruction of

Foreword

the emergence of the Early Church's Christology is any more satisfactory than that of the nineteenth-century "quest." Similar points could be made about Schillebeeckx's understanding of salvation from sin and the role traditionally ascribed to Jesus's death on the cross and, of course, we should mention the resurrection. Other commentators have pointed out that, when reading Schillebeeckx, the name of Rudolf Bultmann inevitably springs to mind. Simuţ does not spend time on such a comparison. However, reading this book we are being invited to think again about whether we can meaningfully accept the idea of Jesus's resurrection without also emphasizing the empty tomb, the body that was no longer there and why it was no longer there. Did the resurrection take place as an actual event in history or not?

As Simuţ points out, in Schillebeeckx's work there appears to be, to say the least, a certain marginalisation of the doctrine of the Trinity, and this applies to his view of the Holy Spirit. This in turn impinges on his view of the Church, traditionally understood as the community of the Spirit. Schillebeeckx's blurring of the distinction between the Church and the world—the relationship between the two has been another of the great themes of his work—adds to the impression that for him both the Spirit's role and his person are superfluous.

This volume is to be commended as a work of theological criticism written by someone for whom engagement with Western theological trends would have been almost impossible until recently. Corneliu Simuţ has shown himself well able to deal with issues circulating in a world very different from the Romanian Evangelical tradition to which he belongs. The freedom which has come to his land and to Romanian Evangelicalism is producing a generation of scholars who have useful insights to share with theologians everywhere, and Corneliu Simuţ should be welcomed as one of these.

Professor Dr. Maurice Dowling
Irish Baptist College
The Institute of Theology
Queen's University of Belfast

Introduction

A Word of Clarification

This book is a compilation of eight independent essays written as part of my interaction with the students enrolled for bachelor and master degrees at the Faculty of Theology within Emanuel University of Oradea. As most of my students are either pastors or in the process of becoming ministers of the Baptist churches in Romania, my research on Professor Schillebeeckx's theology has focused on issues which help the students, but also the ordinary members of the church, to distinguish between traditional theology and its modern counterpart. I am painfully aware that both traditional and modern theology require a minute work of careful definition; nevertheless, in my classes I tend to work with simple concepts which assist the students in their pastoral work.

Thus, when I speak about traditional theology, which is not monolithic in character even if I treat it unitarily, I make reference to pre-Enlightenment theology which works with two levels of reality: the reality of God and of his existence, on the one hand, and the reality of man and of his natural life, on the other hand. Both these levels of reality are equally real, in the sense that both God and man have a real existence in their own particular realms: while man exists in the natural, created world, God exists beyond it in a realm which transcends man's world in every possible aspect. This theology proceeds from "above," from God's special revelation in Scripture as well as in the person and work of Jesus Christ, as testified by the same Scripture. This is why traditional theology takes Scripture word for word, so whenever Scripture mentions events which can be labeled as supernatural, we understand them exactly as the Bible presents them. For instance, when Scripture informs us that God's Logos become incarnate in the historical person of Jesus of Nazareth, we believe this information exactly as it was written in Scripture. Or, to take another example, when Scripture says that Jesus rose again after his death on the

Introduction

cross, then he ascended to heaven in a bodily form, we believe that he actually lives at the right hand of God. In other words, the Bible tells us—or rather God tells us in the Bible—what happened and what we should do, and we believe all his instructions to be absolutely true. Consequently, Scripture informs our experience, so we adjust and correct our experience in accordance with what the Bible tells us.

On the other hand, modern theology is—as far as I am concerned—the Enlightenment and post-Enlightenment attempt either to redefine or disannul the realm of God's existence. In this sense, modern theology is the exact opposite of traditional theology as well as an attempt to present Christianity in a way which reportedly makes sense to the rational, scientific, and secularized expectations of today's people. Therefore, modern theology begins from "below," from the experience of men and women, who use their reason as the final criterion for reading the Bible. This is why modern theology, while reading the Bible, tends to believe it only to the extent that the information presented in it fits the experience of humanity. So, whenever Scripture makes reference to events that can be perceived as supernatural, we should not understand them literally but rather in a way which makes sense rationally and is confirmed by our immediate experience. For example, when we read in the Bible that the Logos of God took human flesh, we should not understand this information exactly as it was written but only to the extent that it can be corroborated with the narrative of Jesus's historical birth. Thus, we should believe that Jesus was born and lived in this world, but not as God's Logos as he was only a mere human being. Likewise, when the Bible tells us that he rose from the dead, we should not accept this literally because our experience cannot rationally accept that people can come back to life. We can and even should accept the concept of resurrection, but not as a historical event; the resurrection is more likely a feature of man's existence which tells us about our desire to transcend our historical existence. In other words, it is not the Bible which transforms our experience but our experience informs the Bible and reads it in way which makes sense to the rationality of today's people.

Having explained what I mean by traditional and modern theology, it is absolutely necessary, I believe, to clarify what this book *is* and what it *is not*. To begin with, I shall briefly outline what my book *is not*.

First, my book *is not* a scholarly monograph. I do not intend to present an analysis of the cultural or the ecclesiastical contexts in which

Introduction

Schillebeeckx developed his theology from his early formation to the present day. This is why I shall not mention anything about his critical approach to Vatican II or the influence of the *nouvelle théologie* on his works. I know for a fact that my definition of modern theology as influenced by rationalism, which I apply to Schillebeeckx, can be harshly criticized because in some academic circles Schillebeeckx is not perceived as a rationalist but rather as an existentialist theologian who is deeply concerned with the historical existence of man. To me, however, Schillebeeckx's existentialist preoccupation is thoroughly rationalistic because he cannot understand, let alone explain, the expectations of modern men and women outside the framework of human reason which is capable of understanding and acting correctly based on man's natural abilities. At the same time, I am painstakingly aware that my interpretation of Schillebeeckx—which, in my view, is conservative and Evangelical—can be seen as unacceptably narrow and even fundamentalist, while my book may appear to be based on insufficient and unclear argumentation. To make things clear, I do not believe in the validity of the historical-critical methods of reading the Bible, neither do I accept them as *the* norm of biblical hermeneutics. Therefore, even though I run the risk of being labeled a fundamentalist, I have to underline that my book is based on my undeterred conviction that the Bible *is* the inspired word of God which must inform as well as transform human experience, and it is from this particular standpoint that I approach Schillebeeckx's theology.

Second, my work *is not* a philosophical dissertation. It is not my goal to present the philosophical context for Schillebeeckx's position, neither do I insist on Western philosophical traditions to which Schillebeeckx may or may not be indebted, such as phenomenology, existentialist philosophy, the Frankfurt school or postmodern philosophy in general. The fact that I use concepts like metaphysics, transcendence, ontology, reality, existence, and history does not turn my book into a philosophical enterprise; I only use them theologically with reference to how I understand the levels of reality involved in my understanding of traditional theology; thus, God exists beyond the realm of created humanity and history in a reality which is totally transcendent. To be sure, metaphysics refers to God's existence beyond the created historicity of our universe, transcendence to the nature of his metaphysical existence in the sense that we cannot know God without his special revelation and ontology to the fact that God is indeed a being, not a concept or anything else. I am aware that

Introduction

such a treatment of Western philosophical categories shows little, if any, sympathetic treatment to the analogical character of Catholic theology but I am equally aware that Schillebeeckx's works are read by ordinary people who uncritically absorb his theology and accept it as they understand it. Leaving aside the fact that Schillebeeckx's theology is not considered Catholic at all in some academic as well as ecclesiastical quarters, my intention was to explain Schillebeeckx's thought in categories which can be easily understood by all those interested in Christian theology in general as well as those preoccupied by their own salvation in particular.

At the same time, it is important to understand what my book actually *is*. I have to underline here once again that my work is only a collection of eight different essays, which ends up with a rather lengthy conclusion. As the overall intention of my book is not scholarly but mainly pastoral, I have to make it clear that the tone of my writing is predominantly polemical. This feature of my book can indeed attract a high degree of criticism, especially the charge that I approach Schillebeeckx with a predetermined set of mind which leaves no room for the fundamental principles of critical scholarship. While my respect for Schillebeeckx's impressive academic achievements remains intact, I have to confess my complete disagreement with his theology and especially with its practical results, which may present my work in an unfavorable light because it can be perceived as dubious, unsympathetic, and tendentious. Such a reading of my work can be applied especially to my critique of Schillebeeckx's concept of resurrection for my conclusion that he does not actually believe in a bodily resurrection of Jesus may be interpreted as a complete misreading of his original intention.

It is very important to understand that my book is not an interaction with Schillebeeckx's entire theological corpus but only with samples of his thought from my own personal perspective. As a result, my work is not a sympathetic engagement with Schillebeeckx's theological enterprise in general but only a critical reaction against some of his major theological insights as reflected only is a very limited number of his publications. This is why it is vital to comprehend that my book is extremely selective because my polemical approach to Schillebeeckx is based primarily on his *God the Future of Man* (1968) and his *World and Church* (1971). I make some references to other works as well but my main concern was to exegete these two particular works. Although I realize I could have also approached works of paramount importance for Schillebeeckx's thought,

Introduction

such as his *Jesus, an Experiment in Christology* (1979), I eventually chose to focus on his *God the Future of Man* (1968) and his *World and Church* (1971) because, in my view, they reflect in an orderly fashion as well as in a clearly delineated sequence some of his crucial theological perspectives. The restricted goal of my work should also account for my decision not to elaborate on Schillebeeckx's relationship with the ecclesiastical authorities of the Catholic Church and his connection with the movement which eventually led to the Second Vatican Council. For the very same reason, nothing is said here about Schillebeeckx's own perspective on the very documents of the council.

One last aspect needs to be clarified. Even if my book consists of eight separate essays which were later put together in an order which, I believe, reflects a possible interpretation of Schillebeeckx's line of reasoning—namely from his perspective on secularization to his redefinition or retranslation of basic theological concepts such as God, man, Christ, resurrection, belonging, the relationship between the world and the church, and then his understanding of the world—the concluding section may appear, at least to some, as a very odd appendix. To put a long explanation into a nutshell, I argue in the last part of my work that what I call Schillebeeckx's theological radicalism bears a wide range of resemblances to Don Cupitt's philosophical non-realism for the very simple reason that, regardless of their distinctive theological backgrounds and scholarly developments, they practically reach the same conclusion which presents God as utterly dependent on man's historical experience. While I am convinced that the theologies of Schillebeeckx and Cupitt, though obviously distinct in many respects nevertheless converge to the same basic conclusion, I am fully conscious that my decision to join Schillebeeckx's position with Cupitt's perspective may seem highly biased, outrageous or even scandalous. It does express, however, my own reading of Schillebeeckx's theology, and of Cupitt's thought for that matter, as an attempt to highlight the necessity of what I believe to be a much-needed return to the values of traditional Christian theology within conservative and Evangelical lines.

1

Re-Branding Christian Theology through Secularization

Edward Schillebeeckx's thought is a tremendous effort to reinterpret traditional Christian theology so that it can be understood by modern people. Schillebeeckx is convinced that Christian theology in its traditional format is no longer useful in explaining the realities of the world to the people living today. This is why he defends the idea of a general re-assessment of the entire Christian theology by putting aside the traditional formulae as well as the traditional way of approaching Christian theology in general. He suggests that we promote a different perspective on Christianity in such a way that it should be relevant to the men and women of today's society. In short, if society and its evaluation of the world have changed, then Christian theology should change as well if it still wants to be useful in today's society.[1] Society has become secularized, so Christian theology should undergo a similar process of secularization in order to find proper answers to the secularized minds of contemporary people.

SECULARIZATION AND RATIONALITY

Schillebeeckx approaches Christian theology from a purely natural—as opposed to supernatural—perspective, in which he draws heavily on the idea of rationality.[2] He notices that the world has changed dramatically and that the people of today face issues which require a specific answer from Christianity, answers which have to be in accordance with what

---

1. Schillebeeckx promotes a theology of historical change. See also Ormerod, "The Times," 834.

2. McManus, *Unbroken Communion*, 85.

their reason tells them.³ This is why he almost takes for granted the fact that Christian theology should take off the traditional interpretation of its doctrines so that it can illuminate the world when it comes to theological issues.⁴ According to Schillebeeckx, traditional Christianity seems to be totally incapable of providing adequate reasonable answers to the problems of today's people and this prevents the church, as well as Christianity in general, from sharing into the construction of today's society.⁵ Thus, Schillebeeckx warns that the men and women of today have questions concerning their existence and, when they turn to Christianity for an answer, the traditional approach to their burning problems is completely unsatisfactory. Modern people also have questions about God, but—if we are to believe Schillebeeckx—traditional Christianity appears to be totally overcome by the burden of an answer which needs to please the ears of today's technologized and rationalized society.⁶ The novelty of contemporary society, given mainly by seemingly unstoppable scientific progress, needs an equally informed reply which should be also characterized by novelty.⁷ This prompts Schillebeeckx to postulate the necessity of a radically different impetus to be given to Christian theology to the point of transforming it into a different theology, namely a theology which is fit to offer answers that meet the rationalized expectations of modern people.⁸ Schillebeeckx is convinced that unless the church does so, the world will detach itself from the church forever and the church will permanently lose touch with the realities of today's society.⁹ In other words, the church will continue to use traditional theology for its own narrow use while the world will lose even the last drop of respect for the church's credibility. Schillebeeckx highlights the fact that the church must not close itself to the realities of the modern world and explain the word of God in a way which turns out to be fundamentally relevant to the men

---

3. Guerriere, *Phenomenology*, 164.

4. In other words, doctrines should develop over time to fit the mindset of every age. For details about the development of doctrine in Schillebeeckx, see Thompson, "Schillebeeckx," 303; Donovan, "The Vocation," 3; Kaczor, "Thomas Aquinas," 283.

5. Borgman, *Edward Schillebeeckx*, 110.

6. Kennedy, *Schillebeeckx*, 45.

7. This is against the theological convictions of Ratzinger, who believes that novelty and innovation must have certain limits. See Modras, "In His Own Footsteps," 12.

8. Hilkert, Schreiter, eds., *The Praxis*, 63.

9. Abdul-Masih, *Edward Schillebeeckx and Hans Frei*, 77.

and women living today.[10] The church's traditional interpretation of the word of God must also be given up in favor of a brand new interpretation which sheds light on modern expectations. Modern people are eager to understand their own world and especially their place in the world and this is why they seek answers in Christian theology.[11] It is very likely that Schillebeeckx refers to Western society in general where the secularization of life due to scientific progress has led to the obvious technological progress which forces people to reconsider religious and theological matters in the light of the newly-established scientific, urbanized and technologized way of life.[12] In spite of the external technological progress, modern men and women seem to have an urgent need to find answers for their inner existential questions which cannot be solved by science and technology. Scientific progress does not necessarily help people existentially and this is why religion or theology is seen as a prospective source for existential answers.[13] Schillebeeckx seems to be acutely aware of the contemporary situation of the modern person who lives in our scientifically dominated society.[14] This is why he recommends that theology adapt in such a way that its traditional message can be turned into a totally new proclamation which is scientifically relevant and existentially appealing:

> It is clear that Christian revelation in its traditional form has ceased to provide any valid answer to the questions about God asked by the majority of people today, nor would it appear to be making any contribution to modern man's real understanding of himself in this world and in human history. It is evident that more and more people are becoming increasingly unhappy and dissatisfied with the traditional Christian answers to their questions. It is their questions about God himself which are involved above all and there is unmistakable evidence of a growing desire everywhere for new answers to be given to new questions concerning him. The situation requires us to speak of God in a way quite *different* from the way in which we have spoken of him in the past. If we fail to do this, we ourselves shall perhaps still be able to experience God in outmoded forms, but clearly our own witness of and discussion of God will be met by most people with headshaking disbelief as

---

10. Rego, *Suffering and Salvation*, 50.
11. Schillebeeckx, *The Eucharist*, 17.
12. Regan, *Experience the Mystery*, 48.
13. McManus, *Unbroken Community*, 25.
14. Ban, *The Christological Foundation*, 175.

mumbo-jumbo. It is partly because we are blind to the "signs of times" that God's word, in all that we say of him, is returning to him void . . .[15]

Schillebeeckx's interest in modern society is commendable and so is his desire to help today's men and women in their quest for existential meaningfulness.[16] It seems, however, that his observation that modern people need modern answers while traditional answers should be left aside as they were good only for people of times past is predominantly empirical, not theological. The fact that modern society has become secularized as well as highly rationalized and technologized due to scientific progress by no means implies a readjustment or even a total re-branding of the entire traditional theology.[17] Society may well change from today's scientific progress to an even greater social progress in future or, one can never know this for a fact, lapse into a total disaster because of the fatal misuse of science. Regardless of whether the world is heading towards scientific progress or a generalized social collapse the inner constitution of humanity seems to remain unchanged. This may also be inferred from Schillebeeckx's own words because modern people still seek answers which can only be provided by theology or religion, not by science and technology.[18] The conclusion can be drawn quite easily, namely that despite his evident progress in science the modern man has remained the same unique being in constant search for non-scientific answers that do not concern his external life in society but his internal state of affairs or his own inner relationship with himself (which eventually defines his outer relationship with society). Therefore, if the essential core of the inner life of modern man has remained unchanged, why should we want to change theology from traditionalism to modernism? Society and science may have reached their "modern" stage of historical development but the inner being of man seems to have remained existentially unchanged. If this is true, then Schillebeeckx is wrong in trumpeting the necessity of changing traditional theology for the sake of the modern man's scientific mind. Or it may well be the case that Christian theology addresses issues that are not concerned with science and technology; they are not anti-science

---

15. Schillebeeckx, *God the Future of Man*, 53.
16. Abdul-Masih, *Edward Schillebeeckx and Hans Frei*, 89.
17. For further details, see Rausch, *Reconciling Faith and Reason*, 22–23.
18. See also Stoker, *Is the Quest*, 31.

and anti-technology, but they are just not preoccupied with providing illumination in scientific matters. Having said that, one could rightly ask whether Jesus died for our future scientific progress. Did he suffer death so that we could enjoy the much later progress of science and technology? Or did he die in order to redeem us from sin, namely from an inescapable state of total transgression and opposition to God? If this is the correct answer—and it is indeed the answer of traditional theology—then the essence of theology is totally irrelevant to the progress of science and vice versa. Man's relationship with himself will be forever a matter which will find proper answers only in theology—traditional theology—regardless whether science progresses or not.

As for Schillebeeckx, he is convinced that this is not the case: man is so anchored in society and its daily reality informed by the almost unbelievable progress of science that whatever he seeks for his inner life must also have an influence or at least a connection with his external life.[19] Thus, he strongly believes that the modern man needs to find a way to make his life meaningful exclusively in terms of the modern science which dominates our secularized world:[20]

> The criticism of the traditional way of speaking of God which is now being voiced within the Christian churches, both Protestant and Catholic, arises, on the one hand, from the deepest values which these churches really aim to embody and, on the other hand, from the new, rational and secular sphere of understanding within which people are now seeking a meaning for human life.[21]

Schillebeeckx is so preoccupied to see Christian theology turn its traditional clothing into modern garments that he loses sight of the fact that the meaning of life may well go beyond a merely and purely scientific approach to life. What if, for instance, some people—even in the West—are never able to find the meaning of life in scientifically informed answers? What if they prefer traditional theology? What if traditional theology not only gives them a satisfactory existential answer for their relationship with themselves but also a powerful impetus to transform modern society? It is very likely to have a scenario in which at least some modern people like traditional values as well as traditional explanations

---

19. For a contrary position see Lefebvre, *Open Letter*, 114–16.
20. Rego, *Suffering and Salvation*, 55.
21. Schillebeeckx, *God the Future of Man*, 53–54.

of life and they would still be more than merely interested in working for the benefit of their fellow human beings. It is possible that this handful of people would never entrust their souls to machines and technology; a "spiritual" answer would therefore suffice in order for their lives to be meaningful, so they would probably never sense any urgency for traditional theology to be changed into a scientifically oriented religious approach to deeper human concerns. What should we make of these people? Do they not use their reason if they prefer to believe non-scientific explanations concerning their existential fears? In other words, which is the correct approach to personal belief or faith? Is it absolutely necessary for us to have a faith dominated by reason, specifically scientifically informed reason? Do we have to profess a faith which is moulded by the scientific reason of our times? As far as Schillebeeckx is concerned, the answer seems to be positive:

> Theology is always the basis of anthropology. We are humans living in the world, in history. On the other hand, faith in revelation is transmitted by the mediation of all human traditions. We are faithful to tradition by making a rupture; there is no such thing as a smooth growth from revelation into theology. The content of revelation is always explained in human concepts, namely is historically conditioned. We always have the revelation of God which is absolute, but religion is not absolute. There is a difference between the living God and our answer to God. Our answer to God is religious and embedded in culture. God is the basis of our faith; our answer is to trust God . . . Trust is the nucleus of faith, but what Jesus means for us today is the result of our thinking. Faith is trust in God *cum cogitatione*, with thinking, with reflection. Without reflection we are fundamentalists.[22]

One important aspect must be clarified here. Schillebeeckx talks about reflection or reason as a compulsory component of our faith.[23] Nevertheless, while faith remains the same as a religious feeling, it constantly changes as it is informed by reflection.[24] Reflection is never the same throughout history; it changes as time elapses and scientific prog-

---

22. Schillebeeckx, Ramona Simuṭ, "Reinterpreting Traditional Theology," 278. See also Simuṭ, *A Critical Study*, 178.

23. Borgman, *Edward Schillebeeckx*, 39.

24. Engelhardt, *The Foundations of Christian Bioethics*, 10.

ress occurs in society.[25] Thus, in the past man had the same faith as a religious feeling but his faith was fueled by a certain type of scientific reflection which was totally unaware of our contemporary scientific discoveries. This is why the faith of people in the past, though genuine and useful for that time, is no longer relevant for today.[26] Why is that? Because today our faith is shaped by the reflection of our contemporary scientific, technological and industrialized society, so our faith is more rationalized than the faith of the past. According to Schillebeeckx, the faith of the past is good for the past while the faith of the present is good for the present; they are both good but the faith of the past does not work in the present because it is totally irrelevant to the present due to its outdated reflection.[27] What happens then if a man who lives today embraces the faith of the past? Is he a fundamentalist? He seems to be so if we are to believe Schillebeeckx because the faith of the past seems to contradict the faith of the present because of the totally different types of reflection that inform the two faiths. Consequently, if the faith of the past seems to contradict the faith of the present, then it follows that the faith of the past is irrelevant to the present and it cannot offer meaningful answers to the problems of the present. Schillebeeckx does not favor the faith of the past because the reflection that informed it was the result of a rationality which had not yet reached its true intellectual capability.[28] This is what Schillebeeckx has to say about the faith of the past, which he associates with traditional Christianity:[29]

> In the biblical, patristic and medieval periods, man viewed and appraised everything directly in the light of the . . . "first and last cause," following the Augustinian world-view. Medieval wisdom and science had little to offer him in the way of improving his life in this world, which was filled with the church's ethical and explicitly religious values and the ultimate perspective of a happy existence hereafter. This was the real horizon of his life. The church tried, of course, to alleviate misery in this world by works of char-

---

25. Borgman, *Edward Schillebeeckx*, 292.
26. See also Mulcahy, *The Cause of Our Salvation*, 342–43.
27. Also check Groome, "Shared Christian Praxis," 218–37, especially 236 n. 32.
28. For details about man's capacity to know God, see Dellavalle, "Feminist Theologies," 333–35.
29. See also Miller, *Consuming Religion*, 196.

ity, but man's intellect seemed not yet to have discovered its special task and its possibilities for the future.[30]

So, in Schillebeeckx, everything pertaining to pre-modern times, namely to pre-industrial, pre-technologized and pre-urbanized—in a word, to pre-scientific—society is, if not bad, at least not worthy of the present.[31] This also applies to faith, so the faith of the past which is the foundation of traditional theology needs to change and readjust in order to turn itself into modern faith.[32] Consequently, traditional theology—which is informed by the outdated faith of the past—needs to turn itself into some sort of scientific theology in order to make sense today. However, it has to be stressed here that no matter how appealing Schillebeeckx's view seems to be, it is way too optimistic and hopelessly overconfident in the rational capacity of the modern man to foster the progress of humanity as well as to confer meaning to modern life.[33] What if the world is destroyed by a nuclear cataclysm so that human society is thrown back into another Stone Age? Regardless of whether such a scenario is likely to happen—even if the theoretical possibility is valid given that the future is hidden to the present, the question still remains: what if, as a result of the misuse of scientific discoveries, modern society is literally swept away? This would definitely annul the state of contemporary progress and personal comfort as well as dramatically enhancing daily misery, suffering, and death.[34] What then? It would be interesting to know how Schillebeeckx would reply to such a question but his answer is unfortunately not available. In the likelihood of such a scenario, however, the modern faith so dear to Schillebeeckx would suddenly become irrelevant to the new disastrous situation. It does not mean that traditional faith would necessarily replace it, but modern faith in progress and the annihilation of human misery would have to find a meaningful answer to a new situation dominated by misery, suffering, and death—all caused by scientific progress.

30. Schillebeeckx, *God the Future of Man*, 54.

31. For the conflict between pre-modernity and post-modernity or the present, see Murray, *Reason, Truth and Theology*, 53.

32. For an excellent analysis of the relationship between traditional faith and the challenges of modernity/post-modernity in Schillebeeckx, see Newlands, *Christ and Human Rights*, 103.

33. For instance, this can be applied to the life of Jesus and its relevance for us today. See, for details, Winter, *The Atonement*, 24.

34. For details about suffering in Schillebeeckx, see McManus, "Suffering," 476.

Re-Branding Christian Theology through Secularization

Resuming Schillebeeckx's undeterred confidence in the possibilities of a new faith, which is not informed by the rationality of the past but by the scientifically based rationality of the present, he believes that the humanity's new situation needs to give reasonable answers to questions that concern man's relationship with the world and with himself.[35] This new faith has to be thoroughly rational in order to be applied effectively in society with a view to improving man's life, present and future.[36] At the same time, it should be noticed that Schillebeeckx equates this new faith to secularization, a social process which he regards as profitable to humanity because it can establish the universal values of justice, peace, and love.[37] Despite his optimistic view of contemporary society, Schillebeeckx does not foolishly believe in a perfect society; he knows that human freedom may be misused, and some people will always be ready to do so:

> As a result of the later developments in the West of rationalization in the service of mankind, modern man began to discover the *world* and thus *himself* as well, in an entirely new way; that is, as a situated freedom which, through the collaboration of men, must give itself its own definite character in a task which gives meaning in this world, within a rational sphere of understanding, so that justice, peace, and love may prevail among men. Man has now begun to plan *himself*, looking towards the future. Although it may or may not be explicitly formulated, it can scarcely be disputed that his is the new pattern of mankind's life today. But we must be critical in our attitude towards the possibility of its total *realization*. It is, after all, obviously marred by equally unmistakable abuses of freedom and ultimately also by the "sin of the world."[38]

Schillebeeckx is convinced that secularization and its new faith based on modern rationality reached an important stage in the contemporary world after the process itself had gone through a series of historical developments which all prove that the rationality which fueled theological faith has gradually widened.[39] Thus, from the Middle Ages and the period of the Reformation to the early pre-modern period and the Enlightenment, human reason acquired step by step a wider range

---

35. Hilkert and Schreiter, eds., *The Praxis*, 31–32.
36. See also De Tavernier, "Love for the Enemy and Nonretribution," 159.
37. Migliore, *Faith Seeking Understanding*, 351.
38. Schillebeeckx, *God the Future of Man*, 56.
39. See also Haight, "The American Jesuit Theologian," 91.

of insights which transformed the original human belief in the vertical and external relationship between God and man into a horizontal conviction which connected men and the idea of God in predominantly internal terms.[40] Schillebeeckx does not harshly criticize the faith of the past with its not so broad rationality—and he clearly refers to medieval[41] and Reformation faith—but rather he takes a condescendent approach; thus, he is magnanimously willing to accept that this represented the beginning of the process of secularization which—like any other starting point—was characterized by certain flaws.[42] According to Schillebeeckx, the first concepts which marked the beginning of the process of secularization in the church were "natural law," the growing importance of "man's conscience," "active intellect," "pure nature," and the Reformation's conviction that the reality of God is beyond the sphere of human understanding—a position that, for Schillebeeckx, is unmistakably secular because it strengthens man's trust in himself when it comes to defining his human position in relationship with God.[43] Then, the Enlightenment came with its belief in "pure reason" and "practical reason," which cemented the idea that God, or the concept of God, cannot be rationally proved by empirical data; God is utterly transcendent and, as his existence cannot be proved rationally, the only reasonable way to speak of God is to consider him, or the idea of God, in the more practical terms of morality.[44] Therefore, theology and philosophy began to manifest an increasingly evident confidence in man's capacity to use his reason as well as his feelings in order to ponder the reality of what had been traditionally called the transcendent, meta-historical and ontologically real God.[45] Traditional Christianity continued nonetheless to exert its influence in the world but not in the newer way of the prevalence of human reason but in the older manner which distinguished between the out-of-the-world reality of God and into-the-world

---

40. After the Enlightenment, Romanticism seems to have diluted man's perspective on marriage, see Kenneth R. Himes and Coriden, "The Indissolubility of Marriage," 453. For details about Schillebeeckx's view of marriage, see Sowle Cahill, "Marriage," 78.

41. Despite his criticism of medieval theology, Schillebeeckx is placed among the theologians who "enhanced the theological comprehension of Aquinas." See O'Meara, "Jean-Pierre Torrell's Research on Thomas Aquinas," 787.

42. Also check van der Ven, *God Reinvented?*, 147.

43. Schillebeeckx, *God the Future of Man*, 57–59.

44. See Abdul-Masih, *Edward Schillebeeckx and Hans Frei*, 57–58.

45. Schillebeeckx, *God the Future of Man*, 60.

Re-Branding Christian Theology through Secularization

reality of man. This situation was perpetuated until the present time even though Schillebeeckx nurtures the hope that it will be changed in the future to the detriment of the church's so-called old way so that the new way of the world can become dominant.[46] Schillebeeckx expresses once again his distrust in the traditional faith of the church, which in his view is oriented towards the past and his utmost confidence in the modern faith of the world, which is reportedly oriented towards the future, a future which—by means of love—permeates the entire rationality of the present situation including the traditional teachings of the church on God:[47]

> The long process of secularization meant, in fact, that religion, the churches and theology suffered a functional loss. A new, independent world came into being alongside the church. But the church continued to live in her old world until she was forced to realize that hers was a totally different world from the one in which very many people now live. The cleavage between the church and the world has thus given the impression that there are two different worlds—the *world of the past memory*, the church and the *world of the future*, that of dynamic mankind living within an all-embracing rational sphere of understanding.[48]

This paragraph is of crucial importance for Schillebeeckx's understanding of reality because, although it presents the possibility of the existence of two different realms of reality—the church of the past and the world of the present but also of the future—it nonetheless contains his evident belief in the objective existence of a singular world only, which is the world of the present and of the future.[49] The church of the past does exist in history but its understanding of the world and of reality in general seems to be fatally flawed. The church's traditional theology, which contained its perspective on reality, was dominant for hundreds of years but this does not mean it was the right belief. Schillebeeckx seems to be convinced that the church did not manage to convey a real image of the world because of the traditional doctrine of God—which influenced every other doctrine. The true and real explanation of reality has always been there even if it was not promoted by the church; in modern times though, due to the broadening of man's rationality which has resulted in scientific

---

46. Ramm, *An Evangelical Christology*, 187.
47. Lewis, *Between Cross and Resurrection*, 116.
48. Schillebeeckx, *God the Future of Man*, 61.
49. See also Walls, ed., *The Oxford Handbook of Eschatology*, 226.

progress, the true perspective on the world—which is exclusively rational and empirical—has managed to make its way out through the traditional doctrines of the church into a belief which is no longer oriented towards the past but only towards the future and its infinite possibilities.[50]

What is the functional loss Schillebeeckx mentions in connection with the church's orientation towards the past as opposed to the world's discovery of the new humanized reality? The functional loss seems to be the church's so-called incapacity to provide reasonable answers to man's growing rational questions about his place in the world. Thus, for Schillebeeckx, as the church lost its capacity to provide reasonable explanations concerning man's increasingly rational awareness, man himself lost his trust in the church and decided to find the answers he needed in the world with its pluralistic religious composition.[51] The world, however, had been so heavily permeated by the idea of God that, despite the church's inability to explain it in rational terms that could have made a difference in the life of the modern man, the idea of God could not be simply given up so it had to undergo a process of dramatic reinterpretation.[52] It so happened that God, who until then had been thought of in terms of theology and religion, began to be seen from the perspective of the non-theological aspects of human culture.[53] Therefore, God lost his transcendental and meta-historical dimension which presented him as a personal being with an ontological status in the above-the-world reality in order to become a mere concept that was approached in scientific, technological, and social terms.[54] God was no longer the sole property of the church which had formally the right to disseminate its interpretation of him; God became privatized in the sense that every other non-theological science had an equal, as well as valid, right to approach and explain God in its own particular way.[55] Schillebeeckx embraces this new situation because it represents a scientific politic oriented to the future with virtually

---

50. McManus, *Unbroken Community*, 21.

51. For a discussion about reasonable belief in pluralistic society, see Moses, "Faith and Reason," 41ff.

52. Kennedy, *Schillebeeckx*, 4.

53. For Schillebeeckx, dedication to human culture does not oppose dedication to God because dedication to God is actually dedication to culture; this means that God can be found in culture. See Borgman, *Edward Schillebeeckx*, 94.

54. Hilkert and Schreiter, eds., *The Praxis*, 69–70.

55. See also Satterlee, *Ambrose of Milan's Method*, 315.

infinite possibilities to present the idea of God in order to make it relevant to humanity, present and future. As far as Schillebeeckx is concerned, the church had formerly had the disadvantage of being the captive of its own traditional interpretation of God, which was vertical and external. Things seems to have changed now and Schillebeeckx is clearly in favor of the new situation, in the sense that the church can break free from its past traditionalism and accept the rational liberation provided by the present and future modernism.[56]

According to Schillebeeckx we must not promote a difficult understanding of God, and he clearly hints at traditional Christianity. Why is traditional Christianity difficult and what exactly makes its approach to God a difficult task for the modern man? The answer lies in the very concept of rationality. Rationality is nothing more than the use of human reason as informed by the surrounding reality. Thus, rationality is man's capacity to perceive and understand the world in accordance with the verifiable realities of the world.[57] Traditional theology did not use this pattern of thought if Schillebeeckx is right, because its presentation of God as a being that exists beyond the limits of perceivable reality left human rationality without the capacity to check the veracity of its claims. If God exists beyond the grasp of reason, it means that he cannot be verified and it follows that he does not exist (at least in empirical terms).[58] This was actually the clash between traditional theology with its vertical concept of God and modern thought with its horizontal understanding of God. As the phenomenon of having God interpreted by various non-theological sciences has gradually intensified, we are now in the situation that God is thought to be more legitimate in the non-theology of the present than he was in the theology of the past.[59] This is why Schillebeeckx himself notices that theology—which suddenly turns into religion if approached scientifically—has reached a particular situation as interpreted by non-theological sciences. Because the traditional interpretation of God given by theology has been recently perceived as being so unreliable in comparison to modern rationality, non-theological sciences began to investigate critically not only the concept of God as reflected in traditional theol-

56. Knitter, "Religion and Globality?," 104–36.
57. Schillebeeckx, *God is New Each Moment*, 109.
58. See Abdul-Masih, *Edward Schillebeeckx and Hans Frei*, 157.
59. For a general discussion about the legitimacy of God and man's quest for God, see Stoker, *Is the Quest*, 205–6.

ogy but also traditional theology itself.[60] In scientific terms, traditional theology—now seen as religion or a dominant feature of the past—has grown to be regarded as utterly suspicious, probably because of its seemingly non-rational or even irrational tenets.[61] To quote Schillebeeckx:

> The confidence that men in need had previously placed in the church was transferred, because of this functional loss, to the sciences, technology, politics, welfare work and so on—all of them activities and institutions realized within a rational sphere of understanding. The traditional way of speaking of God and to God thus became gradually more difficult. Specialists in the new sciences also began to concern themselves with the phenomenon of religion, a field in which previously only the theologian had been held to be competent. The psyche of religious man was scientifically interpreted by depth-psychologists—whose interpretation of faith and religion is, moreover, at its own relative level, quite legitimate. In the same way, sociologists also began to interpret religion. Thus modern man was confronted with a certain ambiguity in his thinking about faith and his practice of religion. Religion had become "suspect."[62]

Unfortunately, Schillebeeckx seems to take for granted the fact that traditional theology is no longer relevant to modern people.[63] At the same time, he also seems to take for granted the right of non-theological sciences to judge traditional theology competently. Last but not least, he is more than willing to accept the interpretation of traditional theology by non-theological sciences as objective, valid, and correct simply because non-theological sciences are more prone to use human rationality than traditional theology. Schillebeeckx is surprisingly optimistic once again concerning the natural capacity of human reason to investigate the not so physically evident aspects of the inner reality of man.[64] While traditional theology does nothing to deny the capacity of human reason but only to highlight its limits because of sin, Schillebeeckx displays an overrated confidence in the power of human reason to investigate the reality which lies both beyond man's physical body and within the inner structure of the

60. Kennedy, *Schillebeeckx*, 37–38.
61. Borgman, *Edward Schillebeeckx*, 130.
62. Schillebeeckx, *God the Future of Man*, 61.
63. See Engelhardt, *The Foundations of Christian Bioethics*, xiv, and Abdul-Masih, *Edward Schillebeeckx and Hans Frei*, 130.
64. Aldwinckle, *Jesus—a Savior or the Savior?*, 95.

individual person. It is clear that Schillebeeckx's approach is fundamentally existential or experiential and psychological as informed by reason;[65] he does not, however, seem to promote the validity of the individual rational experience but rather the sum of personal experiences of each human being. Thus, he trusts that this community of individual experiences—which is in fact the collective experience of society—is perfectly entitled to judge the validity of the traditional claim of theology. The only problem of Schillebeeckx's approach, which also proves to be its fatal flaw, is the very likely possibility that the collective rational experience of society may also be affected by misjudgment, the very same way the misinformed individual experience results in wrong attitudes. For Schillebeeckx, however, this does not seem to be a problem. What he knows for a fact is that society changes and if society changes, then traditional theology should make way for a new understanding of theology which inevitably leads to a new—specifically universalist—understanding of God.[66]

SECULARIZATION AND GOD

Schillebeeckx believes that the increasing distrust in traditional theology fostered by the growing role of reason in modern society led quite naturally to a general situation which made the discourse about God as well as man's personal communication with God rather difficult.[67] Although he does not say it explicitly, Schillebeeckx seems convinced that man's conversation about and with God is virtually impossible given the new faith of modernity which heavily based on rationality. This provides him with a new opportunity to deconstruct the traditional understanding of Christian theology which reportedly felt compelled to abandon its belief in miracles and the efficiency of prayer.[68] Thus, the concept of God as a being which exists by necessity beyond the realm of human reality was left aside just to be replaced in modern society by the experience of human life within the context of human needs. All in all, modern faith in human rationality as the only valid way to understand the experience of today's life has totally changed traditional theology by means of its interpretation in exclusively anthropological terms. The idea of transcendence

---

65. Rego, *Suffering and Salvation*, 202.
66. See also van Beeck, *God Encountered*, 191.
67. For more details, see Ramshaw, "(ii) The Gender of God," 173.
68. Ban, *The Christological Foundation*, 174.

perceived as ontological meta-historicity with view to God's existence was deconstructed to the point that nothing should be conceived as having ontological status beyond the tangible and verifiable realm of human reality. The veracity of the miracles proclaimed by traditional theology is therefore cancelled because nothing can happen outside the rational possibilities of human experience. The traditional theology of prayer was equally subject to this new hermeneutic[69] in the sense that there was no superior reality to supply belief in a powerful and efficient meta-historical intervention in the historicity of the modern man's life. These are the main lines of modernity's approach to traditional theology and there seems to be no doubt in Schillebeeckx's mind about the dethronement of traditional theology by the new modern rationalized faith which will eventually see its firm establishment within society.[70] Schillebeeckx even sounds a bit upset that modern rationality has not yet found a sufficient number of supporters because those who still believe in the old traditional way appear to form a larger community within today's world. Despite this not so convenient situation for Schillebeeckx, he still will not lay down his weapons as he expresses his conviction that churches will slowly but surely be left with fewer and fewer practising Christians who will find it increasingly hard to proclaim the God of traditional theology.[71] What follows is Schillebeeckx's description of how modern rationality affected the traditional understanding of theology:

> All this undermined the traditional way of speaking of and to God. Experience too seemed to confirm the growing doubt—diseases which no prayer or miracle had been able to cure were cured by modern drugs, fields which had remained infertile despite sprinkling with holy water were made fertile by chemicals and human needs were alleviated by various social provisions and economic changes in the structure of society. In view of all this, man ceased to speak of and to God in the way which had previously been taken for granted. Necessity, the "mother of all invention," was rationally conceived and, as experience showed, this approach proved much more effective than prayer in mitigating human needs. The unique "miracle" which might happen to an isolated and privileged person became almost a blasphemy to many others (the majority!)

69. For details about Schillebeeckx's hermeneutics, see Rochford, "The Theological Hermeneutics," 251.

70. Schillebeeckx, *God the Future of Man*, 61.

71. See also Lewis and Demarest, *Integrative Theology*, vol. 2–3, 54.

who had to go on living without miracles. The result is that man today finds it more difficult than he did in the past no only to talk *about* God, but also to talk *to* God. Many people who have been brought up explicitly as Christians quietly leave the church, while those who still continue truly to believe experience great difficulties in speaking of and to God.[72]

The following lines are not intended to be an *ad hominem* criticism but Schillebeeckx seems to have written this text with his heart rather than his head. Emotions appear to have prevailed over reason and the immediate personal experience over the general picture of today's world. Why is this?

First, because Schillebeeckx cannot refrain from noticing—somewhat bitterly—that those who really understand the validity of today's dominant rationality are still a minority.[73] This is a correct assessment of today's situation because even if he writes from the perspective of a man living in the rationalized West, there are still vast regions in the world that have not yet been subdued by rationalism. Asia, Africa, Central and South America, Eastern Europe, and even the West itself still have communities of traditional Christians.

Second, it looks as if Schillebeeckx took for granted the fact that what he says about today's increasingly influent rationality is the definitive interpretation of the world's current situation.[74] To give just one example, Schillebeeckx is undeterred in his confidence that true traditional believers experience great difficulties in talking about and of God. Schillebeeckx is far from being right in this because if he—who is definitely not a traditional Christian any longer—had such difficulties in the past, and now finds it easy to explain God in rational terms this does not mean that traditional Christians share the same difficulties. It is either that Schillebeeckx was sloppy in developing his argument or he really did not have a realistic knowledge of the general picture but there are many traditional Christian communities as well as specific churches that grow in numbers even today despite the fact that a significant part of their members consists of scientists, physicians, engineers etc.

---

72. Schillebeeckx, *God the Future of Man*, 62.
73. Wiley, *Thinking of Christ*, 100.
74. See also Schreiter, "Edward Schillebeeckx," 156.

Third, Schillebeeckx seems to have lost sight of how traditional theology works.[75] Traditional theology is essentially pneumatological, which means that the individual believer is spiritually but nevertheless really indwelled by the person of the Holy Spirit who makes the presence of God the Father and God the Son equally real within the same believer. This is true for all believers who make up a community of the Spirit, where the living, actual, real, and spiritual presence of God is experienced on a daily basis. Traditional Christians may have doubts but their entire life is driven by a power which surpasses any modern rationalistic motivations. This is why traditional Christians have a stricter morality as well as a life which is actively involved in confessing their belief in God. Their faith is the result of God's intervention in their lives as well as the Spirit's continuous indwelling, so there is nothing in the world that can cause them to give up their faith. Wealth or poverty, health or sickness, progress or the lack of it, comfort or hardship, nothing will prompt them to drop their confidence in God. So there is much more attached to traditional theology than Schillebeeckx's surprisingly misinformed conviction that true believers go through considerable pain when it comes to believing in and confessing their God. On the contrary, many of them see absolutely no problem in trusting an ontologically real God who exists beyond our history, wants to save them from their sin and will eventually take them to heaven with him. So, despite what Schillebeeckx thinks about traditional Christians, they will continue to have a confessing life powerfully anchored in a stricter morality which they hold dear as different from the way of life they see in the world.

This brings the whole discussion to the very sensitive point of the identification between the church and the world in Schillebeeckx, who is convinced that the intellect as well as the morality of the world is no different from those nurtured by traditional believers:

> What is more, believers, living in a society which has become increasingly pluralistic in its view of life, have made the initially disturbing discovery that those who do not believe are neither more stupid than they are nor less virtuous. They have found out too that Christians have specific faults and lack understanding in specific respects and that a great deal of injustice has often been perpetrated "in the name of God." All this has meant that the very meaning of religion, of talking about and to God and of appealing

75. For a contrary view, see Häring, "From Divine Human to Human God," 24.

to him, has become obscured. What was once the core of Western Christianity has now become unintelligible—and for many even intolerable.[76]

Schillebeeckx is right when he writes that Christians, in fact traditional Christians and non-Christians are equal when it comes to their intellectual capacity and moral virtue. Even from the standpoint of traditional theology, the situation is presented within the same lines: all human beings are equal in all respects as they were all created by God.[77] There is, however, one huge difference between traditional Christians and non-Christians in terms of practical morality, which Schillebeeckx either ignored as irrelevant or lost sight of as unimportant. Even though traditional Christians are equal with non-Christians in all respects pertaining to their inner constitution as human beings, it will soon become evident that traditional Christians will never tolerate a clearly delineated list of moral issues which they perceive as sinful. Thus, to give just a few examples, unlike secular non-Christians traditional Christians will always reject sex before marriage, sex outside marriage, homosexuality, divorce just for the fun of it, and violence. It is true that the rejection of these practices as well as living a life which excludes them do not make traditional Christians more virtuous than secularized unbelievers but they definitely set them apart as a group of people that is ethically different from the world in terms of the morality of everyday life.[78]

Christians have their own shortcomings and mistakes in their relationship with themselves and the world; as a general observation, Schillebeeckx's remark is correct.[79] Nevertheless, he is far from being right when he says that when secularized people realized Christians were not so special, they almost immediately gave up believing Christianity. To be sure, this is not a proof that Christianity is wrong or that the God of traditional Christians should no longer be trusted; it only means that Christians—not traditional Christianity—can sometimes or even oftentimes be wrong. The truth, validity, and personal relevance of traditional Christianity is not annulled by the mistakes of individual Christians;

---

76. Schillebeeckx, *God the Future of Man*, 62.

77. Kennedy, *Schillebeeckx*, 11.

78. For ethics and ethical norms in Schillebeeckx, see Kaczor, ed., *Proportionalism*, 87.

79. See also Rego, *Suffering and Salvation*, 208.

these can cause trouble to traditional Christianity and its witness in the world but they will never render useless the true value of traditional Christianity, morality, and practice.

Another issue wherein Schillebeeckx is wrong has to do with his observation that the essence of traditional Christianity became unintelligible for today's secularized rationality.[80] Again, the fact that the secularized mind of modern men and women does not understand the values, teachings, and ethics of traditional Christianity, it does not mean that traditional Christianity is in itself unintelligible—it only means that some people think it is unintelligible, and this is very likely their own fault. The fact that at times traditional theology becomes intolerable is one of the saddest realities nowadays which threatens to become tragic despite the secularized man's belief in the universal value of love.

What is the role of God in such a secularized society? Given that he is no longer the ontologically real God of traditional Christianity, it would seem that he lost his importance altogether. In secularized society, however, God did not lose his importance, at least not altogether.[81] People still talk about God and try to express their own lives as well as the meaning of their lives in connection with the idea of God. God may no longer be present in the minds and hearts of secularized people as he was in the soul of traditional believers but he is nevertheless there to inform at least partially an existence which still has to cope with the realities of everyday life as well as with the distressing presence of suffering and death.[82] God has thus become a reference point with which everybody wants to establish a certain connection. Secularized people seem incapable of living without the idea of God even if he is definitely not the God of traditional theology. They realize they have a different kind of life by comparison to the life of traditional Christians, and even if God is not so important to them, they still continue to lead their lives by clinging to the idea of God for a wide range of reasons. God is there to be claimed for various purposes despite the different lifestyle of the secularized man as compared to the lifestyle of the traditional Christian. This is why Schillebeeckx mentions the fact

---

80. Schillebeeckx, *God is New Each Moment*, 68. See also Thiselton, *Thiselton on Hermeneutics*, 457.

81. Abdul-Masih, *Edward Schillebeeckx and Hans Frei*, 57–58.

82. See also McManus, *Unbroken Communion*, 73. Schillebeeckx's insistence on suffering and death seems to be connected to his life experience; see Schloesser, "Against Forgetting," 275ff.

that secularization can also be explained sociologically by means of the concept of differentiation.[83] The modern man realizes he no longer believes in the God of his predecessors and he does not seem to be alarmed by this; he does prefer a rationalized life which he can explain in terms of the surrounding, visible, and tangible reality. In spite of his preference though for this new rationality, the modern man simply cannot get rid of the concept of God because—for some more or less obvious reasons—he feels uncomfortable without God. In this context, secularization becomes "an expression of man's fundamental uncertainty in a new world which he himself has designed."[84]

Schillebeeckx's conclusion seems to confirm the ongoing validity of traditional theology if the modern man is indeed incapable of coming to terms with himself in his secularized world. Schillebeeckx, however, has another explanation which has nothing to do with the truth of traditional theology. For him, traditional theology does not appear to have a bright future and from the way he talks about it secularized society will eventually rid itself of any traditional interpretation of reality.[85] Thus, the distress of the secularized man should be interpreted in a totally different way which does not take into account traditional interpretations of the world such as classical Christian theology. Human society is distressed indeed but not because it gave up or is in the process of giving up traditional values; its distress must be understood in terms of the clash between what man can do in the external world and what he cannot do in the internal realm of his own being. In other words, man can alter the face of the physical world by means of technology but man's inner constitution is much more complex than that so it cannot be approached exclusively on the basis of scientific research. The secularized man can solve the problem of his external life by providing physical safety, comfort, and prosperity. What he cannot do though is fix the problem of the meaning of life, the meaning of his own personal, individual life as well as the meaning of life in general.[86] Again, this situation could highlight the value of traditional Christianity which would be able to offer an answer to such an

---

83. Kennedy, *A Modern Introduction to Theology*, 87. For a detailed study about differentiation see Lawson, *Old Wine in New Skins*, 54–57.

84. Schillebeeckx, *God the Future of Man*, 62–63.

85. See also Borgman, *Edward Schillebeeckx*, 358.

86. Details about the meaning of life in contemporary secularized society can be found in Houtepen, *God*, 325.

internal crisis but Schillebeeckx is not willing to find the solution in the past. He does admit that secular society faces a serious loss of meaning, the real meaning of life as compared to the evident progress of science and technology but this has nothing to do with traditional Christianity. What seems to be going on here according to Schillebeeckx is this: modern society has become increasingly secular and wealthy due to the outstanding progress of science and technology.[87] This secured a high degree of physical comfort for the secular society in general which caused individuals to think only in terms of an external rationality. This means that the individuals of secular society used their rationality only in order to understand the external world, while they lost their capacity to think rationally with reference to their interior world or the realm of the meaning of life.[88] Thus, external rationality which helped man understand his place in the technologized world increased with reverse proportion to the internal rationality that was supposed to explain the meaning of his life. This prompts Schillebeeckx to conclude that secular man developed his vision for the external reality while he almost lost the deeper vision of the meaning of his inner life.[89] This situation which led to a degree of uncertainty made the secular man of modern society cling to the idea of God which was so prevalent in the pre-modern world of the past.

What is Schillebeeckx's solution? The reality of secularization in the modern world and the idea of God can coexist but this will have to happen in terms which have nothing to do with the past or with traditional theology. We live in the present so we must cope with it; we have to develop our thinking, our understanding of the world in terms which are congruent with our rationality, and this is not optional. Schillebeeckx is convinced that progress is vital as part of our culture, so if we are human beings then we have to develop and also understand religious issues in light of this progress:[90]

> I in no sense mean to imply here that scientific and technical culture has been a *choice* on the part of the Western world, a choice of one from many other possibilities, one which could or might have turned out otherwise. I see this scientific and technical development as a necessary, essential part of human culture,

---

87. For a critical point of view see Lefebvre, *Open Letter*, 114–15.
88. Human interiority is approached by means of faith, see Doyle, "Journet," 461.
89. Schillebeeckx, *God the Future of Man*, 63.
90. McManus, *Unbroken Communion*, 108.

Re-Branding Christian Theology through Secularization

in the last analysis part and parcel of humanity itself. By loss of meaning and reality, I mean only the lack of integration of this scientific and technical culture into the *totally human* cultural task. Hominization is not yet humanization. Precisely on the basis of this new situation, the religious question has become relevant in a new way to our society.[91]

It is clear from this paragraph that traditional theology and its concept of God has no chance of being inserted in Schillbeeckx's plan for modern man and his secularized society. Progress is essentially an issue which concerns the future, so it is open to the future in a constantly new way; religion, which has been with man forever given his inner structure and the necessity of finding meaning for his life beyond the physical reality of external progress, must be integrated within this particular modern, secularized, and technologized framework. Religion then must be explained based on the essentials of scientific progress.[92] Thus, the image of the God Schillebeeckx proposes for modern society looks increasingly scientific but it seems the only solution for today's technologized world: a scientific God for a scientific society. Now, Schillebeeckx does not use the phrase "scientific God" but he does mention that religion should be understood against the background of scientific progress. Schillebeeckx realizes that the secularization of society by means of a growing rationality, which explains outer reality in terms of external things that bear no significance or meaning to the inner reality of man, could eventually lead to the total loss of the idea of God. God—seen either as a personal being or as a mere concept—could very well lose his importance for the man of today's secular society.[93] Schillebeeckx, however, does not like this possibility because it would categorically lead to a catastrophic loss of meaning for the majority of secular people. So losing the meaning of God is not an option for modern society; what modern society must do is re-brand the concept of God in terms of the ongoing process of secularization.[94]

What can be done so that modern people do not completely lose the idea of God from their lives? According to Schillebeeckx, the essential thing to be done is realize the necessity of secularization as well as its reality as a globalizing phenomenon. Secularization has managed to go be-

---

91. Schillebeeckx, *God the Future of Man*, 63–64.
92. Depoorter, "Orthopraxis as a Criterion for Orthodoxy?," 176.
93. Schillebeeckx, *God the Future of Man*, 64.
94. See also Rego, *Suffering and Salvation*, 54.

yond traditional Christianity in the sense that it actually broke traditional Christianity as a monological system.[95] Schillebeeckx argues that until the present age of secularization, everything in the world has been conceived in monological terms. In other words, the world was led by various systems which tried to impose their own ideals in the world with total disregard for other systems. Thus, traditional Christianity reportedly attempted to become a leading religious system which was not interested in anything else but itself. The same thing happened in politics, for instance, where Marxists tried the same thing.[96] There was, however, absolutely no connection between the two systems or between them and other systems for that matter. This led to a constant ideological clash which resulted in a ghettoized monological mentality. This means that traditional Christians were interested exclusively in traditional Christianity while Marxists fought only for Marxism. Secularization developed against this ideological conflict fueled by this ghettoized mentality and, if we are to trust Schillebeeckx, it succeeded in overtaking it. Secularization brought about a new rationality, a new way of thinking which went beyond religious and political boundaries. This is why society began to abandon religious and political systems, and their corresponding previously impenetrable boundaries. The new rationality of secularization had therefore a globalizing effect which rendered the monological character of ghettoized religious and political mentality totally useless.[97] Thus, what we have to do in order not to lose the idea of God in the current secularized society is understand that secularization has no room for monologue but only for dialogue. The history of the West has been essentially monological but this stage of humanity has come to an abrupt end. Schillebeeckx is confident that the mistakes of the past can be repaired only if we give up the ghettoized monological mentality of the past, which includes traditional Christianity. In order for our secular society to find meaning in the idea of God for the sake of the lives of today's secularized men we have to turn our back on our monological past:

> Men talk these days about a post-Christian stage of history, but they could just as well talk about a "post-Marxist" stage, since all the values that have been handed down to us in monologue are

---

95. McManus, *Unbroken Communion*, 67.
96. See also Caputo, *More Radical Hermeneutics*, 241.
97. Mueller, *What Are They Saying?*, 57.

> now being called into question. So it is that people everywhere are engaged in dialogue, searching for the fundamental reinterpretation of both Christianity and Marxism. Why else has dialogue become one of the most fashionable words of the twentieth century, if not because this century has witnessed the failure of all *systems* which were totalitarian in that they acknowledged only monologue? It is the failure of monologue which we are now experiencing—the Middle Ages were one great monologue; the Reformation and the Counter-Reformation were two parallel monologues; the Enlightenment was ultimately a secularization of the *rabies theologica*—the *écrasez l'autre* of the Crusades and the Inquisition became *écrasez l'infâme*, but it remained a monologue and as the empirical sciences developed, they took over the dominant role from absolutist metaphysical thought. Always the black-and-white approach of monologue![98]

These words are crucial for Schillebeeckx's understanding of secularization and the new idea of God which should inform it. Secularization is, for Schillebeeckx, dialogical not monological because it succeeds in transcending firmly established boundaries.[99] In Schillebeeckx, everything has to be loose, not fixed, and a bit gray because secularization has no room left for clear-cut black-and-white categories. Dialogue presupposes dual acceptance to the point that everybody should get along very well. Though appealing, Schillebeeckx's approach is utterly reductionistic. To say that traditional Christianity is monological, totalitarian, and absolutistic because it claims and believes in God's ontological reality as the sole, ultimate truth is both unfair and wrong. The fact that during the Middle Ages Catholic Christianity was proclaimed as compulsory does not mean that traditional Christianity is compulsory. The first Christians—who can always be better associated to traditional Christianity—did not take the sword and kill the Jews, the Greeks and the Romans when they rejected Jesus's teachings. On the contrary, the Jews, the Greeks and the Romans felt it was quite acceptable to crush and kill the early Christians because of their convictions. Likewise, if Protestants and Catholics found new ways to kill each other during the sixteenth century, it does not mean that traditional Christianity is compulsory in any way. Taken exclusively in its own terms, traditional Christianity preaches the love of one's enemy which is more than a mere dialogical relationship. The traditional Christian is

98. Schillebeeckx, *God the Future of Man*, 65–66.
99. Wiley, *Thinking of Christ*, 93.

commanded to be dialogical because he has no other way but live out and proclaim his faith. The fact that he believes his faith is the only acceptable understanding of the truth does not turn traditional Christianity into religious absolutism. As a matter of fact, what Schillebeeckx seems to hate about traditional Christianity is not its exclusivistic claims[100] but rather its metaphysical content. Metaphysics is for Schillebeeckx an intellectual reality which escapes the verification process of contemporary secularization.[101] Secularization is essentially rational and its rationality needs physical, visible, and tangible elements in order to assess their role and function. Metaphysics does not allow for such an assessment because its very content is beyond the possibilities of rationality. It is definitely not anti-rational; it is just beyond-rational. By virtue of its own nature, secularization needs non-metaphysical realities in order to be dialogic. Secularization can engage in dialogue provided its dialogue partner shares equally secularized and non-metaphysical convictions.

From this perspective, Schillebeeckx's secularization is equally absolutist and monological because it cannot accept metaphysical realities. A traditional Christian will always be able to engage in dialogue with a secularized man because he understands both physical and metaphysical reality; furthermore, he will understand why the secularized man rejects his metaphysical and ontologically real God. If the secular man eventually decides not to accept the God of the traditional Christian, the traditional Christian will understand why, and consequently he will not force the secular man to believe him. It is true that the traditional Christian can be insistent in the sense that he will try his best to convince the secular man of the veracity of his belief but he will never force him to share in that belief. On the other hand, however, a secularized man will never be able to engage in constructive dialogue with a traditional Christian because he may understand his own secularized reality but he cannot understand the metaphysical reality which informs the faith of the traditional Christian. The secularized man does not understand the reality of metaphysics so he will naturally reject it. This is why secularization in general as well as

---

100. Exclusivism as religious superiority is indeed criticized by Schillebeeckx. See Omar, "Overcoming Religiously Motivated Violence," 77.

101. This means that if we still want to speak of metaphysics and revelation, which discloses metaphysical realities, the only way to verify metaphysics seems to be the indirect agency of praxis. See, for details, Abdul-Masih, *Edward Schillebeeckx and Hans Frei*, 56.

it is presented by Schillebeeckx has no chance to be dialogical. It cannot be dialogical because it is based on physical realities; the secularized man believes in physical realities so his approach to metaphysics will always be monological. Metaphysics cannot be accepted by secularization because it lies beyond the possibilities of human rationality which support secularization. As far as the traditional Christian is concerned, he may not believe in the ultimate character of physical reality but this does not mean he will reject it.

Schillebeeckx will of course resent this criticism because of his conviction that metaphysics cannot be integrated into the rationality of secularization. So there is a sharp distinction between traditional Christianity, which is metaphysical and theistic, and secularization, which consequently is physical and atheistic. The fact that secularization is physical and atheistic does not mean—for Schillebeeckx—that we have to give up the idea of God; what we have to do is just change the way we speak of God.[102] Thus, we should no longer speak of God in the metaphysical terms of theism but in the physical terms of atheism. In other words, secularization is not anti-God; it is merely anti-theistic which makes it atheistic.[103] As a theologian, Schillebeeckx cannot give up the idea of God because this would mean to give up also the idea of theology. This is why he explains that secularization is fundamentally theological in the sense that while it rejects the theism of traditional theology, it embraces the atheism of what he calls radical theology.[104] To be sure, Schillebeeckx is a radical theologian who promotes an atheistic perspective on God as a reality that should confer meaning to the inner life of the secularized man. Secularization is essentially rational, so it is quite natural for Schillebeeckx to abandon traditional theism as binding for the rationality of secularization.[105] Man does not need a theistic God who controls the entire universe; he needs a God that he can control, a God that is fundamentally atheistic, a God that does not prevent him from building his future according to his own rational plans. Secularization helps man understand that there is no reality beyond his reality, there is no God beyond his own rational understanding of God, there is no metaphysical existence beyond the physical existence

---

102. Schillebeeckx, *God the Future of Man*, 66.

103. Kennedy, *Schillebeeckx*, 121.

104. For details about radical theology and its atheistic perspective, see Croken and Doran, eds., *The Collected Works of Bernard Lonergan*, 290.

105. Schillebeeckx, *God the Future of Man*, 67.

of history. For Schillebeeckx, secularization is the end of the theistic God and the beginning of the atheistic God, a God that should always be approached within man's rational sphere of understanding as a meaningful reality for secularized society.[106]

As a representative of secularized radical theology, Schillebeeckx wants to be dialogical to the end. The result is that he wants to turn this atheistic image of God into a meaningful reality for what he calls "the Christian point of view."[107] It is hard to say what he means by this as he does not give any other details but it is clear that he does not refer to traditional Christianity. If this is the case, then his dialogical attitude becomes monological again because he will never be able to turn an atheistic God into a meaningful reality for traditional Christians who cannot accept any God apart from their fundamentally theistic, metaphysical, and metahistorical God. What Schillebeeckx hopes for is probably a future which presents the possibility of the traditional Christian's conversion into a radical secularized believer. Schillebeeckx is hopelessly optimistic if he nurtures such a hope because while he is willing to accept the death of the theistic God and the resurrection of his secularized atheistic deity, the traditional Christian does not have this option. The traditional Christian will always find the ultimate meaning of life in his theistic metaphysical God; as for Schillebeeckx, a God "manufactured" by man's secularized rationality seems to confer sufficient meaning to modern society.

---

106. Schillebeeckx, *God the Future of Man*, 68–69.
107. Schillebeeckx, *God the Future of Man*, 69.

2

Re-Defining the Concept of God

God in the world and God for the world are two complementary images of God which can be found in Schillebeeckx. The discourse about God or explicit statements about God is associated with traditional Christianity, which thus proved its faith in the meta-historical, specifically transcendent, ontological reality of God. Contemporary secularized society, however, has revised its thinking about God, so it no longer needs to have a God which exists above history and physical reality, but only a God which is essentially human and open to new possibilities due to the openness of our future as compared to the present. As this God is fundamentally human, the traditional discourse about God specific to classical Christianity becomes useless and is replaced by a silent approach to God which is consistent with the modern man's secularized confidence in his rationality. Thus, God is seen as being part of the world due to our humanity, which must reflect itself in the ethical practice of doing good as a confirmation of the fact that God is not only present in the world but also an active reality that helps us improve the world.

GOD IN THE WORLD

In order to construct the image of God for the modern man, Schillebeeckx needs to resort to the reality of contemporary society.[1] The society that we live in is fundamentally different from the society that we left behind. Our society is a society of the present and similarities with past society are scarce if any.[2] Schillebeeckx likes to believe that contemporary society has become secularized by means of a process which gave up the traditional understanding of God as ontologically real and transcendent

1. Borgman, *Edward Schillebeeckx*, 201.
2. Schillebeeckx, *God is New Each Moment*, 91.

in favor of an explanation that stresses the importance of man's natural self-awareness as well as his rational sphere of understanding.[3] The secularization of today's society implies the disposal of traditional views both with respect to God and the role of man in society. The man who lives in today's world is a rational being.[4] He builds his entire life on rationality, namely on his capacity to use his natural reason in order to understand his role in the world as well as his relationship with himself. Reason investigates nature, or the reality of the world, in a way which is constantly checked and re-checked; this means that human reason verifies the reality of the world—both human and non-human—against its own claims.[5] This informs the human being that his life is historical and terrestrial; thus, whatever he does needs to be thought of in physical terms of historicity. The modern man realizes that he needs a new image of God because the old image of God, the transcendent and ontologically real God of traditional theology, no longer serves his rational aspirations.[6] So the modern secularized man should no longer look for a God outside the world but for a God in the world.[7]

Therefore, the old image of God needs to be abandoned in favor of a new image of God. This new image of God, which is supposed to be rational in accordance with the rationality of today's secularized society, cannot be built just like that in a very facile manner because for some people, who have an earnest secular understanding of life, giving up the idea of God could be interpreted as a potential death of God.[8] Traditional Christianity has been strong for centuries and its belief in the metahistorical reality of God's existence has been influential as well as authentic for those who believed it. Schillebeeckx, however, does not bother too much about the long history of traditional Christianity; with the strike of a pen, he postulates the demise of traditional Christianity which has turned into a useless and irrelevant belief that does not answer the demands and expectations of modern man.[9] One thing is clear in Schillebeeckx: he does

---

3. See also Avis, *God and the Creative Imagination*, 154.
4. Abdul-Masih, *Edward Schillebeeckx and Hans Frei*, 79.
5. Schillebeeckx, *Christ, the Sacrament of the Encounter with God*, 4.
6. Rego, *Suffering and Salvation*, 50.
7. For details, see Morrill, *Anamnesis and Dangerous Memory*, 90.
8. See also Nichols, *Catholic Thought*, 166.
9. Engelhardt, *The Foundations of Christian Bioethics*, xiv.

Re-Defining the Concept of God

not like traditional theology for a number of reasons but two of the most important are these: first, traditional theology professed ideas and concepts which had the potential to manipulate people due to their lack of connection with physical reality; and second, traditional theology—due to its potentially manipulative content which does not reflect the rationality of the physical world—is theoretically and practically incapable of explaining the meaning of life to the secularized mind of today's men and women. This is why, for Schillebeeckx, traditional theology is outdated and needs to be replaced:

> What in the first place characterizes our new image of man and the world is that our old image of God has evaporated. We can no longer live by it because it is associated with our old image of man and the world. But even more characteristic is our apparent inability to form for ourselves a new image of God, an inability that is clearly reflected in the books and articles that have been written about the "death of God." In the past, Christian thinkers have always been clearly conscious of the fact that God was unapproachable, that he could not be described and that man was fundamentally incapable of putting his knowledge of God into words or forming any adequate image of him. In the usual theology, spirituality and preaching of the past, however, God was often presented and experienced as someone who intervened in the world and ideas of God derived from the qualities theologically predicated of him were too often manipulated as if they were adequate concepts of God. In all this, man's religious experience continued to be authentic; yet it was contained within a social and culture context which colored man's inward religious experience then but has now been superseded.[10]

So the concepts of traditional theology were inadequate, which means that the concept of God understood as metaphysical, meta-historical, and ontologically real was fatally flawed by its lack of rationality with view to the physical reality of the world.[11] Despite the inadequacy of traditional theology and of traditional concepts, Schillebeeckx is willing to accept the idea that the religious experience of the outdated traditional theology was nevertheless authentic.[12] Why is that? Because religion is an integrative

10. Schillebeeckx, *God the Future of Man*, 69.

11. For more details about the so-called inadequacy of traditional theology as confronted with the modern situation, see van der Ven, *God Reinvented*, 41–42.

12. Borgman, *Edward Schillebeeckx*, 341.

aspect of society and its fundamental essence, which is faith, is a natural component of man's apprehension of reality. Man understands his place in society and his relationship with himself as living in society by means of religion.[13] Thus, in Schillebeeckx, religion as well as its faith—or, to be more specific, traditional theology as well as its metaphysical faith—must be approached sociologically in order to be meaningful.[14] The concepts of religion can be more or less adequate but religious experience is definitely adequate as long as religion is a constant of human social life.[15]

For Schillebeeckx it is important to know that concepts may change but experience is forever the same. Thus, theological concepts are not there to stay for eternity; they can and will change given the open reality of the humanity's future, but human experience, religious or non-religious, is a permanent reality of every human individual and it will never change. This is why religious and theological concepts must be rooted in experience, not the other way around.[16] In other words, the classical concept of God as metaphysical, meta-historical and ontologically real should not be binding for our experiences. The concept of God may be defined in various ways throughout history, so—as it changes constantly—it is useless to the unchanging religious experience of men and women.[17] As a matter of fact, things should be the other way around if we are to believe Schillebeeckx: our experience of the present helps us understand our lives in light of what happens within society, so instead of relying on changing concepts we should reinterpret these concepts in order to make sense for us today. Schillebeeckx displays a very sympathetic attitude to the people in the past who had inadequate concepts of God.[18] They believed that God was metaphysical and ontologically real because they had a wrong

---

13. It should be said at this point that, in this respect, Schillebeeckx is backed by Küng. See, for details, Valkenberg, *Sharing Lights*, 145. Their theological cooperation, however, met staunch criticism. See, for instance, Grootaers, "An Unfinished Agenda," 305 n. 87. Furthermore, Küng and Schillebeeckx are seen—at least in some quarters—as unimportant thinkers who will eventually prove to be "largely irrelevant to the future of Catholic theology." Reno, "Theology after the Revolution," 15. For others, however, they are theologians of "caliber." See Komonchak, "The Church in Crisis," 11.

14. The starting point should be the experience of the disciples; see Breyfogle, "Religious Mystery and Rational Reflection," 266.

15. Schillebeeckx, *God the Future of Man*, 69–70.

16. Abdul-Masih, *Edward Schillebeeckx and Hans Frei*, 6.

17. See also Boeve, "Theology and the Interruption of Experience," 23.

18. Fatula, *The Triune God*, 27.

understanding of physical reality. They evidently lacked our scientific perspective on the world, so it is no surprise they expected help from a God beyond history if they did not know that help does in fact come only from history. Despite their wrong concept of God, they still had an authentic religious experience because their lives were part of the reality of the world. In other words, Schillebeeckx's rule concerning the understanding of reality is this: if it happens in the world and is of the world, then the object in question is authentic; if it does not happen in the world and is not of the world, the object is not authentic. This authenticity must be verified rationally in order to be established as such.[19] Whenever the claim to authenticity cannot be checked rationally it becomes a pretence to inauthentic ideas. Experience—religious or other—is conditioned socially; this means that it can be verified rationally and have its claims to authenticity firmly established. This has always been the case with religious experience, so the religious experience of the past and the religious experience of the present are equally authentic.[20]

So the religious experience of the past and that of the present are both authentic. It is clear, however, that the religious experience of the past was based on a different understanding of religious concepts. The religion of the past and the religion of the present can have the same set of concepts but they definitely have fundamentally different understandings of those concepts. Schillebeeckx explains that the religious experience of the present is different from that of the past because of science.[21] The development of science prompted humanity to reconsider the traditional concepts of theology, so even if religion itself did not change, the understanding of concepts did, and this also resulted in a different religious experience.[22] To be sure, the religious experience of the present is not different from that of the past in authenticity or in concepts; it is different only in the understanding of concepts, which have been reconsidered in the light of modern science. What does Schillebeeckx mean by that? The religion of the past was traditional and unscientific, so its concepts—most notably the concept of God—were understood as anchored in metaphysics. After

19. Details about the rational approach to authenticity can be found in Marsh, *Process*, 334.
20. Schillebeeckx, *God the Future of Man*, 70.
21. See also Wicks, *Handbook of Spirituality for Ministers*, 75.
22. For details about Schillebeeckx's theology of development, see Talar, "The Synthesis of All Heresies," 491.

the rise of modern science, the perspective on these traditional concepts changed so they were no longer understood as presenting a metaphysical reality but only a reality that can be assessed rationally. The authenticity of religious experiences as socially and rationally conditioned makes all religious experiences—past and present—equally valid in such a way that they are all part of what Schillebeeckx calls "the history of the authenticity of Christian faith within the life of religious mankind."[23] Therefore, if there is any difference at all between the non-scientific religious experiences of the traditional past and the scientific religious experiences of the modern present, that difference is only in quality.[24] Schillebeeckx does not say whether the non-scientific religious experiences of the past were of a poorer quality while the scientific religious experience of the present are better in quality; it is evident though that he prefers the present and science, so one can conclude in his view that the scientific religious experiences of the present are better in quality then the non-scientific experiences of the traditional past.

But as concepts are reassessed in the light of science, there is no guarantee that today's reassessed concepts will not be reconsidered in future. This, however, is not a problem for Schillebeeckx. He even concedes that concepts will undergo a constant process of reassessment, so that certain concepts which are valid for a certain time in history will be later reconsidered based on new scientific findings.[25] This cycle of scientifically informed conceptual reassessment will affect religion forever; in other words, the concept of God will change constantly.[26] No one can say for a fact how the concept of God will be understood in the more or less distant future; Schillebeeckx, though, is pretty sure that the idea of traditional metaphysical and meta-historical transcendence as applied to God has been dethroned for good. Nobody, however, can confirm this beyond any doubt. This lack of objective certainty—which definitely does not torment Schillebeeckx—makes his approach rather limited and overconfident.[27] For one thing, his approach is undeniably based on what happens in the industrialized West, so his theory cannot be applied to the entire world.

---

23. Schillebeeckx, *God the Future of Man*, 70–71.
24. Rego, *Suffering and Salvation*, 392.
25. Abdul-Masih, *Edward Schillebeeckx and Hans Frei*, 75.
26. See Kotva, *The Christian Case*, 86.
27. Culbertson, *The Poetics of Revelation*, 14.

Re-Defining the Concept of God

Schillebeeckx may speak as if the whole world shares his interpretation but his radical theology is far from being accepted everywhere. Then, even if it seems that traditional transcendence has met its doom, Schillebeeckx cannot provide sufficient proof that the infinite possibilities of the future do not include a resurgence of traditional transcendence. So it may well be the case that, in general, the West does not accept the idea of a theistic and transcendent God but the West is not the world and the world is not the West. Schillebeeckx's theory does not even apply perfectly to the West either because at least some of the Western churches are still traditional in all respects and especially with view to the definition of God.

As for Schillebeeckx, he cannot think outside the secularized West.[28] He takes for granted the influence of the West on human society in general but he also seems much too confident in the capacity of scientific progress to determine humanity to give up the idea of a transcendent metaphysical God. If this is the case in the West, it does not mean that the entire world will follow in its footsteps. The West itself is not entirely secularized but this does not matter to Schillebeeckx. What matters to him is the process of secularization which reportedly and inevitably leads to the transformation of the traditional concept of God from the traditional theism to the modern atheism.[29] Schillebeeckx at least does not see any other option. According to him, this movement from theism to atheism is absolutely necessary because the rational secularized world must change the traditional perspective on God who has oppressed humanity by promising it a better future beyond time and history.[30] For Schillebeeckx, this concept of God is tyrannical and leads to dehumanization. Therefore, today's secularized society must abandon traditionalism in favor of a new concept of God: a God that is no longer metaphysical and transcendent but physical and immanent, a God that is devised by the secularized mind of modern man and is meant to be relevant for his life. Schillebeeckx's theology is so radical that it does not have any room left for the traditional understanding of God; such a God is a dehumanizing force which must be replaced by the humanized power of the atheistic secularized God:[31]

---

28. Check also Kennedy, *A Modern Introduction to Theology*, 89 90.
29. Vergote, *Religion, Belief and Unbelief*, 15.
30. See also Rego, *Suffering and Salvation*, 233.
31. Bergin, *O Propheticum Lavacrum*, 212.

> The attempt to make a meaningful distinction between the "God of religion" whom the process of secularization has killed and the *living* God or the "God of faith" seems to me to be impossible, in a secularized world, unless it can be shown that our secular experience of existence itself contains elements which inwardly *refer* to an absolute mystery. If this were not so, even this *secularity* itself would collapse, or else it would have to be given at least a substructure of ideologies which would sacrifice the human person to a better future and thus result not in humanization but in dehumanization. It seems to me that in a secularized world fideism inevitably leads to the death of faith in the living God—in other words, to *atheism*, whatever the form this may take.[32]

It is clear then that for Schillebeeckx God is not the absolute reality. Any belief in God as the absolute reality will inevitably build an image of God which has only a few things—if any—in common with the reality of the world. In Schillebeeckx, the concept of God must be connected to the reality of everyday life in such a way that the human being can find meaning for his existence based on his life experience. Thus, Schillebeeckx's concept of God is conditioned by the idea of meaningfulness seen in human terms.[33] For him there is no such thing as meaningfulness in connection with the metaphysical reality of the traditional God; meaningfulness can be defined properly only from an exclusive anthropological perspective. Things are simple for Schillebeeckx: if secularized man does not find any meaning in the idea of a metaphysical and transcendent God, then his existence is not existentially satisfactory so the traditional understanding of God as metaphysical and transcendent must be abandoned.[34] Schillebeeckx's theory is almost unbelievably reductionistic because he makes the idea of meaningfulness utterly dependent on the reality of man's secularized experience of the world and of himself. This is why even the concept of God must be approached within these lines, namely in direct connection with how modern man understands the external reality of the world and the internal reality of his own being.[35] Thus, the concept of God is existentially trapped between secularized man's approach of surrounding reality and his inner experience:

32. Schillebeeckx, *God the Future of Man*, 71.
33. Lane, *The Experience of God*, 25.
34. Schillebeeckx extends his existential approach to the New Testament; see Viladesau, *The Beauty of the Cross*, 24.
35. See also Borgman, *Edward Schillebeeckx*, 96.

Re-Defining the Concept of God

As the absolute reality, God by definition eludes direct experience. Because of this, a humanly meaningful faith in God is only possible within a rational sphere of understanding if our human reality *itself* contains a real reference to God, which is therefore part of our experience. The facile assertion that it is precisely this datum which no longer appeals to modern man and no longer corresponds to his understanding of himself can, in my opinion, only be called a pseudo-scientific slogan which elevates, in a very uncritical manner, certain emphases which perhaps—or rather, manifestly!—catch the eye now onto the level of a *ne varietur* of man. Because man is a being whose essence is to exist by way of understanding and self-understanding, he can only speak meaningfully about God if this affirmation is inwardly connected with his understanding of himself, it is impossible to formulate any statement about God which does not at the same time say something meaningful about man himself, or any statement about man which does not say something meaningful about God. This means that as soon as the historicity of man's existential experience had been discovered in reflection, we realized that our language about God must grow and change with the development of our existential experience. If this did not happen, what we said about God would, viewed in the light of linguistic analysis, become irrelevant, meaningless and empty.[36]

It seems that in Schillebeeckx the idea of meaningfulness is defined by the concept of positivity.[37] If man perceives something as positive then it is meaningful; if not, that something is not meaningful. This is evidently applied to the concept of God. If Schillebeeckx does not approve of the idea of the traditional metaphysical God which he dismisses as oppressive and therefore negative, then it follows that the traditional idea of God as metaphysical and transcendent must be abandoned as lacking meaningfulness.[38] This means that every individual has the right to build his own image of God in accordance with what he feels or experiences as positive and meaningful for his life.[39] The immediate result of this theory is the proclamation of a frenzied "godology," in which everybody sees God as he pleases. If a certain individual feels that he should build a certain concept of God which is relevant for himself today, he will do so. However,

---

36. Schillebeeckx, *God the Future of Man*, 71–72.
37. McManus, *Unbroken Communion*, 164.
38. For details, see Fackre, *Christology in Context*, 174ff.
39. Boeve, "Experience according to Edward Schillebeeckx," 204.

what happens tomorrow? What if that same individual goes through a different experience which he also finds positive and meaningful or, on the contrary, negative and painful? He will have to change his concept of God again in order to adjust its meaningfulness or meaninglessness to his experience.

Schillebeeckx's reductionistic perspective on God is best seen in his connection between the existential meaningfulness of God and linguistic analysis.[40] According to Schillebeeckx, it is actually linguistic analysis which makes our discourse about God relevant.[41] This connection reduces from the very start any possibility to describe God in the ontologically transcendent terms of traditional theology. It is quite evident that traditional theology is not primarily preoccupied in offering a linguistically relevant perspective on God but rather an image of God which presents God within certain categories.[42] These categories—which are essentially transcendent and metaphysical, but also pneumatologically immanent and personal (because the ontologically transcendent and metaphysical God become, through the active work of the Holy Spirit in the believer, spiritually present within the physical reality of the believer's person)—may or may not be linguistically relevant but they definitely present God as he is understood to exist in his metaphysical reality which Schillebeeckx translates phenomenologically.[43] It is obvious that Schillebeeckx takes for granted the necessity of God's meaningful revelation of himself for the human being as well as his relevance for man's situation.[44] One could ask—quite rightly—at this point why is it absolutely necessary for the discourse on God to be relevant to man. Since when is relevance a must for man's perception of God? Traditional theology presents God exactly the other way around, in the sense that relevance should not be an issue when we approach the reality of God. God himself is God himself and nothing can change this reality. We learn from Scripture about the reality of God which is presented to us in certain terms. These terms may

---

40. See also Kerr, "The Reception," 257.

41. Abdul-Masih, *Edward Schillebeeckx and Hans Frei*, 87.

42. See also Viviano, *Trinity*, 76.

43. Especially with a view to the Eucharist; so he does not advocate the traditional metaphysical presence of Christ but the reality of his symbolic presence as Lord. See Fitzpatrick, *In Breaking of Bread*, 78–79.

44. For the origin of Schillebeeckx's preoccupation with relevance, see Krieg, "Karl Adam," 432ff.

or may not be linguistically relevant but they do present the reality of God's existence. Human perception in general and human perception of God in particular is highly subjective, so certain persons would find the language of Scripture relevant for their lives while others would be utterly displeased with the same presentation of God. This fundamental duality, however, which presents human perception as fundamentally non-objective does not change the objectivity of God's existence. The reality of man's perception is subjective because it is manifested within the reality of history—which in traditional theology is essentially sinful or opposed to God's purposes—while the reality of God's existence is objective because it exists within the meta-physical reality of meta-history. Therefore, there is absolutely no connection between the reality of God and the reality of man without God's revelation in Scripture.[45] Thus, there is no way in which the reality of God could ever be relevant to the reality of man. The reality of God and the reality of man are so categorically different as well as distant and separated that man simply cannot understand the reality of God, let alone find it relevant. God's revelation though does not seek to present God's reality as relevant but only as existent. Whether man finds this reality relevant or not is a totally different thing but revelation itself does not present God in relevant terms. The very core of traditional theology's soteriology—the death of Jesus for our sins—is utterly irrelevant and meaningless.[46] Why would God himself in human form decide to die for his creatures? There is no relevance or meaningfulness in such a decision. Why would he become incarnate in the first place in order to die for us? Again, nothing seems to be relevant in this. The Scripture explains that he become incarnate and died so that we could be liberated from our sinful existence but this explanation does not make God's action more relevant. It definitely explains God's action but it does not make it relevant. The Scripture tells us that God raised Jesus from the dead, confirming him as his Christ, who later ascended to heaven to make intercession for us. The same Jesus, who is the Christ, will eventually return to take his church with him into heaven. What is relevant in all this theology? Nothing at all is relevant here but this does not make the reality of God's action any less existent. The reality of God's existence has nothing to do with the so-called relevance of his work. According to traditional theology, man is

---

45. Details about Schillebeeckx's understanding of revelation can be found in Hilkert, "Revelation and Proclamation," 1.

46. Rego, *Suffering and Salvation*, 53.

not called to assess God's work in order to find it relevant or irrelevant; he is called to accept God's work in his life.

As for Schillebeeckx, he cannot accept the idea of God unless it is relevant for man's life.[47] This is why he presents it in terms which are relevant to man's mind; these terms, though, cannot be metaphysical and transcendent because metaphysics and transcendence are fundamentally irrelevant to the secularized mind of the modern man who can only accept and understand physical and immanent realities.[48] Schillebeeckx's problem is his overrated confidence in the present situation of modern man. He is convinced that, in comparison to the past, we are in a better by far position—if not the best—in terms of the development of our own humanity. Thus, the present is finally secularized and fundamentally based on science, technology, and reason. This situation allows us to see ourselves through our own eyes without any interference from the patronizing reality of a metaphysical and transcendent God. The discourse about God's metaphysical and transcendent existence belongs to the past, when such a theology was still relevant and meaningful to people.[49] For us, however, the categories of God's transcendence and metaphysics are totally irrelevant given our secular perspective on the world which teaches us that the only ontological reality is our own history. Thus, our history is the only relevant and meaningful reality which informs the secularized mind of the modern man. In other words, the key difference between the past and the present is progress—scientific, technological, industrial etc.—so it is progress which establishes the objectivity of the realities that supply man's need for relevance and meaningfulness.[50] For Schillebeeckx, progress makes modern secularized people say they do not understand the things of the past. This is why the secularized mind of the modern man will never accept the tenets of traditional theology; they simply do not match because of progress.[51] It has to be said here that Schillebeeckx's view of progress is much too optimistic and unrealistic. If we are to believe him, then the mere existence of progress leads automatically to

---

47. Kennedy, *Schillebeeckx*, 32.
48. See also Wiley, *Thinking of God*, 91–92.
49. Schillebeeckx, *God the Future of Man*, 72.
50. Newlands, "Christology," 107.
51. Borgman, *Edward Schillebeeckx*, 88.

Re-Defining the Concept of God

the rejection of traditional theology.[52] This is true of course in connection with the traditional theology of God as metaphysical and transcendent; thus, the fact that man has progressed in science and technology is by necessity a condition which makes modern man totally incapable of understanding metaphysical and meta-historical categories. Schillebeeckx's theory though is too narrow when he establishes an absolute relationship of necessary causality between the idea of scientific progress and the modern man's inability to believe in a metaphysical God.[53] Things, however, could be the other way around. What if a certain scientist, having studied various technological realities, reaches the conclusion—based on rational judgment—that it is entirely reasonable to believe in the possibility of a metaphysical and meta-historical realm which is ontologically real much the very same way our historical world is described as real? Then, the idea of an ontologically real, transcendent, and meta-historical God, so traditionally part of the past in Schillebeeckx's thought, would no longer appear beyond the reach of the modern man, secularized or not. To be sure, this idea would not be necessarily relevant or meaningful but it would be—and it is—rationally possible.

Schillebeeckx, though, prefers his narrow and reductionist understanding of reality which is based on the necessity of the connection between rationality on the one hand, and relevance and meaningfulness on the other.[54] A certain reality or concept cannot be accepted in Schillebeeckx unless it is at the same time rational, relevant, and meaningful.[55] This is a proof that Schillebeeckx'x theology is thoroughly existentialist, so the concepts which make up his theology have to be able to solve the problems of modern man's interior unrest. Schillebeeckx's solution is simplistic: modern man has existential issues and the only way for him to sort things out is to accept concepts which are rational, relevant, and meaningful.[56] At the same time, these concepts will have to be valid for his life in order to be accepted. To quote Schillebeeckx:

---

52. For more details about the radical theology's rejection of traditional values, see van den Brink, *Almighty God*, 1–6.

53. It seems that Schillebeeckx's dismissal of traditional theology is general is strongly related or even dependent on his rejection of the traditional Catholic theology of the Eucharist in particular. See also Watson, *The Breaking*, 157.

54. Boeve, "Theology," 21.

55. Kennedy, *Schillebeeckx*, 32.

56. Whalen, *The Authentic Doctrine*, xii.

> What we say about God, in preaching and teaching, still frequently makes use of categories derived from an existential experience which belongs to an earlier stage in man's development—when *that* kind of language about God was still meaningful and relevant—an impasse inevitably results, now that we are in a more developed stage of human experience and reflection: people no longer understand what we are taking about. If speaking of God really means that we are at the same time saying something meaningful about man, then talking about God in categories that belong to an earlier stage of man's experience simply cannot involve anything that is meaningful either about—or to—modern man. This kind of talk will appear to him to be completely irrelevant to his contemporary experience and even as contradicting his deepest existential desires. It is difficult to avoid giving the impression that being a believer involves accepting absurdities as true and maintaining an image of man and the world that cannot be regarded as valid in everyday life.[57]

Unfortunately, Schillebeeckx does not take his theory to the practical level of everyday life. He merely talks in philosophical categories which may sound rational and relevant, but which lack any reference to morality whatsoever.[58] This is a huge setback for Schillebeeckx because he obviously fails to integrate morality into his highly rational, secularized, and existential system.[59] For a better understanding of Schillebeeckx's failure to include moral elements in his definition of secularized theology, one may wish to consider the possibility presented by a modern man who considers leaving his wife. His marriage no longer meets his deeper existential desires, so he does not have second thoughts about his divorce. It he is existentially dissatisfied, then it is completely rational to leave his wife in order to recover the existential meaning of his life. Furthermore, it is entirely relevant for him to consider finding another woman with whom he may go on in life. He may or may not marry this new woman but everything depends on whether he will find it meaningful or not. This is just one example which practically shows that Schillebeeckx's rational and existential approach to theology makes morality very lax, if not entirely superfluous. Another example would be that of a woman—married

---

57. Schillebeeckx, *God the Future of Man*, 72–73.

58. See also Abdul-Masih, *Edward Schillebeeckx and Hans Frei*, 57.

59. For the importance of existentialism in Schillebeeckx's thought see also Haight, *Christian Community*, 4.

or not—who considers abortion. She may well find it inconvenient to continue the pregnancy because it may not be the right time for her, which would turn the pregnancy into a reality that does not make her life meaningful and relevant. So the only way to restore the relevance and meaningfulness to her life is to rid herself of her undesired pregnancy. The third and the last example is that of a male who feels sexually attracted to another male. He rationally thinks about it and realizes that unless he engages in a homosexual relationship with the other male, his life will be meaningless and irrelevant. This is why he will rationally decide to make his life existentially relevant and therefore engage in a homosexual relationship. These are all practical realities that prove Schillebeeckx's lack of concern for a moral dimension when it comes to establishing his radical theology. In other words, Schillebeeckx's rationality fuels a secularized existentialist theology which—at the very practical level of everyday life—loosens morality and legitimates adultery, abortion, and homosexuality. To make things clear: Schillebeeckx does not discuss or even mention the three above-mentioned practical examples; his theology, however, does allow for them as long as he dismisses traditional theology. As for traditional theology, things are clear: do not commit adultery, do not kill, and do not engage in homosexuality. It does not matter that these commandments sound irrelevant or even idiotic to the modern man's secularized mind and existentialist desires; from the standpoint of traditional theology, which is morally legitimized by the ontological reality of the metaphysically transcendent God, things are crystal clear. The traditional believer would even find them rational, relevant, and existentially meaningful for his own life.

For Schillebeeckx, theology can be exclusively historical—in the sense that it is definitely not meta-historical—so God is no longer to be sought outside our world but only in the world.[60] This prompts Schillebeeckx to express his adherence to natural theology but natural theology should not be understood as defined by traditional Christianity; it is only a secularized theology.[61] If in traditional Christianity natural theology is concerned to find natural, historical arguments for the meta-historical existence of God, in Schillebeeckx the idea of natural theology

---

60. Rego, *Suffering and Salvation*, 25.
61. Deporteer, "Orthopraxis," 176–77.

has to do with the legitimacy of the idea of God.[62] Whether the idea of God is legitimate or not is an issue which has to be investigated from the perspective of man's existential situation:[63]

> What must, in the first place, be sought is what the linguistic analysts call the "disclosure"—the existential situation in which what can be directly experienced empirically discloses and evokes something deeper than that which is immediately experienced, something that reveals precisely the deeper basis and condition of possibility of the secular event. What must be disclosed in the real basis of the "underground," existential trust in life that many people possess, not reflectively but nevertheless quite unmistakably, despite moments when absurdity forces itself on them—that fundamental trust that the future has meaning on the basis of the unspoken assumption that being man—the impossible—is nonetheless possible.[64]

We are therefore invited to find God in the world and not only in the world generally, but also in the world specifically, namely in the inner world of our existential situation.[65] Schillebeeckx seems to be aware that the world or the external reality of the world is not always existentially meaningful. The world itself as nature is not necessari to modern man's existential meaningfulness, so the idea of God—which has traditionally conferred meaning to humanity—should be sought in a different realm. In the same way that surrounding nature, no matter how beautiful, cannot provide us with existential meaningfulness, we will have to look within our own beings for an existential resurgence.[66] In other words, the idea of God has to be reconsidered in existentialist terms, which seem to be the only ones capable of instilling trust in the idea of God. Thus, Schillebeeckx admits—in a somewhat concealed way—that we need the idea of God but we have to legitimize it in order for it to be meaningful to us.[67] We cannot legitimize the idea of God by looking at the outer world because neither

---

62. Schillebeeckx, *God the Future of Man*, 73.
63. See also Borgman, *Edward Schillebeeckx*, 103.
64. Schillebeeckx, *God the Future of Man*, 73–74.
65. Boeve, "Thinking Sacramental Presence," 12–13.
66. Schillebeeckx's early theology sounds very traditional although the historical and existential element is still there due to his emphasis that we have to turn to the world and ourselves in order for us to understand religion. See, for details, Schillebeeckx, *Christ, the Sacrament of the Encounter with God*, 3–6.
67. See also Bergin, *O Propheticum Lavacrum*, 192–93.

Re-Defining the Concept of God

history nor nature can provide us with meaning for our lives. Quite the contrary, external life presents us with situations which seem rather absurd so life itself would appear absurd as well.[68] Therefore, in order not to reach the misfortunate conclusion that life is utterly meaningless having searched the external world, we have to make sure that we investigate the world of our deep existential feelings, which is actually the only possibility left for the legitimization of the idea of God. Now it becomes even clearer why Schillebeeckx searches for God—or the legitimacy of the idea of God—in our inner existential existence;[69] this is in fact the only realm which can be rationally investigated without external influences. In a way, Schillebeeckx seems to cut off the individual's existential world from the external world of history but this is only the case when it comes to finding the legitimacy of the idea of God. Schillebeeckx knows that we live in time and we have to influence history for the benefit of humanity but it is seemingly easier to legitimize God when the "investigation field" is reduced to our inner existence and its existential expectations.[70] For Schillebeeckx the idea of God is legitimate if we search it within ourselves but then we have to make it meaningful for the world.

GOD FOR THE WORLD

The fact that the idea of God is legitimate only if it is understood exclusively in human terms means that something which is found in the human being must explain the essence of God. As far as Schillebeeckx is concerned, the essence of humanity as well as of the idea of God as anchored in the reality of mankind is the idea of goodness.[71] Human life finds its accomplishment and meaning in the idea of God understood as man's decision to apply the idea of goodness practically for the benefit of humanity in general.[72] Thus, the concept of God becomes in Schillebeeckx some sort of ethics as commitment to the world because God is legitimate and meaningful for our lives only if we decide to choose the application of goodness in our lives for the improvement of the lives of others. The

---

68. Hilkert, *Naming Grace*, 35.

69. For further details about Schillebeeckx's existentialist credentials see Murnion, *The Catholic Priest*, 253.

70. See also Caputo, *More Radical Hermeneutics*, 224.

71. McManus, *Unbroken Communion*, 166.

72. Iraola, *True Confucians, Bold Christians*, 93.

association between the idea of God and man's decision to do good to his fellow human beings pictures God as a universal value of humanity which is encapsulated in the notion of goodness. God is relevant to us only when we decide to do good no matter what happens but we have to realize that this is a conscious option. Schillebeeckx is keenly aware of the reality of evil in the world but this reality is ultimately the application of an idea, namely evil. Thus, in order to counter both the idea and the reality of evil, man must willingly choose the idea of goodness as well as its practical enforcement in the world. God is meaningful for us only if he is understood in terms of the idea of good with its absolutely necessary application. It has to be said here that Schillebeeckx proposes a non-ontological God, which has no metaphysical existence. Schillebeeckx's God is a mere idea, which belongs to the historical reality of humanity and is essentially existential. Moreover, his teaching of God is evidently dualistic because man can choose between God, namely the idea of God and evil. The idea of God and the idea of evil are equally powerful at least in theory, and we take a decisive step towards God only when we choose to do good. Schillebeeckx even insists on the necessity of man choosing good in order not to let evil disseminate itself throughout the world.[73] This promotes an almost mechanical view of God because man is somehow forced into choosing God because his other option is embracing evil. Thus, lest he should engage in evil and suffer the consequences, man has to choose God and do good. For Schillebeeckx, this is to be a believer, namely to decide that evil cannot have the upper hand in the world, so we need to do something to stop evil.[74] The only thing we can do is to do good. These are Schillebeeckx's main ideas about the way he understands God:

> What must be investigated are the implications of the fact that there are people—whether believers or not—who have definitely opted for goodness and who therefore affirm that they regard human life as ultimately meaningful; people who, in spite of everything and above all in spite of man himself, refuse to be shaken in their conviction that it is not evil but goodness which has the last word. Is not this factual datum, which often presents itself before people have asked themselves the religious question, already a decision in favor of or against God; or rather, does it not ultimately justify the religious question and the objective urgency of this question,

---

73. Rego, *Suffering and Salvation*, 226.
74. Fackre, *Christology in Context*, 197.

because this trust cannot be justified when it is viewed only within the perspective of man himself taken as a whole?[75]

Schillebeeckx's position is far too optimistic because he postulates the idea of good as meaningful to humanity.[76] Then he connects it to the idea of God in order to support the practice of goodness and the rejection of evil. Schillebeeckx, however, is inconsistent with his own methodology. For instance, he rejects the traditional interpretation of God as metaphysical and meta-historical in favor of his radical view that God is an idea which helps humanity cope with its search for meaning.[77] The problem is that the idea of goodness is traditionally tied to the reality of God and while Schillebeeckx rejects the traditional interpretation of God he nevertheless keeps the idea of goodness as essential for his definition of God. Unfortunately for him, nothing in this world can legitimize his association between goodness and the idea of God. In traditional theology, this association between the reality of God and the idea of goodness is legitimate because goodness is seen as one of God's fundamental attributes as a metaphysical and meta-historical being with a clearly defined ontological status. Thus, due to the reality of God's existence, we know for a fact that goodness also exists in the world and beyond it or, if there is no trace of goodness left in the world because of sin, the idea as well as the existence of goodness is perfectly legitimate because God exists beyond the world as a metaphysical and meta-historical being. In Schillebeeckx though this is definitely not the case, because his God is historical and so is his idea of goodness.[78] The only option for Schillebeeckx to legitimize his idea of God—to which he mechanically attaches the idea of goodness—is to hook it to man's need to find meaning for his life. He assumes that every single human being is in search for meaning, so this particular search for meaning must be a universal human feeling. Therefore, if it is universal then it follows that it can be connected to the universality of God but this is again a traditional idea. At any rate, Schillebeeckx borrows the essence of his concept of God from traditional theology, at least with respect to God's goodness and universality, but he radically reinterprets it so that his God is no longer metaphysical and meta-historical, but historical and

---

75. Schillebeeckx, *God the Future of Man*, 74.
76. Depoorter, "Orthopraxis," 175.
77. Scirghi, *An Examination*, 129.
78. Kennedy, *Schillebeeckx*, 11.

existential. God is effective only if his existence is legitimized and the only way to legitimize the idea of God is, at least for Schillebeeckx, to connect the idea of God to man's conscious option for the application of goodness for the benefit of all people.[79]

Schillebeeckx's radical reinterpretation of the idea of God turns the traditional God of believers into his modern God of non-believers. If God is legitimate based on man's universal need for meaning, then it does not really matter whether those who seek a meaningful life are believers in God or not. It is actually unimportant to be a person who believes in God; what really counts is to be searching the meaning of your life which then legitimizes the idea of God.[80] In other words, unlike traditional theology where man's existence is totally dependent on God's reality, in Schillebeeckx the very existence of God is dependent on man's quest for meaning or even on his decision to choose the good. What happens if or rather when people choose not to do the good? Does God lose his legitimacy? Apparently not, because Schillebeeckx seems to have foreseen such critique. Nevertheless, the legitimacy of his God is saved by the traditional notion of universality which in his case is not applied to God but rather to man's universal humanity as well as his quest for meaning. Thus, the determinative factor for Schillebeeckx's doctrine of God is man. Every human being who exists in the world has his own life, so every single human being must have his own approach to life. As far as Schillebeeckx is concerned, people either manifest trust in life or they believe life is not worth living. For him, man's dichotomic approach to life is specific to humanity so it goes undisputed. Schillebeeckx sees man's relationship with his own life as a human reality which cannot be denied, so everything that is related to God needs to be understood in human terms. The traditional idea of salvation is no longer connected to the metaphysical and meta-historical approach to God, but to man's existence. Human existence itself or the very fact that man lives in the world is a reason to expect salvation. We should know for a fact that salvation does not come from above, or from an ontologically real, metaphysical, and meta-historical God, but it comes from within ourselves, from the world.[81]

---

79. Schillebeeckx, *The Eucharist*, 130.
80. Zuidberg, *God the Pastor*, 98.
81. Valkenberg, *Sharing Lights*, 145.

Re-Defining the Concept of God

When Schillebeeckx talks about humanity, he does not mean individual human beings but rather society in general, the idea of humanity which is based on the reality of individuals but which at the same time transcends individual existence. This is why the promise of salvation has nothing to do with a certain individual existence in particular; in light of humanity, one single existence cannot be fundamentally meaningful. Schillebeeckx does not mean that individual existences are not important; he wants to say though that the idea of salvation is relevant only if approached from the standpoint of humanity in general.[82] When we accept that life is meaningful as a reason to expect salvation from the perspective of humanity, then it means that we have already accepted the universal idea of love as embodied by the idea of God. We do not have to look for the proofs of God's existence; these proofs are utterly irrelevant because once we decide life is relevant as well as worth living for the benefit of humanity we have already accepted the idea of universal love.[83]

Schillebeeckx is convinced that we do not need proofs of God's existence. What we need is to search our inner self in order to find meaning for our lives. Once we do this, we may know for a fact that the idea of God has already been legitimized based on our own existential quest for meaning.[84] This quest for meaning though is not seen by Schillebeeckx as a subjective reality; on the contrary, the individual experience of man is an objective existential reality which confirms the equally objective physical and historical existence of the human being in the world. Thus, the idea of God as based on man's existential desire to find meaning for his life is not only legitimized by our decision to do good once we established that life has a meaning, but also proved objectively by man's experience in the reality of the world. We should not forget that in Schillebeeckx the man who searches for the meaning of his life is not exclusively an existential being; he is also a secularized person who trusts his own rationality.[85] Thus, he will understand that God does not exist as a person; in this particular sense, God is absent. Nevertheless, the personal absence of God due to his non-personal existence does not cause any trouble to the secularized mind of the modern person. The secular man does not need

---

82. Mulcahy, *The Cause of Our Salvation*, 18.
83. Hick, *The Metaphor of God Incarnate*, 22.
84. See also Stoker, *Is the Quest*, 31.
85. Peter McEnhill and Newlands, *Five Key Christian Thinkers*, 224.

a personal God; rather he needs a God which legitimizes his quest for meaning which is in turn a legitimizing action for the very idea of God in secular society.[86] Thus, modern man understands that God is absent because he is not personal; at the same time, having established the legitimacy of his existence in existential terms, God is present in our lives due to our continuous quest for meaning:

> Anyone who disregards this datum will be falling prey to an enormous historical naiveté. This manifest trust in life which many people have and the fact that others categorically deny it is a datum which I, as a believer, am bound to interpret in this sense: every man either accepts or denies that the fact of human existence is a *promise of salvation* which cannot be explained in the light of man's concrete being and he makes this decision before he explicitly asks himself the religious question. Thus faith in God's unconditional love, in God as man's future, has already been either accepted or refused. The so-called proof of the existence of God which is based on the experience of contingency is therefore only the reflective justification, made afterwards, of the conviction that this unconditional trust in the gift o a meaningful human future is not an illusion, not a projection of frustrated wishful thinking—the reality in which the God who is to come manifests himself and in a very intimate manner, as the one who is absent, but approaching nevertheless.[87]

To make things clear: in Schillebeeckx, God is the future of man but not in the traditional sense that the metaphysical and meta-historical God will eventually save humanity from its sinful existence with view to a new life with God. In Schillebeeckx's theology, God is the future of man in terms of man's temporal and terrestrial future.[88] The reality of the future is God and as the reality of the future is not available to the present, it means that God is absent for now but he will eventually come. We are believers if we trust this God, or our own future; we are believers if we trust that human existence and especially our future existence is relevant and meaningful.[89] This is why Schillebeeckx proposes what he calls the "natural knowledge of God,"[90] which is nothing but his proposi-

86. McManus, *Unbroken Communion*, 24.
87. Schillebeeckx, *God the Future of Man*, 74–75.
88. See also Schults, *Reforming the Doctrine of God*, 193.
89. Rego, *Suffering and Salvation*, 50.
90. Schillebeeckx, *God the Future of Man*, 75.

Re-Defining the Concept of God

tion that God should be approached exclusively in natural terms, or in terms which are intrinsically connected to our existential and historical existence. Thus, for Schillebeeckx, Christianity is no longer traditionally soteriological but existentially ethical. The essence of Christianity is no longer man's redemption from sin by a metaphysical and meta-historical God who hates man's sinful attitude, deeds, and nature, but wishes to restore his life to a new existence; in Schillebeeckx, Christianity is man's desire to understand himself and others as well as act accordingly. Once we understand ourselves and the meaningfulness of our lives, we realize that life is worth living with view to the improvement of life on earth. We know that there is no life beyond this life and there is no individual future beyond one's physical death; this is why we have to do whatever it costs to have this life improved and made worth living. Thus, we have to fight injustice and evil,[91] so Christianity is not only essentially ethical, but also incisively social and even actively political.[92]

Schillebeeckx's Christianity though radical still draws on the traditional notion of transcendence. It is not the transcendence of God but rather the transcendence of man.[93] Actually, Schillebeeckx defines transcendence as self-transcendence, which is man's "attitude of fundamental trust in reality" despite what he sees in everyday life. Man has to be open to God, namely he has to be open to reality because future reality itself is God, so man must be willing to rise above the disconcerting reality of the present in order to practise the good he has chosen.[94] Choosing the good and doing the good is for Schillebeeckx the life of faith and we all have to justify this particular life of faith by accepting the existential value of our own lives. Schillebeeckx uses some traditional terms at this point in order to illustrate his concepts; thus, we have to understand the "revelation of salvation in Christ." This revelation, however, should not be approached by faith as in traditional theology but rather by reason.[95] As God cannot be conceived in ontologically transcendent metaphysical and meta-historical terms any longer, what we have to do now is transcend ourselves, or step outside our inner existence, in an attempt to understand

---

91. Abdul-Masih, *Edward Schillebeeckx and Hans Frei*, 71.
92. Kennedy, *Schillebeeckx*, 111.
93. Schillebeeckx, *God is New Each Moment*, 110.
94. See also Borgman, *Edward Schillebeeckx*, 184.
95. Brown, *The Divine Trinity*, 67–68.

Critical Essays on Edward Schillebeeckx's Theology

rationally "the gratuitous revelation of salvation in Christ." We know that Christ is not the preexistent Logos of God who became incarnate, died, was raised and then ascended to heaven for our salvation from sin perceived as offense to God; Christ is the spiritual embodiment of the idea of Jesus's meaningful life and death. Thus, what Schillebeeckx says here is that we must understand—rationally of course—that our lives are meaningful just like Jesus's life was meaningful. The idea of Christ helps us comprehend the meaningfulness of Jesus's life and we have to accept it by rationally self-transcending ourselves. When we do this, our life is personally justified as a life of faith. All this is possible if we accept the fact that this radical reinterpretation of traditional theology by means of secularization has to be done in order for humanity to acquire a new sense of hope and meaning in our society based on Christ's example. This is why Schillebeeckx uses the phrase "Christian secularization" which is man's rational and radical reinterpretation of traditional Christianity in order to make man's existential desires meaningful both for himself and for society in general.[96] For Schillebeeckx, traditional Christianity is ideology and ideology is harmful because it deceives people as well as oppressing them.[97] Traditional Christianity reportedly gives man a false sense of hope by luring him into a faith which is essentially non-historical because the God of this faith is meta-historical. Man is deceived by being told that he should not expect good things on earth because this world is utterly sinful and needs to be redeemed sometime in future but this future is meta-historical as well. Modern man, though, knows for a fact that there is no such thing as meta-history, so nothing which is connected to the idea of meta-history—God, Jesus, salvation—is true. This is why these traditional meta-historical notions must be radically reinterpreted in order for them to lose their meta-historical content and present their essence in purely historical terms. A secularized person—or a "secularized Christian" if we are to accept Schillebeeckx's terminology—will therefore believe in a historical God, a historical Jesus and a historical salvation. History, however, needs to be approached from the perspective of man's inner search for meaning, so the historical God, the historical Jesus and the historical sal-

---

96. See also Haight, "The American Jesuit Theologian," 91–92.
97. Abdul-Masih, *Edward Schillebeeckx and Hans Frei*, 58.

Re-Defining the Concept of God

vation become the existential God, the existential Jesus—which is in fact Christ—and the existential salvation.[98]

For Schillebeeckx, this is the God we have to accept, a God which is existentially meaningful for humanity, a God that triggers man's desire to be committed to the world.[99] Thus, Schillebeeckx's historical and existential God is essentially an ethical God that promotes commitment to the world.[100] We have faith in God if we are willing to fight injustice and evil, so our faith is profoundly ethical.[101] Schillebeeckx is convinced that faith in God is faith in man and we have to do everything in our power in order not to lose our trust in man. Losing trust is man is losing trust in God, in our humanity and future. This is why the only chance left for us is to work for the improvement of life in the world with view to a promising future of "absolute Goodness." If we believe in our future, we believe in God—not of course not the traditional metaphysical and meta-historical God—but in man's capacity to make the world a better place. This inner conviction of man is constant throughout history which means that we are right to believe in and expect a bright future for humanity.[102] Schillebeeckx uses again traditional concepts which he reinterprets so that they fit his radical understanding of theology; thus, he writes that when we believe in our better future we actually believe in the resurrection.[103] It is clear that that resurrection should not be taken literally as the return of corpses to life but existentially as our belief in man's capacity to act in relevant and meaningful human terms.[104] If revelation is understood as a "truly *human* act," as suggested by Schillebeeckx, then it becomes truly meaningful for our present existence as well as humanity's future life.[105] Another traditional concept dramatically reinterpreted by Schillebeeckx is the kingdom of God.[106] The kingdom of God is actually the world of man since God must be reinterpreted in human terms and

---

98. Schillebeeckx, *God the Future of Man*, 76.
99. Bergin, *O Propheticum Lavracum*, 208.
100. Heyer, *Prophetic and Public*, 50.
101. Schillebeeckx, *God the Future of Man*, 76–77.
102. Rego, *Suffering and Salvation*, 176.
103. For details about Schillebeeckx's doctrine of the resurrection, see Prusak, "Bodily Resurrection," 64.
104. McManus, *Unbroken Communion*, 121.
105. Schillebeeckx, *God the Future of Man*, 77.
106. See also "From the Humanity of Christ," 252.

it is based on universally valid human values such as love, peace, and justice.[107] We all have to accept these values for ourselves first and foremost in order to make them relevant and meaningful for our own lives. Then, we have to apply them practically in the reality of everyday life for the benefit of all mankind. Schillebeeckx also reinterprets the idea of grace, which is no longer the benevolent attitude of the traditional metaphysical and meta-historical God to sinful humanity, but the possibility that the universal values of love, peace, and justice should be applied in the world.[108] We are Christian, Schillebeeckx thinks, if we believe that society can be changed for the better based on the application of love, peace, and justice. We cannot be sure what the future holds for humanity; the future is open to possibilities but nonetheless obscure because we do not know how it will eventually turn out. At this point, reason—understood as knowledge of present facts—loses its capacity to help us establish the kingdom of love, peace, and justice; nevertheless, reason does not lose its capacity to envisage the eschatological—namely future—possibility of a better humanity. Thus, in Schillebeeckx, the traditional idea of God's eschatological kingdom of God accepted by faith becomes man's future society based on love, peace, and justice accepted by reason.[109]

To be sure, Schillebeeckx's radical theology is fundamentally humanized and humanizing: God is human, faith is human, participation in God is human, hope is human, the future is human, and the presence of God is human. The idea of humanity and its—for Schillebeeckx—humanizing force perspires through all the pores of Schillebeeckx's theology from one end to another and carries with it the message that God is fundamentally human, existential, and ethical:

> Commitment to the world, experienced as *faith*, thus forms as essential part of the Christian faith in God. But—and this is the vitally important complement—it is in and through our *active* trust in faith that *God's gift* is realized in history. On the one hand, it is possible to say that the church, as the community of believers, ... *participates* in God's activity in this world through her active hope, ... "articulates" this activity of God, that is, gives it a *name*, as a testimony to the whole of the world, ... proclaims the unconscious hope of the world and ... must play a leading part in humanizing

---

107. Migliore, *Faith Seeking Understanding*, 351.
108. Pollefeyt, *Incredible Forgiveness*, 67.
109. Schillebeeckx, *God the Future of Man*, 78.

> the world, must be in the vanguard in caring for man. On the other hand, however, it must be stated that the church cannot carry out these functions and this mission if she does not also lead her *own* life, the distinctive life of the church which nourishes these functions; in other words, if she does not celebrate in gratitude that from which this world may live—the reality of Jesus Christ, the Lord, the absolute and gratuitous presence of the living God.[110]

The church Schillebeeckx mentions here is definitely not the traditional church that believes in the metaphysical and meta-historical reality of God who is spiritually and pneumatologically—but nevertheless truly—present in its members; Schillebeeckx's church is the sum of all those who choose to believe in the human reality as well as in the relevance and meaningfulness of the idea of God. This is the church which then chooses to become involved in the world by enforcing the rule of justice, peace, and love for the benefit of humanity, present and future.[111] This church is basically at least part of the world because there is no specific need to be a Christian—or a traditional Christian—in order for these values to be applied in society. Thus, Schillebeeckx blurs the boundaries of the traditional church by inserting it in the world. Such a church, which is not considered in traditional terms, will find it easier to believe in Schillebeeckx's humanized God.[112] Only this church, a human church which is actually the world, can be relevant to the world.[113] This is why only a human God, which is actually man himself, can be relevant to humanity.[114] Schillebeeckx is convinced that the idea of God is far from being perfect and it is also far from being cleansed of all historical misunderstandings. If we want to be responsible, we have to restore the idea of God and make it human because—for Schillebeeckx—this is the only way to make it relevant and meaningful for the world.[115] At the end of the day, Schillebeeckx's idea of God is just another way of saying that man has the natural capacity rationally to understand his life as relevant and meaningful as well as get involved in an ethical endeavor to transform the world and make it a better place in a future which is open to all good

110. Schillebeeckx, *God the Future of Man*, 78–79.
111. Doyle, *The Church Emerging from Vatican II*, 213.
112. Thompson, *The Sacraments*, 75.
113. Schillebeeckx, *God the Future of Man*, 79.
114. Häring, "From Divine to Human God," 3.
115. Schillebeeckx, *God the Future of Man*, 88.

possibilities. Thus, in Schillebeeckx, it is not only the church which has a human face given its identification with the world; God too has a human face and, even more than that, he is thoroughly human, a God created by man in the image of man.[116]

---

116. Schillebeeckx, *God is New Each Moment*, 73.

3

Re-Kindling the Natural Awareness of Man

THE TRADITIONAL DOCTRINE OF man in Christian theology is, according to Schillebeeckx, notoriously irrelevant to the people of today's society because man is seen as the creation of a God who has his own existence beyond the realm of humanity. In order to make Christianity relevant again, Schillebeeckx denounces the traditional interpretation of man's existence as connected to God in favor of a view which pushes man and his existence towards the sphere of humanity in general. Schillebeeckx is more than willing to keep the traditional language of Christian anthropology but he insists that man should not be understood in relationship with an existence which is beyond his own but rather in connection with his own existence; thus, man must be aware of his natural essence, and not so much of his divine origin. Schillebeeckx's solution is applied by means of the phrase "humble humanism" which defines Christian theology as firmly anchored in man's humanity (through the concept of humanism) as well as specifically different from other philosophies (through the idea of humility, which is specific to Christianity).

HUMBLE HUMANISM AND MAN'S FIGHT AGAINST SIN

Schillebeeckx is critical of traditional Christian theology which promotes the idea of man's creation out of nothing[1] as well as of his salvation from the nothingness of his sin, which is depicted as an affront to a God living outside the realm of mankind. Such theology causes serious damage to man's perception of himself because, as Schillebeeckx himself argues, it makes man totally unaware of his own self. Christian theology should be concerned with how man sees himself and it should nowadays

---

1. Kennedy, *Schillebeeckx*, 88.

trigger a renewed interested in man's existence.[2] In other words, Christianity should be preoccupied with humanism; nevertheless, Schillebeeckx does not advocate any sort of humanism but that type of humanism which is informed by the essence of Christianity which he identifies as humility.[3] Humility should not be understood as contempt towards one's own self or towards others but a preoccupation with those who are neglected by society.[4] Thus, humble humanism is basically the preoccupation with those who are oppressed by various factors within society.[5] Resuming the idea of humility, Schillebeeckx criticizes the fact that humility grew into a religious feeling in connection with the reality of God when it was, in fact, a social condition or the state of being poor.[6] Schillebeeckx is convinced that Jesus understood how humility should be understood—namely not as an inner religious condition but rather as a social state—because he reportedly preached the salvation of the poor.[7] In Schillebeeckx, the poor are those who suffer because of their state of poverty or those whom society rejects because they do not live up to the standards of the ruling class.[8] This is why he writes that Jesus's message of salvation was only for the poor, while the rich were not taken into account. Thus, salvation becomes a social idea which is meant to help the poor transcend their condition in order to have a better life. Humble humanism is therefore the essence of Jesus's salvific message which sought to help the poor be liberated from poverty in order to find a new meaning in life.[9] Schillebeeckx is aware that his theory needs to be supported by Scripture in order to stay within the limits of Christian theology, so he resorts to the Old and the New Testament for enlightening details:

> In the Old Testament, humble man was originally poor man, in the material, economic, and social sense. Humility and poverty were practically identical. The humble were the poor who were oppressed by the ruling class. There were two possible attitudes towards this social misery—it could be accepted in gentle resigna-

2. See also Borgman, *Edward Schillebeeckx*, 261.
3. Guerriere, *Phenomenology of the Truth proper to Religion*, 150.
4. Schillebeeckx, *World and Church*, 19.
5. Borgman, *Edward Schillebeeckx*, 87.
6. Check also Mize, *Joining the Revolution in Theology*, 220.
7. Rego, *Suffering and Salvation*, 267.
8. Schillebeeckx, *God is New Each Moment*, 104.
9. Yewangoe, *Theologia Crucis*, 304.

Re-Kindling the Natural Awareness of Man

tion or it could be opposed in bitter revolt. Resignation and gentleness came gradually to form the moral background to the concept of "social humility" ... It was in this way that the religious ideal of humility and poverty came about. God was experienced as the only way out in all cases of misery. To be poor or to be humble became a religious attitude—it was "good to be humiliated and poor." Humility was thus a *definite attitude towards* God. Finally, the concept of humility and poverty came, in the last books of the Old Testament, to be completely dissociated from its original social and economic context and humility, whether one was rich or poor, oppressed or not, was an inward religious attitude, the religious sense of one's own impotence and need of God's intervention, bestowing grace ... Christ brought the message of salvation to the poor and humble ... It was to those who felt a deep need for God and who confessed their own moral impotence that Christ brought the glad tidings. The rich—those who, in their self-satisfaction, had no need of God—were ignored.[10]

If Jesus was right—and Schillebeeckx seems to agree with him—then his message was not only religious but also social, economic, and even political in nature. It is clear that Schillebeeckx does not like the exclusively religious interpretation of humility, which he associates with traditional Christianity, because it promotes a low attitude towards humanity and towards man's natural capabilities.[11] Exclusive religious humility makes man unconfident in his own power, so this attitude must be avoided. Social, economic, and political humility is different because it does not describe an inner condition but an outer, external reality. Thus, it seems that in Schillebeeckx, if a certain man is convinced he is humble on the inside, then he will lose his self-esteem regardless whether he is socially poor or rich. On the other hand, when a man perceives himself as humble only on the outside, he can still retain his confidence in his own capabilities despite his precarious social situation. As far as Schillebeeckx is concerned, Jesus did not teach us to be humble on the inside in order to lose our self-confidence; on the contrary, he preached that we should be fully confident in ourselves despite our external humility, which can be virtually any kind of social, political or economical oppression.[12]

---

10. Schillebeeckx, *World and Church*, 20–21.

11. For details about religious humility in Schillebeeckx, see also McManus, *Unbroken Communion*, 57.

12. Hilkert and Schreiter, eds., *The Praxis*, 40.

It will quickly be evident while reading Schillebeeckx's argument concerning humble humanism that he tries to stay within the lines of traditional theological language as much as he can. Thus, he admits that early Christianity opposed Greek and Roman philosophy in general by insisting on the notion of humility, while pagan philosophies highlighted the idea of nobility.[13] Schillebeeckx though asserts that a synthesis is indeed possible between Christian humility and the idea of the nobility of the soul—which he does not seem to ascribe exclusively to pagan philosophies—in the sense that there cannot be "genuine humility without humane nobility of the soul."[14] This is why he criticizes what can be termed ignoble or even foolish humility, namely a humble attitude that denies any human value whatsoever, which seems to be promoting at the same time an exclusively divine approach to humanity. Schillebeeckx underlines the fact that true humility should never be a means to deny or to lower the values which a human being possesses. While trying to maintain an obvious connection with traditional theology and its divinely oriented approach, Schillebeeckx nonetheless subtly asserts his essentially human perspective on theology by observing that true humility should never minimize the importance of the things which man thinks in his heart are good.[15] The phrase "in his heart" is an affirmation of man's capacity to exert his own authority in matters pertaining to the establishment of his own values.[16] In other words, there is no authority outside a man that can tell him to value or scorn something. If man decides that a certain thing is good for him, then that particular thing possesses value in itself and is good for man. If man is his own final authority in judging what is valuable and what is not, then it means that man has an inner greatness of his own which must be acknowledged as such.[17] It should be stressed again at this point that Schillebeeckx makes a considerable effort to continue his argument within the lines of traditional theology and especially of traditional theological language because he insists that the greatness of man should be approached from the perspective of what traditional theology calls the doctrine of creation. In traditional theology, man was created in

13. Rego, *Suffering and Salvation*, 269.
14. Schillebeeckx, *World and Church*, 22.
15. McManus, *Unbroken Communion*, 166.
16. Cote, *Re-Visioning Mission*, 83.
17. For details about Schillebeeckx's view of authority, see Newlands, *Christ and Human Rights*, 103.

Re-Kindling the Natural Awareness of Man

history by a God who exists outside history but who actively gets involved in history. Thus, for Schillebeeckx, man's divine dimension should never be denied because his specific human values are to be complemented by his divine values. This means that while admitting he is a created human being, man himself should be constantly aware that his value is given not only by his inherent qualities but also by realities which lie beyond his own being. This is why man should always look inside and outside himself, at God, in order to find his true sense of humility. In this particular context, humility means self-awareness given by self-knowledge as well as the knowledge of his outer reality.[18] Man must be aware of his own valuable features which are precious because he is a creature:

> Humility is not a diminution or denial of human values, pusillanimity or smallness of soul, or a compulsive denigration as evil of something which man regards, in his heart, as nonetheless inwardly valuable and precious to him. True humility presupposes a loyal acceptance of human greatness, but it regards this precisely as a *creaturely* value. Humility does not consist of a denial but of a *confrontation* between divine and human values, in which the humanly beautiful and civilized is accepted as God's gift. Humility includes experience and awareness of self, but awareness of ourselves as God's gift. The sensitive point of humility is to be found in the delicate attitude of the humanist who, while being aware of his own value, keeps his gaze fixed on God. Humility is man's sense of being a creature, the *religious respect* which man has when he accepts something that is naturally valuable. Awareness of being a creature is thus the basis of humble humanism.[19]

Schillebeeckx's text looks fairly traditional but it has to be re-interpreted in light of his doctrine of God. In his theology, God is not the ontologically real Trinity that is confessed by traditional theology. For Schillebeeckx, God is not a person and it does not have an existence outside the world and humanity. God is our own future,[20] so God is humanity.[21] God is only a projection of humanity which helps human beings rise above their condition. It is within this specific interpretation of God that we should understand Schillebeeckx's theological anthropology.

---

18. See also Martin, *The Feminist Question*, 81.
19. Schillebeeckx, *World and Church*, 23.
20. Hilkert and Schreiter, eds., *The Praxis*, 56.
21. Schillebeeckx, *God the Future of Man*, 180–81.

In traditional theology, man is created by a God who exists beyond humanity and history, and it is this God that gives man his inner value. Thus, for the traditional theologian, man has value but only in the sense that it was given to him by God. Schillebeeckx tries to "redeem" traditional theology in keeping its language while reinterpreting its content. This is why he writes that we must see ourselves as creatures or as beings who have creaturely value.[22] This, however, does not mean that man is created in history by a God who exists beyond it. Man has always been part of history and will stay for ever like that; what he needs to know, however, is the fact that he is a creature, a creature that should constantly perceive itself as having inner value. This inner value is to be regarded as the gift of God, namely as something which is valid, good, and useful even beyond the physical reality of the human being. What Schillebeeckx attempts to do here is to establish the universal value of humanity which not only resides in every human being but also in humanity as a whole.[23] Man is a creature not because it was physically created by a God who is superior to him; man is a creature because he has values which are universally precious as well as valid for the entire human race. Schillebeeckx also talks about the traditional doctrine of creation and the idea that God has a plan with his creation.[24] This, however, should not be understood in traditional terms but in the sense that man has a religious component which is universally present in humanity in general. In other words, the fact that the idea of the world's as well as man's creation has been part of humanity's cultural legacy does not actually mean that the world and man were created by God; it only means that man is a religious being whose values transcend his own physical body. This religious sense which teaches man that his inner value does not reside in his physical body but also in the greatness of humanity in general makes man conscious of his own capabilities as well as responsible in his relationship with the world. In other words, man's religious feeling is not an indication of the actual existence of God but a spiritual reality which makes man conscious of himself and his role in society.[25] Here is how Schillebeeckx presents his theory of man's religious dimension:

22. Borgman, *Edward Schillebeeckx*, 226.
23. Valkenberg, *Sharing Lights*, 146.
24. Cf. also Yaghjian, "Flannery O'Connor's Use of Symbol," 268ff.
25. McDermott, *Word Become Flesh*, 274.

Re-Kindling the Natural Awareness of Man

> Christianity is the vehicle of this central saving dogma of God's good creative power which conceived in love a beautiful plan of the world, which numbers the sun, the moon and the stars, creates the history of the world and buttresses and creatively supports man's ascent in civilization towards community-building love in justice. Simply from the point of view of the creation, the Christian humanist is conscious, in deep humility, of the religious dimension in depth of his humanism. Trust in himself . . . , the tense spring of Hellenic humanism, is introduced by the Christian humanist into the reverent and dedicated atmosphere of his sense of God and of being a creature . . . reliance on himself, but on himself as God's gift . . . The Christian humanist thus accomplishes his task in society in humility and in humble awareness of himself.[26]

It is truly surprising how many times Schillebeeckx uses the word Christian to build his argument if we consider his overall thought which promotes the humanization of theology and especially of the doctrine of God.[27] It is as if Christianity had some sort of superior standing as compared to other religions. To make things clear, this is definitely not the case in Schillebeeckx. Christianity may appear to be superior but in fact it is more than willing to borrow ideas from other religions and philosophies.[28] Thus, the idea of trust in oneself was appropriated by Christianity from Greek philosophy as if the traditional theology of man's creation by God did not support man's confidence in himself. It is true that in traditional theology man's confidence in himself is informed by his confidence in the God who created and saved him, but this seems to be too much for Schillebeeckx. Man does not need God to be confident in himself; he only needs himself and the awareness of himself to have such a confidence in his own being. This confidence is enriched by man's religious feeling which is proved by the idea of creation but this is not exclusively Christian. Thus, the humble humanism promoted by Schillebeeckx is categorically not confined to Christianity alone. Humble humanism or man's awareness of himself and of his universal value is religious but not exclusively Christian. The universal value of man transcends both Christianity and any other religious or philosophical system. The idea of creation which helps man understand his inner as well as his universal

---

26. Schillebeeckx, *World and Church*, 24.
27. See Borgman, *Edward Schillebeeckx*, 13.
28. Viviano, *Trinity, Kingdom, Church*, 84.

value does not individualize either Christianity or non-Christian systems of thought as having preeminence in fostering the right perspective on man.[29] To be sure, Schillebeeckx does not discriminate when discussing the idea of creation; Christianity and non-Christian religions/philosophies are the same because they all have to understand that man has a universal value which needs to be understood from the standpoint of the idea of creation perceived as anthropology.[30] In other words, everybody—Christian or non-Christian—must realize man's value as universal because it transcends every individual human being as well as every religious and philosophical conviction.

In addition to the traditional idea of creation, Schillebeeckx uses the equally traditional tenet of participation in God with a view to God's glory.[31] Again, it is not the God of traditional theology that Schillebeeckx has in mind here but the God of modern man, the God made in the image of modern man's present expectations and thinking. This God is our own future as well as our own humanity; this God is us or our universal value which runs throughout history and helps us move forward. We participate in this God, which means that we participate in our universal value as human beings and it is for the glory of this God, i.e., the glory of humanity, that we are challenged to participate in this particular God. What is the glory of humanity? Schillebeeckx does not use this phrase as he continues to talk about the glory of God; nevertheless, if God is our future and ourselves, then it is pretty clear that the glory he points to is our own glory.[32] The glory of man is nothing but man's progress which should be the goal of every human being as well as of humanity in general. We participate in God, namely in our own universal value and we have to work for the glory of God, or for the glory of our universal value, which is clearly seen in progress. God inspires us to progress, which means that our universal value prompts us to press forward in order to change society through progress.[33] Once again, Schillebeeckx has to be given credit for his effort to explain these ideas using the language of traditional Christian theology:

29. Abdul-Masih, *Edward Schillebeeckx and Hans Frei*, 70.
30. Borgman, *Edward Schillebeeckx*, 261.
31. Schillebeeckx, *Christ, the Sacrament of the Encounter with God*, 180.
32. Valkenberg, *Sharing Lights*, 145.
33. Lefebvre, *Open Letter*, 115.

> The idea of creation is thus the basis both of the humility of the humanist and of the humanism of the humble Christian. Humanism must be humble, religious, in order to be fully itself. Humility acts as the norm for Christian humanism, because it leads and directs this humanism, as a human participation in God, towards God's glory, which must radiate from this humanism. The Christian knows and the philosopher must realize, that God, the loving creator who distributes values, is inwardly concerned with human progress, of which he, the creator, is the great inspirer and promoter and in which we, the creatures, are the humble collaborators.[34]

Schillebeeckx may well speak of God to prove his point but we have to understand that God is only a pretext for as well as a means to underline man's universal greatness. Humility is part of the larger picture because it counterbalances greatness. The humility of man is nothing without his greatness and it is equally true for Schillebeeckx that man's greatness is nothing without humility. In other words, man must realize his universal value while at the same time being fully aware of his constitutive limitations. Humility in this context is nothing more than self-awareness or the awareness of man's natural essence. Man cannot and should not act as if he were unnatural; the full realization of his natural constitution is critical for Schillebeeckx's concept of humility. Thus, humble humanism is man's understanding of his human condition as part of natural reality. When man finally realizes he is in the world and of the world, he also develops a sense of responsibility towards himself and the world. This sense of responsibility acquires a concrete manifestation in man's desire to achieve progress.[35] This is why Schillebeeckx's discourse about humble humanism is not only a way to dig out man's religious feeling but also a plea for human progress in all areas of human activity.[36] As far as man's progress is concerned, this needs to be developed based on man's conviction that he is created, namely on his religious feeling which makes him aware of both his natural constitution and his universal value. Therefore, in Schillebeeckx, the idea of progress is religiously informed in the sense that man's move towards progress must be done in full awareness of his universal greatness and humility, which is just another way of saying

---

34. Schillebeeckx, *World and Church*, 24.
35. McManus, *Unbroken Communion*, 164.
36. Kennedy, *Schillebeeckx*, 89.

that progress must be achieved responsibly.[37] Man must always be fully conscious that he is a creature; not a creature of a superior God but a being who is aware of his inner value as well as his universal importance. In Schillebeeckx, progress has nothing to do with the traditional understanding of God and it definitely does not help man understand his own being from the perspective of an ontologically real God. It is actually the other way around. Progress is for man and is meant to help man build a community which is based on man's universal values of love, justice, and morality.[38] These universal human values were not instilled in man by a superior God; they are inherent to human individuals as well as humanity in general. Schillebeeckx knows very well that human beings also have a bunch of notorious shortcomings but the idea of humble humanism is there to counter them. Despite his natural flaws, man must be aware that the way to responsible progress is the only possibility of changing the world for the better, and this cannot be done without what Schillebeeckx calls humble humanism: a responsible awareness, in humility, of his natural constitution and universal greatness for the benefit of the entire human race.[39] To quote Schillebeeckx:

> This humility does not paralyze the courageous action of the Christian humanist whose aim is to build up a technical, economic, socio-political and artistic world order in which justice and vital moral and religious action is promoted. It simply covers all this activity with ardent reciprocal love for and gratitude to the creator of so much that is beautiful. The Old Testament hymn of the religious people of nature, "Praise the Lord, all you works of the Lord . . . praise the Lord, you sun, moon, and stars," is sung endlessly by the Christian humanist, who completes it, making it a mighty "Praise the Lord, you art, science, and culture . . . praise the Lord, you just and community-building love!"[40]

Schillebeeckx's "technologized" version of the old Biblical hymn may seem hilarious at first glance and thus escape theological criticism, but it is in fact a very serious deconstruction of traditional theology. This is clear when one notices that the "works of the Lord" are actually the "sun, moon, and stars," namely things which are way beyond man's own capac-

---

37. Schillebeeckx, *Christ, the Sacrament of the Encounter with God*, 202.
38. MacNamara, "The Distinctiveness," 159.
39. Hennelly, *Theology for a Liberating Church*, 51.
40. Schillebeeckx, *World and Church*, 24.

Re-Kindling the Natural Awareness of Man

ity of creation. In traditional theology, the entire universe—including the sun, moon, and stars—were created by God, seen as an eternal being that exists in himself and is capable of creating entities out of nothing. This is why the Biblical hymn is recognition of God's capacity to create things which lie beyond human possibilities. Schillebeeckx turns this traditional argument upside down by turning the Biblical hymn into a pretext which praises man's achievements. Schillebeeckx's Lord is not the God of traditional theology, the one who created the universe out of nothing or the one who created things beyond man's natural capacity, but man himself who creates things out of other things or things that lie within his natural endowment: art, science, and culture.[41] Likewise, in traditional theology, the works of the Lord—namely the sun, moon, and stars—are meant to confirm his capacity to create incredible things as a confirmation of his omnipotence for his own sake. In Schillebeeckx, the Lord is man, so man is his own God, because he creates things which are meant to confirm his natural capabilities for the benefit of the human race in general. Thus, exactly as the Lord works for himself in traditional theology, the same way man works for himself in Schillebeeckx's theology.

The social orientation of Schillebeeckx's humble humanism is confirmed by his social interpretation of the traditional doctrine of sin.[42] Thus, sin is no longer perceived as man's rebellion against an ontologically real God in thought, deed, and even in his own nature but as a reality which destroys the harmony of society. This is why sin is associated with death and suffering as the main "sinful" aspects of human society in general. Schillebeeckx does not understand sin as evil in opposition to God who punishes it but rather as tragic in relationship with humanity that suffers from it. The presence of sin—namely suffering and death—in the world of men is pervading and all-encompassing; there is no place in this world where sin is not present.[43] Suffering and death infiltrate all the spheres of human life, so there is no escape from them. The duty of man is to fight sin, understood as suffering and death, in order to transform society in a better place for mankind.[44] Schillebeeckx's perspective on sin is again a deconstruction of traditional theology. Whereas in traditional

41. Fackre, *The Christian Story*, vol. 2, 234.
42. Borgman, *Edward Schillebeeckx*, 60.
43. Johnson, "The Word Was Made Flesh," 159–60.
44. For details about suffering and how it can be overcome in Schillebeeckx, see McManus, "Suffering and Salvation," 230.

Christianity sin is essentially moral because it is directed against God, in Schillebeeckx sin is fundamentally social as it disrupts the welfare of society. If the essence of the development of society is Schillebeeckx's humble humanism then sin appears to be the opposing factor which destroys society by hindering it from progress. Thus, sin is counter-humanism, sin is against man because it prevents him from developing into what he can be.[45] As the essence of humble humanism is universal love, sin is the absence of universal love because it destroys it. Sin, understood as suffering and death, puts an end to the development of individual human beings and definitely hinders humanity from fully accomplishing its natural capabilities. When confronted with sin, or suffering and death, human society as characterized by humble humanism and freedom finds itself in a difficult position, and Schillebeeckx is fully aware of this. The progress of society, which is anchored in human freedom, can be endangered by the tragic reality of death that marks the terminal point of every individual human being.[46] Thus, social progress is hindered with the death of every individual human being that does not have the chance to accomplish and develop its natural possibilities.[47] In short, this is how Schillebeeckx depicts sin:

> The history of man and our own experience of life does, after all, teach us that this social task, directed towards the ultimate ideal of a moral and religious community of persons, is always threatening to fail and does in fact partly fail again and again. Sin flourishes in the heart of every human being. Human society "lives in a state of mortal sin." The "prince of this world" who gains support through *uncontrolled* human passion brings about, in addition to this humble humanism, an anti-humanist power. Just as creation develops towards a community-building love as a distinctively human glorification of God, so too does the power of evil grow at the same time. Sin is like a malignant growth which is constantly trying to break down *charis*, gratuitous love ... The ideal of creation peculiar to humble humanism implies a hard struggle against sin and its consequences ... Humble humanism has to take the reality

---

45. Therefore, man must liberate himself from sin and this is what Schillebeeckx understands by redemption. See, for details, Moniz, "Liberated Society," 279.
46. La Due, *The Trinity Guide*, 7.
47. Fuller and Westberg, *Preaching the Lectionary*, 580.

of sin into account. Human freedom, the sovereign gift of creation, is also the center from which humanism is threatened to death.[48]

It should perhaps be mentioned here that Schillebeeckx's predominantly social perspective on sin understood as suffering and death as well as opposed to humble humanism is an excessively optimistic view of humanity.[49] His confidence in man's capacity to exercise freedom is quite unrealistic. It is obvious that his model for ideal society is the technologized, urbanized, and industrialized West, which is free of political oppression. Moreover, Schillebeeckx seems to be under the impression that the lack of political oppression—which does not presuppose the lack of economic oppression or of other types of oppression[50]—allows men and women to live in freedom, which means that they are free to conceive and implement their own decisions. These decisions, however, do not necessarily have to be essentially free if their society is free of political oppression. Economic hardship can be present in a politically free country so man's decisions are still influenced by external factors which make them un-free. In other words, if sin is understood exclusively as suffering and death, the human freedom that Schillebeeckx describes as the core of the society built on the principle of humble humanism is not only threatened by death, it is actually annulled by death.[51]

Schillebeeckx's understanding of sin and humanity in general is too optimistic also because he believes in the eradication of sin.[52] Man has a duty to fight sin, which means that he must fight against anti-humanism. As humanism is informed by the idea of God, anti-humanism is the lack of the idea of God, and such a philosophy is detrimental to humanity. To be sure, Schillebeeckx does not mean the ontologically real God of traditional Christian theology; it is more than clear by now that his God is actually the future of humanity, so God is humanity expecting to perfect itself in the future. Humanism is belief in the possibility that humanity can reach perfection, in the sense of building a society where life is meaningful. Anti-humanism is the opposite view, namely the

---

48. Schillebeeckx, *World and Church*, 25.
49. Rego, *Suffering and Salvation*, 43.
50. Abdul-Masih, *Edward Schillebeeckx and Hans Frei*, 3.
51. For details about Schillebeeckx's perspective on death, see Borgman, *Edward Schillebeeckx*, 179.
52. Mueller, *What are They Saying?*, 60.

conviction that there is no bright future for humanity because oppression in its different forms will be forever present in the world. Despite this, Schillebeeckx is convinced that evil can be fought and even eliminated if every person who embraces the idea of humble humanism confesses his own sin, namely acknowledges his human condition as well as the general situation of human society.[53] Schillebeeckx is so concerned with his social definition of sin that he believes in the possibility of eradicating the "naturally moral aristocracy," probably a hint to traditional Christians who believe in the superiority of their trust in an ontologically real God. The traditional belief in God is highly exclusivistic as well as morally strict because sin itself is seen in moral terms, so it is clear that it is opposed to Schillebeeckx's social perception of sin. Thus, there is no moral aristocracy for Schillebeeckx[54]; there is only an "aristocracy of grace," namely the community of those who understand humble humanism and fight for the social progress of human society. Schillebeeckx's idea of the "aristocracy of grace" seems a bit too Gnostic in nature but it does help him in his attempt to present his vision of humanistic society informed by the knowledge of the self as well as of humanity in general. It is evident that Schillebeeckx is thoroughly existentialist here because humble humanism re-kindles man's natural awareness which makes him cope with himself and others in order to find his place a society which is marred by the constant presence of sin, namely suffering and death.[55] Once man knows himself by means of humble humanism, then he is ready and able to contribute to the building of a society which can stand against suffering and death.[56] Schillebeeckx reinterprets the traditional doctrine of original sin—which says that sin is perpetuated from parents to offspring by means of man's inner nature so that sin is permanently present in individuals as well as in society—in the sense that he only retains the idea of sin's constant presence in society.[57] For Schillebeeckx, sin is not moral and is not transmitted; it is only present permanently, and for this reason it must be fought against constantly:

53. Yewangoe, *Theologia Crucis in Asia*, 323.

54. Moral aristocracy can refer to priestly or clerical aristocracy, see Portier, *Tradition and Incarnation*, 327.

55. Borgman, *Edward Schillebeeckx*, 267.

56. Depoortere, *A Different God*, 119.

57. See also Haight, *The Future of Christology*, 67.

Re-Kindling the Natural Awareness of Man

> It is certain that, in the kingdom of good and the kingdom of evil, heaven and hell already have their beginning here on earth—the sense of God and humanism, the loss of God and anti-humanism. *Man* is the commencement of those warring powers. The first task of any genuine humanism, in which full justice is done to all that is distinctively human, is therefore the struggle against sin—evil—through which the great anti-humanist power has to be eliminated. The humanist himself has first of all to strike his breast in penance and confess his guilt. If he is a sober realist, he will not believe in a naturally moral aristocracy ... The humble humanist confesses that there is in fact only an aristocracy of grace which illuminates the feeble conscience and gives it strength. Contemporary existentialist writers have made the fallacious idea of the naturally moral hero go up in smoke and have depicted man's tendency towards sin, the "fatality" of *free* sin, in colours which inevitably remind the Christian of the dogma of original sin.[58]

The language of traditional theology is a prop for Schillebeeckx in his attempt to connect humanism to a reality which is higher than us. If sin, suffering, and death, is in us then is it possible to fight it effectively? If sin is in us, and it seems that it is there to stay, then sin is indeed us and we are sin. To make things clear: Schillebeeckx does not say that we are sin, he only says that we are sinful, but if suffering and death are so deeply connected to our human lives, it follows that the identification between sin and humanity is almost total.[59] Schillebeeckx is aware that there is no reasonable way to explain man's fight against such a catastrophic sin apart from a reality which is higher than man himself. This is why he mentions God as man's last resort in his fight against sin. There is a problem, however, because in Schillebeeckx God is humanity and its future; therefore, invoking God in man's fight against sin is nothing but man's self-invocation and if man asks himself to fight against himself, the probability of success appears to be very low. What seems to be the case here is the fact that Schillebeeckx resorts to the idea of God not as a means to return to the traditional concept of God but only to retain the higher status of the traditional God. In other words, God is not the ontologically real God of traditional theology; God is a stylistic device meant to highlight man's universal value in face of adversity, sin, suffering, and death.[60] This is to

---

58. Schillebeeckx, *World and Church*, 26.
59. Schillebeeckx, *Christ, the Sacrament of the Encounter with God*, 27.
60. Borgman, *Edward Schillebeeckx*, 268–69.

say that in order to fight suffering and death, man must indeed look at himself for a better awareness of his natural constitution but he must also look above, or beyond himself, to the universal values of mankind which would hopefully assist him in fighting suffering and death with a higher degree of success.[61] In Schillebeeckx's words:

> Is it not true that sin is the greatest danger with which humanism is threatened, because it crushes its very heart—its humility and sense of being a creature—and deprives the social task of humanism of its moral and religious dimension and therefore makes humanism recede in an ebb . . . instead of rising in a tide? It is not also true that sin is the great possibility for every human being who is caught up in the great catastrophe of sin and who contributes himself to its ever-increasing power? In view of this situation, the humanist is bound to ask God, in all humility, for the help of his healing grace if he sincerely wishes to achieve his legitimate social task on earth. It is only in humbly receiving God's grace that humanism can ever be itself and be humanism in the fullest sense. Humanism that is left entirely to itself can only be a destructive obstacle to the ultimate success of this social task.[62]

Humanism is not complete if it only takes an inner perspective on humanity; in order for it to find its effective completion, humanism must seek an outer perspective which—according to Schillebeeckx—would be able to support him in his fight against sin. Thus, full knowledge of man's internal constitution accompanied by an encompassing and comprehensive knowledge of humanity in general could stand a chance of winning in man's constant fight against suffering and death.[63]

HUMBLE HUMANISM AND MAN'S SALVATION

The goal of humanism is the utmost benefit of humanity and it is now that Schillebeeckx chooses to discuss the issue of man's salvation.[64] Schillebeeckx's way of explaining what salvation is and what it entails is based once again on a very traditional theological language which needs to be translated in terms of his general theology. In order to explain what salvation is, Schillebeeckx picks his words in a very personalized

---

61. See Hilkert and Schreiter, eds., *The Praxis*, 11.
62. Schillebeeckx, *World and Church*, 26.
63. Depoortere, *A Different God*, 103.
64. Borgman, *Edward Schillebeeckx*, 208.

Re-Kindling the Natural Awareness of Man

and even personal manner which presents God as having the initiative in creating man out of his love. Thus, God's purpose in creating man was the deification of man.[65] This all sounds like traditional theology but even while speaking in traditional terms which resemble the language of classical Christianity, Schillebeeckx already begins to deconstruct it. To give just one example: unlike traditional theology which professes a huge gap between creation and salvation which is given by the reality of sin, Schillebeeckx links creation and salvation by means of God's love which is manifested to humanity from the beginning to the end, namely in a permanent and universal way. We already know that in Schillebeeckx God is not a meta-historical being with an ontological status but is only a symbol[66] for the universality of humanity, especially from the perspective of man's hopefully bright future. So God could not have created man as in traditional theology; the motive of creation is used here to draw attention to man's perennial values which transcend time and history as if they had been given to man by a superior being that encapsulates all these values.[67] Schillebeeckx explains that salvation does not correct creation, which is true even in traditional theology. Nevertheless, unlike traditional theology which explains why man needs salvation in spite of his perfect creation by God—and the concept of sin as offense to God is crucial at this point—Schillebeeckx leaves aside the idea of sin and insists on God's saving love.[68] By placing creation and salvation at the same level through God's love while eliminating the role of sin—which separates creation from salvation in traditional theology—Schillebeeckx conveys the idea that God's love is has nothing to do with the reality of sin. God's love seems to be some sort of a value which is at man's disposal to be used for the benefit of humanity. This seems to be true when Schillebeeckx equates creation with humble humanism, which implies that man is "created" when he understands the essence of humble humanism, namely universal love based on his natural self-awareness with view to his higher purpose of transforming society for the better.[69] Then, through the idea of humble humanism Schillebeeckx ties creation to man's duty to get involved in

---

65. Schillebeeckx, *Christ, the Sacrament of the Encounter with God*, 41.

66. This also applies to sacraments in Schillebeeckx, see Seidler, "Contested Accommodation," 864.

67. Fennell, *God's Intention for Man*, 12.

68. Borgman, *Edward Schillebeeckx*, 175.

69. Abdul-Masih, *Edward Schillebeeckx and Hans Frei*, 69–70.

changing society, which is depicted as a saving endeavor. In other words, man is "created" during his own life when he understands the essence of humble humanism and then he is "saved" when he applies the essence of humble humanism, namely universal love, in order to change society.[70]

It is quite clear then that, in Schillebeeckx, both creation and salvation are acts of man, so his references to God as the author of creation and salvation are nothing but an attempt to confer a universally binding validity to man's inherent qualities. According to this theory, man can be saved in many different ways if he applies universal love to his fellow human beings in order to transform society into a better realm for men and women. Thus, salvation comes through art, technology, economy, and even politics if these crucial human activities are performed in the spirit of universal love for the benefit of humanity; man is saved when he is complete as a social being.[71] Moreover, man is saved, namely he rises above himself and his natural condition—in fact, he rises above his own sin as well as the sin of society, meaning the pervasive and tragic reality of suffering and death—whenever he chooses to act in such a way that he implements the core of humble humanism. For Schillebeeckx, salvation is supernatural in the sense that acting in the spirit of love in order to improve one's life places man in a better condition compared to the natural reality of suffering and death. Man transcends his natural status and consequently gets "saved" when he changes society for the better based on the principle of universal love as the essence of humble humanism:

> God's loving initiative, his act of love in creating man, is only one aspect of his one great plan of salvation directed towards the *deification* of created man. He did not correct his work of creation by conferring grace. The creation itself was the first evidence of God's saving love. Creation is thus, together with its acme, humble humanism or humanism as the conscious glorification of God, inwardly directed towards the life of grace. This means that the humanist task in society, economically and politically well ordered community in which science and art, love and justice can prevail, is not simply a demand of creation, but also a commission which has been imposed upon us by the life of grace itself. Humanism thus becomes a part of our saving task. If, moreover, the supernatural gift of salvation is intimately connected with the religious dimension in depth of the humanism of creation which, of its very

---

70. McManus, *Unbroken Communion*, 112.
71. Mulcahy, *The Cause of Our Salvation*, 18.

nature, possesses a powerful tendency towards God, then it follows that supernatural deification can also be accepted in the very name of humble humanism.[72]

This text is a clear deconstruction of traditional theology in spite of its traditional language. Man's religious dimension is a mere human feature, and this is to be put together with what Schillebeeckx calls the humanism of creation, namely man's rekindled natural awareness.[73] The result of this juxtaposition is salvation or deification, which in Schillebeeckx is just another way to say that man rises above his natural condition when he reaches full knowledge of his natural capacity as well as implementing it in order to bring about positive change in the world.[74]

Schillebeeckx continues to use traditional terms in discussing the issue of salvation and especially man's need to accept it. He is convinced that the reception of salvation presupposes an even higher degree of humility as compared to what he has already defined as humble humanism. It has been shown that humble humanism is actually man's knowledge of himself through the rekindling of his natural awareness in view of transforming the world, so the acceptance of an even higher humility should perhaps be understood as a deeper knowledge of one's self accompanied by a more powerful sense of the need to change the world. Schillebeeckx resumes the idea of a superior reality as compared to the reality of creation and humanism; this superior reality is of course God and his wealth. Most assuredly Schillebeeckx does not make reference to the God of traditional Christianity, the God who exists in a personal manner as a Trinitarian being; his God is humanity in its entirety from the perspective of its future, so the superiority of God by comparison to the realm of man and humble humanism is in fact the preeminence of humanity's future as compared to man's actuality of the present. Schillebeeckx even mentions the fact that God has a value which is absolute and at the same time greater than creation and humanism; the absolute though unveils itself throughout history.[75] This means that the future of humanity is far more important for humanity in general than man's present awareness of himself and of his universal values. If the future is permanently terrestrial—and it is

---

72. Schillebeeckx, *World and Church*, 27.
73. See Borgman, *Edward Schillebeeckx*, 435 n. 196.
74. Schillebeeckx, *Christ, the Sacrament of the Encounter with God*, 42.
75. Kennedy, *Schillebeeckx*, 3–4.

definitely so—then it follows that the future should be the accumulation of man's knowledge throughout history so, in comparison to the present, the future will be wealthier in human knowledge and awareness than the present. Man's natural awareness of himself as a being as well as of humanity in general and of its universal value will increase as time elapses, so the future will be in a permanent state of continuous enrichment by means of man's growing natural awareness throughout history. At this point, Schillebeeckx contrasts humanism as part of creation with grace which is connected to deification or—even if Schillebeeckx does not use the word here—salvation.[76]

At first glance, the contrast between creation and salvation sounds traditional because creation is permeated by sin while salvation is God's intervention by grace in the sinful creation. Nevertheless, in Schillebeeckx, this statement needs heavy translation. Creation and humanism concern man's growing awareness of himself as a natural being who is endowed with universal value. In time, man realizes he is not just another being but a being that has the natural capacity for progress. This is creation: when man understands his own condition and his capacity to move forward by means of progress due to his inner universal value. Man is "created" from the very moment he knows for a fact that life is worth living because progress can make it so and even better. This sort of creation is compared by Schillebeeckx to the state of grace which is seen in terms of deification or salvation.[77] Being saved for Schillebeeckx means participation in God's inner being, which is again a sample of traditional language. What does it mean though? It simply means that, once "created" or once aware of his natural capacity and value, man needs to move forward in order to share in "salvation" which is marked by his decision to use his natural capacity and value in order to change the world and make it a better place for humanity.[78] This, however, is not a task which has a definite end; it is rather an endless process which will grow in the future. This is what Schillebeeckx means by participation in God's interiority: humanity's future involvement in the transformation of society and of the world due to the individual man's growing natural awareness of himself as a creature that possesses universal value.

76. See also Bergin, *O Propheticum Lavacrum*, 209–10.
77. Schillebeeckx, *World and Church*, 27.
78. Walls, *The Oxford Handbook of Eschatology*, 226.

Re-Kindling the Natural Awareness of Man

The future though is unknown to the present and whatever happens in the future is a matter of mysterious dealings because we simply do not have knowledge of the future as it unfolds in space and time.[79] Future is essentially mysterious in contrast to the present because it lies beyond the grasp of the present. For Schillebeeckx the future is God so God is mysterious and, as the future is God and a totally different world from the present situation, the future is the kingdom of God which is essentially a mysterious realm when compared to the present.[80] Schillebeeckx does not refrain from using traditional concepts again when he says that this kingdom of mystery, namely the future of humanity, is transcendent because it lies beyond any possibility of the present reality.[81] The man who lives in the present knows what he can do in the present, or during his lifetime, but he does not have any firm knowledge of the future, or of what happens after he dies. The future is ultimately transcendent because man cannot tell for a fact what will happen beyond the present situation. What he can do, however, is manifest his love in the present—even to the point of sacrifice—in order to hope for a better future for those who come after him. Schillebeeckx is clear about the fact that there is no future without the present in the sense that the future is built on man's present manifestation of love and sacrifice for the better state of humanity in future. If this is the case, Schillebeeckx's theology pictures man in a desperate search for individual and communitarian meaning both for the present and for the future.[82] Nevertheless, the ultimate meaning of man and humanity in general seems to be a matter pertaining to the future, so man's meaning should be judged eschatologically—from the perspective of the future—when the reality of sin will hopefully be eradicated. This makes the individual human person a mere pawn on the universal stage of humanity's existence—past, present, and future—which must contribute to mankind's search for meaning by allowing himself to be "created" and "saved." Thus, the individual man is invited to "create" himself by rekindling his natural awareness of himself as a creature that has universal value and then "save" himself by agreeing to use his inner universal value for the transformation of the world in a continuous present which

---

79. See Kennedy, *Schillebeeckx*, 44.
80. McGonigle and Zagano, *The Dominican Tradition*, 95–96.
81. Borgman, *Edward Schillebeeckx*, 280.
82. See also Hilkert and Schreiter, eds., *The Praxis*, 5.

will hopefully lead to a better future for humanity in general. This is why humanism—and Schillebeeckx again uses traditional categories—is part of God's reality and, at the same time, is oriented towards God. In other words, humanism or man's rekindled natural awareness of himself is essentially of the future, it is something which happens in the present but it becomes ultimately relevant in the future.[83] Humanism is also oriented towards the future as a task which must be pursued by man in order to find the meaning of life for himself and humanity. Every human being must do this during the span of his lifetime; this is man's continuous present which is also the future for those who come after us.

Schillebeeckx is aware that his is not an easy task but man must look to his inner resources and find a way to push through. Rekindling one's natural awareness seems to be an act of utmost humility for Schillebeeckx because it involves one's self-knowledge which is the first step for progress—progress to find the meaning of life both in one's individual existence and in mankind's existence in general. This becomes man's pride—or rather his "humble pride"—namely his desire to be what Schillebeeckx calls a child of God.[84] Schillebeeckx's traditional formula is probably meant to confer a personal touch to man's endeavor to find the meaning of life. As man strives to "create" himself by rekindling his natural self-awareness and then "save" himself and others by applying what he knows for the progress of humanity, he may realize that even if he finds the meaning of his life the world will not change much—if at all. This could theoretically lead to despair, so Schillebeeckx invites us to be humbly proud and become children of God or children of our own future hoping that the ultimate meaning of life and the eradication of sin will eventually be achieved in the future.[85] At the end of the day, we have to be proud of God which, in Schillebeeckx's terms, translates as a challenge be proud of our own future as human beings, who agreed to be "created" and "saved" by the rekindling of our self-awareness.[86] To use Schillebeeckx's words:

> Man's acceptance of the gift of salvation also means that an even deeper humility is imprinted on what is already a humble human-

---

83. Rego, *Suffering and Salvation*, 50.
84. See also Abdul-Masih, *Edward Schillebeeckx and Hans Frei*, 127.
85. Dietrich, *God and Humanity in Auschwitz*, 93.
86. Harrington, *Seeking Spiritual Growth*, 22.

ism. Man's consent to grace, that is, to God as God, to God's inner wealth, includes his humble confession of God's absolute greater value, greater than his work of creation, in other words, than humanism. Humanism remains a work of creation, but grace is deification, by which creatural non-being participates in God's interiority. In this participation in grace, humanism is taken up and drawn into the *kingdom of the mystery*, in which the divine possibility absolutely transcends all human possibilities, with the result that humanism, in joyous surrender and inner readiness to sacrifice, lays itself open to the mystery's unsuspected tasks of love. It is here that humility, humanism's being "of God" and "for God," celebrates its supreme triumph . . . This humility is the basis of the most audacious human pride—the pride of the child of God, being proud of God![87]

Schillebeeckx knows very well that life is meaningless without "creation" and "salvation" as described by means of his theory about humble humanism.[88] Man will never come to terms with his own existential fears unless he engages in a personal self-knowledge of his being and then puts the inner value he finds within himself into daily practice. Humble humanism is a fight against sin, understood as suffering and death, but the only way to wage such a war is constantly to use man's natural self-awareness for the benefit of humanity in its entirety. Schillebeeckx realizes this is not easy and it will never be easy; to fight against suffering and death involves in most—if not all—cases personal suffering and even death.[89] Therefore, humble humanism is not only agreeing to fight against suffering and death but also agreeing to suffer and perhaps die for this ideal to come true.[90] Schillebeeckx resorts once more to the language of traditional theology to explain the reality of the presence of evil in the world. For him, evil—namely suffering and death—is not from God.[91] The creative love of God has nothing to do with suffering and death because evil is essentially human. But as God is not an ontologically real and personal being in Schillebeeckx, we should understand that God is the symbol of humanity's universal values which are essentially good. These universal values, which are themselves essentially human, seem to be

---

87. Schillebeeckx, *World and Church*, 27–28.
88. See also Borgman, *Edward Schillebeeckx*, 265.
89. See also Mulcahy, *The Cause of Our Salvation*, 18.
90. Draulans, "The Permanent Deacon," 203–4.
91. Kennedy, *Schillebeeckx*, 92.

"above" the reality of man's individual existence. This means that while an individual person can be evil and cause suffering to others, the reality of man's universal goodness is by no means anulled by individual evil acts. It is in this particular sense that God—or humanity's universal values—is utterly transcendent in comparison to individual lives. In other words, it seems that evil is mainly personal while goodness is predominantly communitarian: individual persons can cause suffering to others but they can be "created" and "saved" by humble humanism based on humanity's universal goodness. This is probably why Schillebeeckx writes that "evil is simply the destructive work of human freedom"[92] with the clear intention of underlining that evil is not transcendent but utterly immanent. Evil does not go beyond the individual reality of man in order to become some sort of universal counter-value; Schillebeeckx will never accept such an idea. Thus, in contrast to the pessimistic anthropology of traditional Christianity which connects evil and sin to man's inner nature manifested in every human being so that man sins by necessity, Schillebeeckx is a bit more optimistic when he says that evil is caused by human freedom, not by human nature.

So the world is evil and the only way to find a way out of this tragic situation is a dramatic intervention in the history of humanity. Traditional themes are present again in Schillebeeckx's presentation of salvation: God turned the world of evil into an oasis by choosing the church. Salvation is presented as a gift from God to humanity and the means whereby man is delivered from evil.[93] These traditional images though should not be mistaken for a theology which proclaims the meta-historical intervention of an ontologically real God in the historical realm of humanity with a view to man's deliverance from his sinful nature. For Schillebeeckx, the situation is different: God is again just another way to point to mankind's universal value which is the only resort man has against evil. Man's universal value is practically seen in the application of love for the benefit of others. This love transforms man's present situation into a means of grace because every human individual has the chance to be created and saved based on the values of humble humanism. Creation and salvation are daily realities for every human being because they are triggered by human freedom, the same human freedom which can be the cause of

---

92. Schillebeeckx, *World and Church*, 28.
93. Schillebeeckx, *God is New Each Moment*, 26.

evil.[94] Thus, everything which pertains to creation and salvation is a manifestation of human universal values which have to be used for the benefit of the whole of mankind. For Schillebeeckx, human freedom is indeed a universal value but the evil which can result from it is definitely not. Nevertheless, the tragic reality of evil becomes a way to achieve salvation because it forces human beings to reconsider their natural powers as well as use them to fight evil.[95]

This is confirmed by what happened to Christ—even if it seems that Schillebeeckx should have used the word Jesus instead of Christ—who was sent by God to transform the reality of suffering and death. Of course Jesus was not sent by a meta-physical God to rescue man from sin; Jesus was a mere man who understood man's universal values and decided to apply them in his life in order to transform the world for the better. Christ surrendered himself to God, in other words he accepted the universal values of humanity in his own life for the benefit of other people. Schillebeeckx is convinced that Jesus failed in his mission because the world did not accept his message and even killed him but this was only a personal failure.[96] He failed as an individual person, who could not convince the world of the value of his message. Nevertheless, the example of his life was not a failure because it inspired others who proclaimed his triumph as if he had returned to life from his tomb. Jesus did not come back to life but what he did during his life and even in his death remains a model for every man and woman who wants to be created and saved by the universal love which confers meaning to life.[97] Jesus though was fully conscious that he fought against evil and that this could mean personal suffering and even death. Like him, we must be equally aware that our fight for personal and communitarian progress may well include the reality of personal suffering and death. Humble humanism is both success and failure because some people will be created and saved by universal love while others will remain unchanged or even retaliate. Humble humanism, however, is a must for man's quest for a meaningful life.[98]

---

94. Borgman, *Edward Schillebeeckx*, 267.
95. Schillebeeckx, *World and Church*, 28.
96. Tupper, "Theology," 117.
97. Scirghi, *An Examination*, 139–40.
98. Schillebeeckx, *World and Church*, 29.

Creation and salvation as manifestations of humble humanism are heavily informed by experience. For Schillebeeckx, they cannot be detached from the experience of everyday life.[99] Their application in society may cause personal detachment from society because those who want to create and save others will always be rejected by people who refuse the offer of universal love. The reality of one's detachment from society due to the rejection of humble humanism has to be approached in humility, or in full self-awareness. We have to realize that this is no easy task, and if it involves suffering and sometimes even death, then we have to come to terms with the fact that retaliation is possible. Jesus learned this during his own life experience but the idea of personal suffering and death should never stop us from applying the principles of humble humanism.[100] It should be stressed at this point that Schillebeeckx' militant approach to humble humanism must be appreciated despite the fact that it is informed merely by man's existential fight to know himself in order to help others find their own existential tranquility.[101] This is because there is no such thing as life after death; if we want to find the meaning of our existence then we have to hurry and find it during our lifetime and for our life. For Schillebeeckx, however, there is no personal meaningful life without personal involvement in society so that the lives of others may also find personal meaning. This definitely involves personal sacrifice[102] which is presented by Schillebeeckx as meaningful only if helps others find meaning for their lives.[103] Whoever finds meaning in life by means of humble humanism is a "new creation" because he allows himself to be created based on the principle of universal love which is active inside and outside the individual life of the human person.[104] This is confirmed by Jesus's death; he himself became a new creation because the example of his life not only created himself but also turned others into "saved" new creations. The "creation" and "salvation" of individual persons through humble humanism is eventually and essentially a "resurrection," a new return to life—not to any life but to the authentic, meaningful life that

---

99. Abdul-Masih, *Edward Schillebeeckx and Hans Frei*, 6.
100. See also Schillebeeckx, *God Is New Each Moment*, 113.
101. See also McManus, *Unbroken Communion*, 52.
102. Borgman, *Edward Schillebeeckx*, 300.
103. Schillebeeckx, *World and Church*, 30.
104. Rego, *Suffering and Salvation*, 50.

understands the value of personal love and sacrifice in order that others should find meaning for their lives.[105]

To be sure, in Schillebeeckx, creation, salvation, and resurrection happened on earth and within history;[106] they are all existential endeavors that help man rekindle his natural self-awareness in order to find the meaning of life and transform society by progress for the benefit of every human being. It is clear once again that Schillebeeckx's theory of humble humanism is in fact a deconstruction of traditional theology. If in traditional theology those who find salvation in history and await resurrection with God beyond history make up the church which is fundamentally different from the world, in Schillebeeckx those who are created, saved, and resurrected by humble humanism form "the community of men on earth" that "has reached completion as community of saints."[107] Schillebeeckx does not refer to the church in the traditional sense of the word but to all those who found the existential meaning of life and decided to take a stand for the world. Actually, it does not really matter if they are from the church or from outside the church; what it matters is that they should accept the universal love of humble humanism which helps them be self-aware of their natural powers as well as of their capacity to change the world based on the universal human values embodied by the image of Christ.[108]

---

105. Schillebeeckx, *World and Church*, 30–31.
106. Wood, *Spiritual Exegesis*, 113.
107. Schillebeeeckx, *World and Church*, 31.
108. See also Hick, *The Myth of God Incarnate*, 22.

4

Re-Shaping Christology from Jesus to Christ

Edward Schillebeeckx's Christology leads to the separation of the traditional image of Jesus Christ into the Jesus of history, who lived in Palestine and the Christ of faith, which is a representation of Jesus in the faith of the church. Because Jesus of Nazareth is dead as he was a mere human being, there is no binding hermeneutic which could cement a relatively steadfast doctrine of the church. This results in an inclusivistic perspective on the church which pictures a dead Jesus who is relevant only as a mere psychological Christ meant to quench existential fears.

THE ROLE OF EXPERIENCE AND THE DEAD JESUS

The first aspect which must be stressed in connection with Schillebeeckx's approach to Jesus is the paramount importance of the concept of experience. Actually, Schillebeeckx's theology cannot be properly understood without his perspective on the idea of experience. Why is experience so important? Because it explains what it means to be human and defines God's revelation.[1] In Schillebeeckx, experience is crucial because it connects theology to the idea of humanity which is in fact the foundation of theology.[2] Thus, theology is not something which comes to humanity from above, namely from a transcendent God as defined by classical theology, but is the way humanity understands the idea of God based on its own perception—reflected in experience—of the reality of God.[3] It is quite difficult to say whether for Schillebeeckx God is an ontological reality or a mere idea but the fact that human experience is so vital for the way people understand God could mean that God is primarily an idea which

---

1. Abdul-Masih, *Edward Schillebeeckx and Hans Frei*, 101.
2. See also McManus, *Unbroken Communion*, 85–86.
3. Rego, *Suffering and Salvation*, 111–12.

should be understood ontologically. In other words, God is an essential concept for all people because people need to relate to it in order to have their lives explained in such a way that they make sense of this world.[4] Regardless whether God is an idea or an ontological reality, it is clear that what we call God comes to us from ourselves, not from outside humanity.[5] Schillebeeckx wonders what our discourse about God would look like if the word God had not been introduced to us. How could humanity talk about God if the word itself had not been introduced? What is the starting point of defining God? Schillebeeckx can only think of one such starting point which could be "*the* event in a normal human conversation,"[6] so God is—in a way—the result of human hermeneutics and, as hermeneutic belongs to or is essentially a part of human experience, the idea of God is clearly shaped by what humanity thinks of such a concept.[7] Therefore, experience is crucial because is also explains what Christianity is and how it should be understood. A small but significant note should be made at this point: when he insists on experience, Schillebeeckx does not have personal experience in mind but rather the experience of all human beings and especially the experience of the entire Christian tradition which must necessarily be coupled with the religious experience of all men and women.[8]

This observation is essential for what Schillebeeckx means by Jesus, in the sense that Jesus should not be exclusively approached in Christian terms (namely in terms which are fundamental to the Christian tradition) but in terms of general human religion, which evidently goes beyond the outer limits of Christianity.[9] In other words, our experience of Jesus must not necessarily be Christian but religious. It could even be argued that our experience of Jesus can be both Christian and non-Christian.[10] This means that in order to understand Jesus properly, we have to reinterpret what we know of him in such a way that we also actualize again and again the information we have about Jesus. Thus, Jesus becomes a con-

---

4. For details about Schillebeeckx's concept of God, see also Borgman, *Edward Schillebeeckx*, 101–2.

5. Kennedy, "God and Creation," 56–57.

6. See Schillebeeckx, *Christ, the Christian Experience in the Modern World*, 64.

7. A. Depoorter, "Orthopraxis," 176–78

8. Boeve, "Experience according to Edward Schillebeeckx," 218.

9. See also Brown, *The Divine Trinity*, 139–40.

10. Aldwinckle, *Jesus—a Savior or the Savior?*, 59–60.

stant hermeneutical exercise because this re-actuality is the very norm of our present lives. The present must be defined hermeneutically and this means that we can only understand the present and ourselves if we try to understand God—and of course Jesus—in terms which are relevant to our present experience. Our present must be linked to the past of humanity but this connection should be made exclusively on the basis of experience.[11] So, in order to understand Jesus today, we should definitely know what has been said about him in past history but the final understanding must be marked by our own present experiences. This is to say that Jesus must not be understood as he was presented in the past because such a presentation only worked for the past and it would be utterly irrelevant for the present. Jesus—although a figure of and from the past—should be presented in actual, present, and relevant terms which are defined by our own present experiences.

Consequently, the idea of revelation as the only source for the understanding of Jesus is demolished because there is no such thing as a defined set of doctrines stemming from a divinely-inspired revelation in the past. The past is almost by definition rendered irrelevant in Schillebeeckx because it is fundamentally detached from the present. The past, however, cannot be ignored but it is definitely not the norm for the understanding of Jesus. For Schillebeeckx, a correlation has to be made between the past and the present in order to understand Jesus but this correlation—although based on information from the past—must necessarily be relevant to the experience of the present and to the experience of the people living in the present.[12] Thus, the past must not be brought into the present—this is why revelation is utterly futile if divinely inspired in the past—but the past must be reinterpreted in such a way that it fits the experience of the present. A revelation which comes from an ontologically transcendent God as in traditional theology is of no use to Schillebeeckx; such a revelation cannot be used or useful for contemporary people because it cannot be reinterpreted so that it fits our present experiences. This is why his correlation between the past and the present presupposes the use of the information from the past in order to make it relevant to the present but also to make the present relevant.[13] In other words, we can use the texts

---

11. Mbogu, *Christology and Religious Pluralism*, 245.
12. See also Hermans, *Participatory Learning*, 84.
13. Valkenberg, *Sharing Lights*, 146.

of the Holy Scripture, both the Old and the New Testaments, but they should be understood based on what we know of the present.[14] The Bible must be accepted based on our present experience, not on what it meant originally. So the information of the past must be translated again and again because human experiences change constantly and there is no way to understand our present unless we reinterpret what we know from the past so that it matches our experience:

> I have always said that the theology of experience is the foundation. Human experiences are the basis, not my own experience, all the experience of the Christian tradition, the religious experience which has been accumulated over time. We have to let this go through our lives and reactualize everything—this is the norm, the norm of our actuality of the moment. The present time is a kind of criticism of tradition but there is a mutual confrontation, a correlation between the past and the new experience of the present. We must always be very sensible with the proportionality of what comes from the past and our own experience. We cannot transform the Christian tradition into ecclectism. There is no such thing as a set of revelation placed in culture, in the times of the Scriptures, Hellenism, Patristics, the Middle Ages and so on. We must take these experiences and place them in our times by mutual criticism. We cannot absolutize either the past or the present. This revelation is embedded in culture, in historical situations. We must not replicate the past but interpret it. I am busy with hermeneutics. This means we can read the text of the Gospel, either the Old Testament or the New Testament. The meaning of words is always embedded in our image of the world and of ourselves. These experiences change and we must re-translate past experiences for our present experiences.[15]

Schillebeeckx's theology of experience is based on the idea of change. Man changes and so does the world as well as man's perceptions of the world. This is a *datum* which automatically prompts Schillebeeckx to the conclusion that human experiences concerning salvation follow the same pattern, namely they change because man changes.[16] He nevertheless ad-

---

14. See also Bernier, *Ministry in the Church*, 4.

15. Ramona Simuț, "Reinterpreting Traditional Theology," 275–76. See also Corneliu C. Simuț, *A Critical Study*, 175–76.

16. Abdul-Masih, *Edward Schillebeeckx and Hans Frei*, 103.

mits the existence of some "anthropological constants"[17] which remains the same but the basic human experience of salvation changes so—in light of this theory of experience—the explanation of what salvation means should change in order to be relevant to the present experience of humanity.[18] At this point, it should be stressed that Schillebeeckx offers a very brief though critically relevant definition of salvation: salvation is in Jesus but this means nothing but the very important question why we need Jesus now, in the present time.[19] In other words, being saved in Jesus is to understand why we need Jesus today. We should not be concerned with what salvation meant in the past because man's understanding of salvation changes constantly so man's needs over time are different from age to age, so there is no single answer to the question of man's salvation. Thus, to be saved could mean one thing in the past and a different thing in the present.[20] The world today has a certain expectation of salvation, and this must be reflected in the way we explain salvation. This salvation, however, must be explained in such a way that the world benefits from it. The only way for the world to benefit from salvation is to have salvation explained in such terms that the world understands it and people feel their own expectations are met. This implies a drastic change of language; we must drop the early theological language of the past in order to make room for new explanations of salvation which are relevant to the mind of contemporary people.[21] Schillebeeckx is convinced that the church must serve the world but this service must be effective, so in order for the church to render an effective service to the world it must re-evaluate its teaching as well as the language used for the proclamation of this teaching:

> The problem for many Christians, their crisis, is not so much that times have changed and that Christians might be accused of moving with the times and the new questions that they pose. On the one hand, the crisis lies in the fact that Jesus is still regularly explained to us as salvation and grace in terms which are no longer valid for our world of experience, i.e. in terms of *earlier* experiences; and on the other hand in the fact that we seem no longer capable in words or actions to "make a defence for the hope that is

17. Donna Teevan, "Challenges," 582.
18. Wiley, *Thinking of Christ*, 91.
19. Kotva, *The Christian Case*, 85.
20. For the relationship between the past and the present, see Pecklers, *Worship*, 25.
21. Mueller, *What Are They Saying?*, 58.

Re-Shaping Christology from Jesus to Christ

in us" (1 Peter 3:15). Are we really what we confess in our creed of faith and hope? Is there not a false adaptation here? For the service of Christians to the world is a divine service. In other words, only insofar as we give form to our specifically religious, Christian task do we *ipso facto* give a specifically Christian service to the world instead of merely duplicating what the world already does and perhaps does well.[22]

It is clear that Schillebeeckx uses the traditional idea of church mission and the proclamation of the Gospel[23] of Jesus to the world but this traditional doctrine is dramatically reinterpreted in the sense that the meaning of the Gospel must be actually revised to the point that it meets the expectations of today's people.[24] Therefore, it is not the expectations of contemporary men and women that must be changed in order to fit the Gospel but the Gospel which must be changed in order to match our present expectations. Thus, the Gospel is no longer the constant and unchangeable reality which shapes the lives of all Christians from generation to generation as in traditional theology. The idea of the unchangeability of the Gospel based on the immutability of Jesus as God and of God himself does not work in Schillebeeckx's equation. An immutable Jesus reflects an immutable God and an immutable God gives an unchangeable revelation which contains an unchangeable Gospel. Such a Gospel is totally irrelevant for Schillebeeckx because it does not meet the needs and expectations of people in the present. So, the interpretation of the old Gospel must find a new way to be presented and perceived as relevant to the present.[25] The traditional idea of the transcendence of God, Jesus and the Gospel is demolished by Schillebeeckx in order to make the message of the Gospel relevant to contemporary times.[26] Nothing and nobody is transcendent: the Gospel does not disclose a transcendent God and it definitely does not talk about a transcendent salvation. Jesus himself is a mere man so

---

22. Schillebeeckx, *Christ*, 63.

23. The Gospel can be seen in the synoptic Gospels and in the Gospel of John but one must pay attention to Schillebeeckx's differentiation between the two. For details, see Coffey, "Quaestio Disputata," 900ff. To be sure, the Gospel of John is very important to Schillebeeckx, see Bonsor, "History, Dogma, and Nature," 295ff n. 27.

24. Viviano, *Trinity, Kingdom, Church*, 84.

25. Rego, *Suffering and Salvation*, 318.

26. For details about the message of Jesus, see Schreiter, *The Schillebeeckx Reader*, 136ff.

his message can only be human.[27] His message becomes divine only when the church realizes that it must preach a Gospel according to the needs of the present. It does not actually matter what earlier Christians believed; the only thing that matters is our present experiences and how they shape our understanding of the Gospel. The Gospel, however, as well as Jesus himself, is fundamentally human:

> Jesus was thinking as a Jew, but there cannot be any transcendent elements in what he said, because one prophet criticized what another prophet said before him. As an eschatological prophet, Jesus was not transcendent, he was rather a messenger of the kingdom of God. The message was the salvation of humankind—this is the most important aspect of the Gospel; the salvation of the poor, the salvation for those who have no voice; it is a kind of liberal theology. There may be an absolute revelation through Jesus, but our interpretation of it is not absolute, as it goes through the filter of our experience and interpretation. We are restrained by language but this is not all. The New Testament was written by Jews who became Christians and spoke Greek. Their perspective on the world was different from what had been before, for instance, from those who translated the Septuagint. We must be true to the deepest meaning of the Gospel. In order to be faithful to this tradition we have to make the proper translation for our times. In this sense, the present time enters within our vision of the Gospel. It is not only that we know what the Gospel is; we are able to know the meaning of the Gospel for us today only through our experience of the present moment.[28]

It has to be admitted here that Schillebeeckx does indeed make reference to the possibility of an absolute revelation in Jesus but he does not seem to be convinced of its actual existence.[29] It seems rather that he struggles to remain within the boundaries of traditional theology or at least stay connected in some way to classical Christianity but his conviction that there is no "set of revelation" would suggest that the "absolute revelation" to which he alludes should be reinterpreted as a mere theoretical possibility. This possibility appears to be rather an impossibility because

---

27. Kennedy, *Schillebeeckx*, 137.

28. Schillebeeckx, Ramona Simuț, "Reinterpreting Traditional Theology," 276–77. See also Corneliu C. Simuț, *A Critical Study*, 175.

29. For details about the relationship between transcendence and immanence with view to revelation, see Geldhof, *Revelation*, 11.

while an absolute revelation in Jesus *may* exist, Schillebeeckx is unshakeable in his belief that the alleged absolute revelation is useful to humanity only if interpreted in such a way that it always meets the expectations of the present. Such an interpretation renders the absoluteness of revelation utterly useless, so it seems that the phrase "absolute revelation in Christ" was a mere stylistic device which helped Schillebeeckx underline—by contrast—the human character of Jesus, his Gospel, and the way it should be understood today.[30]

In Schillebeeckx, revelation can exist as a concept only if translated through and explained by experience.[31] In other words, it is not the divinely inspired and objective revelation of an immutable and ontologically real God which explains what salvation is and what we should do, but rather our experience which helps us understand Scripture according to our present expectations—once we understand the Gospel based on our experience so that our life acquires meaning, then we can say that this is actually revelation. Therefore, revelation does not come from above, from God, but from below, from men. Or, more precisely, it does not come from outside humanity but from within it. With respect to Jesus, it should be said that given this definition of revelation as molded by our human experience Jesus is totally disconnected from us, so there is no direct link between humanity and Jesus. Salvation is not an act of God but a perception of the good by men and women with reference to Jesus.[32] Thus, people experience the reality of goodness in connection with Jesus and they believe this experience is actually salvation from God. Schillebeeckx is convinced that Christians cannot have a direct liaison with Jesus; our connection with Jesus is utterly mediated by experience. This is what Schillebeeckx terms the experience of faith which is essentially an interpretative experience because each generation of people relates itself to Jesus based on what and how it understands the message of the Gospel.[33] It means that the experience of Jesus over time can change drastically in accordance with the experience of various people throughout history. Schillebeeckx is fully aware that his theory can be accused of subjectivity, so he insists that despite the diversity of subjective human experiences there is a con-

---

30. See also Haight, *The Future of Christology*, 191–92.

31. Schreiter, "Edward Schillebeeckx," 156–57.

32. For details about salvation as perception, see Avis, *God and the Creative Imagination*, 134–35.

33. Rush, *The Reception of Doctrine*, 223.

stant element which is always present. At this point, Schillebeeckx talks about salvation in Jesus which he does not picture as an event but as an experience. So, in the midst of the plurality of human experiences, the constancy of Christianity is the experience of God's salvation in Jesus. The experience of salvation in Jesus is the basis of human experience and in this respect, Schillebeeckx believes, humanity does not face any crisis.[34] Should any such crisis appear, it will happen in connection with concepts and interpretations not in connection with the experience of salvation in Jesus:

> What the Christian community will be concerned to say in constantly changing situations, through constantly new forms of expression, even in philosophical concepts of a very complicated kind, is ultimately no more than that in Jesus Christ it experiences decisive salvation from God. When the old concepts or interpretative elements no longer relate to new situations and when needs and necessities change, interpretative concepts also change. But the original experience persists through these changes: in their own different situations people still continue to experience God's salvation in Jesus. These changes do not themselves cause a crisis. As long as the basis of experience—experience of salvation in Jesus—remains, any possible crisis takes place above all on the level of conceptual interpretation.[35]

The problem is that the experience of salvation in Jesus is still a human experience because what we understand by salvation is given by our apprehension of the Gospel based on our present expectations and experiences. So, even if *the* experience of salvation in Jesus as a constant expectation of humanity can remain the same over time, its appropriation by people will definitely be anything but unique.[36] Nevertheless, Schillebeeckx does not explain why humanity should have the need to experience salvation in Jesus if human experiences are fundamentally subjective and there is no objective revelation as a set of prescriptive doctrines.[37] Despite this, Schillebeeckx is convinced that salvation must be *in Jesus* otherwise faith vanishes from human experience. But who is Jesus?

---

34. Mertens, *Not the Cross, but the Crucified*, 118.

35. Schillebeeckx, *Christ*, 63–64.

36. For details about the experience of salvation, see Greene, *Christology in Cultural Perspective*, 22.

37. See also Nasr, *The Need for a Sacred Science*, 164.

Re-Shaping Christology from Jesus to Christ

This is a blunt affirmation and even if a greater amount of sophistication had been perhaps needed to formulate it, Schillebeeckx himself is equally blunt in openly promoting the death of Jesus.[38] For instance, due to his program of reinterpretation of traditional doctrines, he suggests that as we are under no obligation to believe certain dogmas, we could and actually should reinterpret the classical Christian doctrines so that they fit our contemporary experiences and beliefs. Therefore, as no mentally sane person believes today in resurrection, something needs to be done in connection with the traditional doctrine of the resurrection of Jesus. In other words, there is no present correspondence which would allow us to believe that Jesus came back to life after he died on the cross.[39] Based on this presupposition, Jesus died for good and he never rose from the dead because none of the people who die today come back to life.[40] Schillebeeckx is at times very confusing because he writes that he does believe in bodily resurrection but this should not be understood in terms of a dead body being brought back to physical life. To quote his very words:

> A reinterpretation of what we call dogmas is very important and must occur. We must not be busy with what we believe. There is no obligation to believe this or that. For me, the creed has always been the foundation of life but we must always interpret the doctrines of the creed—the resurrection, for instance. I believe in bodily resurrection, but this has nothing do to with corpses coming to life. The corpse of Jesus Christ did not leave the tomb and whoever holds this believes in a fairy tale. I believe in the bodily resurrection of Jesus but not as a dead body coming back to life again.[41]

If physical life is not given back to dead bodies but the resurrection of Jesus must be believed—even though reinterpreted—the only logical solution is a different kind of life given to dead bodies; if physical life is out of the question, then the only reasonable option is spiritual life, which is in fact a spiritualized resurrection.[42] Therefore, according to

---

38. O'Boyle, *Towards a Contemporary Wisdom Christology*, 254.

39. For further information about the significance of the cross in Schillebeeckx, see McManus, "Reconciling the Cross," 638.

40. Caputo, *More Radical Hermeneutics*, 223.

41. Schillebeeckx, Ramona Simuţ, "Reinterpreting Traditional Theology," 281. See also Corneliu C. Simuţ, *A Critical Study*, 171.

42. For details about spiritualizing the resurrection, see Wedderburn, *Baptism and Resurrection*, 164ff.

Schillebeeckx, Jesus died physically, his body was put in a grave and never left it. This is to say that Jesus is buried to the present day. Nevertheless, he is alive spiritually and Schillebeeckx insists that we should believe in resurrection with reference to the idea of body which is not physical but spiritual:

> Here, however, I must mention that there are two major points of interpretation. Firstly, those who believe there will be a bodily resurrection in the sense that life will be given to dead bodies. Secondly, Paul says we have a new body coming from heaven, a pneumatological vision; there is no such thing as a corpse coming out of the tomb. The corporality, the completeness, the wholeness of being a human with God eschatologically is something which cannot be expressed by a representation. We are not souls only; the resurrected body will be spiritual. I believe in the resurrection of the body, but it has nothing to do with a corpse coming to life from the tomb.[43]

This explanation, however, does not manage to dissipate the confusion created by Schillebeeckx with reference to his understanding of bodily resurrection. One thing is sure though: Jesus is dead and after his death his dead body did not come back to life. If we are to believe in bodily resurrection, we will have to resort to pneumatology and eschatology in order to explain it spiritually. So, if Jesus is alive, he is alive spiritually because of the spirit of those who believe and his spiritual presence—although he is physically dead—must have a sort of eschatological significance for believers.[44]

So, Jesus is dead and this also comes from a slightly more subtle presentation of the major events of his career. According to Schillebeeckx, what really counts in connection with Jesus is his death because this put an end to his work but also triggered some crucial events, such as the reassembling of the disciples once they came to terms with his death,[45]

---

43. Schillebeeckx, Ramona Simuț, "Reinterpreting Traditional Theology," 281–82. See also Corneliu C. Simuț, *A Critical Study*, 171.

44. Houlden, *Jesus in History*, 756.

45. Details about the reassembling of the disciples in Schillebeeckx can be found in Guerriere, *Phenomenology*, 153.

the Easter experience,[46] and the sending of the Spirit.[47] These three major events are presented by Schillebeeckx in order to explain what he calls "the formation of the church." Then, more light is shed on his argument because these three separate events are seen as nothing other than mere aspects of one singular event. This event is saving, we are told by Schillebeeckx, because it is fundamentally based on a crucial experience, the experience of Jesus rising from the dead. Taking into account Schillebeeckx's entire perspective on Jesus, it should be said that these three events or the threefold saving event should be interpreted, or rather reinterpreted based on the human experience of the disciples who perceived Jesus as risen.[48] It is by now common knowledge that Jesus did not come back to life from the dead, but his disciples were convinced he had escaped death one way or another, so it could be argued—according to Schillebeeckx—that they were convinced that they had experienced Jesus as being alive. Thus, the reassembling of the disciples was not made because Jesus came back to life having been resurrected by God the Father as in traditional theology but the disciples eventually gathered again after they all accepted that Jesus had died and that he would never come back to life in bodily form. Nevertheless, they must have come together because of Jesus's teachings, encouragements, and promises, which were so important to them that they had a totally new experience, which made them believe Jesus had defeated death since they were all together proclaiming his teachings and remembering his deeds.[49] Schillebeeckx does not offer many details on the Easter experience which in traditional theology is associated to the bodily resurrection of Jesus. For Schillebeeckx it is clear that Jesus did not come back to life in flesh but his disciples were convinced he was alive in their midst.[50] It is very likely that this led to the experience of the sending of the Spirit which should not be taken literally—in the sense that the Holy Spirit of God as ontologically part of the Godhead came in their lives—but rather experientially, because the disciples had the experience

---

46. For more information about the Easter experience in Schillebeeckx, see McDermott, *Word Become Flesh*, 115.

47. The sending of the Spirit in Schillebeeckx is also analyzed by Kristiaan Depoortere, *A Different God: A Christian View of Suffering* (Leuven: Peeters, 1995), 119.

48. William P. Loewe, *The College Student's Introduction to Christology* (Collegeville: Liturgical Press, 1996), 136.

49. See also O'Collins and Kendall, *Focus on Jesus*, 106.

50. Cf. Tilley, "Remembering the Historic Jesus," 3 n. 43.

of being powerfully bound together by the same spirit, probably urged by Peter.[51] Even if what Schillebeeckx had to say about this threefold saving event is constantly open to interpretation and re-interpretation, one thing is sure: Jesus died and never came back to life in bodily/physical form but his teachings produced such an impact in the lives of his disciples that they came together and started a movement which Schillebeeckx terms "the Jesus movement."[52]

It is crucial to notice at this point that in speaking about Jesus after his death, Schillebeeckx gives up ontological categories. Moreover, Jesus and theological concepts about Jesus should be understood in light of his death. The "Jesus movement" began after Jesus's death, so it is the reality of his death as well as the reality of what happened to his disciples after his death which really shapes our understanding of Jesus. In traditional theology, Jesus is presented not only as living on earth but also as being pre-existent and incarnate and, after his death, risen from the dead and ascended to heaven in bodily/physical form. All these ontologically transcendent categories (preexistence, incarnation, resurrection, and ascension) are found in the Christological hymn presented by Paul in Philippians 2:5–11.[53] Despite the complexity of the hymn itself as well as the very complicated issues related to its wide range of exegetical and theological interpretations, it is generally accepted in traditional theology that the *morphē theou* refers to Jesus's preexistence, *ekenōsen* (*kenōsis*) to his incarnation, *etapeinōsen* to his death, and *hyperypsōsen* to his resurrection and ascension. Schillebeeckx, however, refutes the traditional interpretation and suggests that ontological categories are obsolete.[54] His mean reason for this is the lack of any literal reference to Jesus's resurrection (strangely, he is right, there is no literal reference to Jesus's resurrection in the hymn but the Gospels are full of such references). Thus, Jesus's preexistence[55] should not be taken protologically but eschatologically;[56]

---

51. Macquarrie, *Jesus Christ in Modern Thought*, 311.

52. Schillebeeckx, *Christ*, 65.

53. For other details about Schillebeeckx's interpretation of the hymn, see Scirghi, *An Examination*, 135.

54. This is also the case with transubstantiation, for instance. See McGrath, *The Christian Theology Reader*, 594.

55. In radical theology, the idea of ontological preexistence is seen as a "grave embarrassment." See Byrne, "Christ's Pre-Existence," 308.

56. Check also Geldhof, *Revelation*, 129.

in other words, he did not have a real existence prior to his ministry but, after his death and in view of his eschatological teachings, his disciples understood his paramount importance for their community which led to the idea of preexistence.[57] There is, however, no ontological preexistence, but only an eschatological preexistence which is fundamentally non-ontological (it can be moral or didactic or virtually anything else depending on the interpreter's present expectations). With reference to Jesus's incarnation, Schillebeeckx prefers to connect *ekenōsen* (traditionally associated to Jesus's incarnation) to *etapeinōsen* (the reference to his death). Thus, he eventually annuls Jesus's incarnation by integrating it within the more encompassing reality of his death, so Jesus did not actually become a man having previously existed as God; he was just born as a man, lived as a man and died as man in perfect humility and understanding of his mission, which was to teach us true humility.[58] The subsequent references to Jesus's exaltation should not be taken literally as references to his physical/bodily ascension but only as means used by his disciples to extol Jesus's crucial importance for them and their community. Schillebeeckx is deeply convinced Jesus has always been a man and remained a man until his death; any discourse referring to him must not go beyond his human condition. Thus, Jesus never wanted to be God or *'elōhîm* and if he did not want to be God, why should we ascribe him deity?[59] Of course his disciples believed he was a god and they preached he was a god but this is understandable given the fact they had known him personally and their lives were so powerfully influenced by his humble life.[60]

Nevertheless, it must be stressed here that, as far as Schillebeeckx is concerned, Christianity is not about abstract ideas or noble ideals. He insists that God is a God of men and Christianity is about the real significance of Jesus as a person.[61] Jesus, the human person, is of course dead but he is alive as he embodies the values he lived and died for. At the end of the day, the hymn is not so much about Jesus as about the noble character of humanity resulting from the ignominious death of Jesus. The whole idea of preexistence is connected to the concept of *kenōsis* (traditionally

---

57. See, for more information, Hayes and Gearon, eds., *Contemporary Catholic Theology*, 154.

58. Lewis, *Between Cross and Resurrection*, 346.

59. See also Kemball-Cook, *Is God A Trinity?*, 170.

60. For details, see Schillebeeckx, *Christ*, 172–77.

61. Mbogu, *Christology and Religious Pluralism*, 269.

representing incarnation), so that both preexistence and *kenōsis* (ontological categories in traditional theology) are interpreted in a modern fashion[62] to refer to Jesus's self-acceptance of his human condition as well as to the fact that the reasons he suffered were totally unjust.[63] Thus, for Schillebeeckx, the hymn seems to be fundamentally moral because it has to do with the condition or behavior of a man who accepted his life and lived a special sort of existence. This is important because it is within this particular context that Schillebeeckx strips God's salvation from its ontological reality. Therefore, salvation is no longer seen as external to man but it resides in human life and especially in the special character of human existence as reflected in Jesus's own life. Here is what Schillebeeckx has to say:

> Although salvation comes from God it must lie in a particular kind of life and a particular way of being a human being. For all the idea of preexistence in the hymn, the emphasis on the one hand on the *self-emptying* and *unjust suffering* of the historical manhood of Jesus and on the other, on the fact that *this* is in no way the last word. Such a way of life has a definitive, irrevocable value, in and of itself. A man does not live in this way for the sake of a reward; that would contradict the unconditional nature of the gift in *kenōsis* and *tapeinōsis*. On the other hand, to be dead is to be dead . . . This even human irrevocability cannot be the last word—at least, if one is interested not only in "values" but also *in the living man* who embodies them. In that case God's affirmation of the inner irrevocability and decisive, final attitude of Jesus must have some real significance *for the person of Jesus himself* . . . God is a God of *men* . . . This Christian hymn . . . is an ode to God's mercy towards men precisely in their most grievous human condition. It is at the same time a hymn of praise to the true greatness of men, concealed in the unattractive form of humiliation.[64]

In other words, we have to understand that if we want to be saved by God we should be seeking salvation outside the human condition; what we have to do is find significance for our lives in the life of Jesus and predominantly in the type of life he lived as characterized by sacrifice, humiliation, and self-acceptance. Salvation from God actually comes from

---

62. Hebblethwaite, *The Incarnation*, 86.

63. Rego, *Suffering and Salvation*, 363.

64. Schillebeeckx, *Christ*, 175–76.

us, from human beings, because Jesus himself was a human being who lived a special kind of life so that he became a model to all people.[65]

The pattern of Jesus's life is available to everybody, Christians or non-Christians. Thus, if we follow this pattern of life we can all be Christians even if we do not believe in Christ or in God. Secular society in its entirety can be essentially Christian even if it is not only unbelieving but also against God and Jesus. All it takes to be a Christian is follow the pattern of life offered by Jesus. Therefore, if we act in a just manner and we give our lives for others, then we are fully-fledged Christians because we lead a life which contains the essence of the Gospel, even if we are totally secularized:[66]

> Secularism is not evil. Human beings are secular, but this does not mean they are evil. Secularization will go on forever. I do not believe in a new age which is to come and all these things. Humanity is one thing. Believing in the church, in love, doing good to others and being capable to stick to an ideal, which for a Christian is the kingdom of God, is the most important thing of all. Freedom for every human being, solidarity, and above all justice, are the most relevant aspects of humanity. When people do good things they have the kernel of the Gospel even if they do not believe in Christ. Many people see this reality as a fairy tale. Our judgment, however, will be on the basis of our facts, on the basis of doing the good (Matthew 25). Giving our lives for others (not suicidally) is what really counts. When somebody is a victim of evil, we must give our lives for the sake of the good. When we do this, we are Christians. If you do the will of God even if you deny the existence of God—then you are a Christian.[67]

It is easy to notice that Schillebeeckx turns the traditional "logic" of Christianity on its head. If in classical Christianity, salvation is from sin, and sin is perceived as the constant and inescapable reality of being against God in nature, thoughts, and deeds (this is precisely why we need God's intervention in Christ and then the indwelling of the Holy Spirit), in Schillebeeckx salvation is not from sin but from bad behavior. Thus, in order to be saved, we have to be Christians and in order to be Christians

---

65. See also Yewangoe, *Theologia Crucis in Asia*, 319.

66. For the relationship between secularized society and Catholic Christianity, see Bosco, *Graham Greene's Catholic Imagination*, 83ff.

67. Schillebeeckx, Ramona Simuţ, "Reinterpreting Traditional Theology," 282. See also Corneliu C. Simuţ, *A Critical Study*, 172.

we have to do what the life of Jesus teaches us. It does not matter whether we believe in God or not, it does not count whether Jesus is dead or alive—even if, according to Schillebeeckx, we know he is dead—all that matters is to have faith in Jesus's life and apply his life to our own in such a way that we do good things to others. So, the essence of Christianity according to Schillebeeckx is to follow the pattern of the life of a dead person called Jesus, whose corpse is probably somewhere in an unknown Palestinian tomb and do the things he did in spite of the fact that we do not believe in him or even hate him. Thus, we become Christians implicitly.[68] Schillebeeckx's "logic" leads to numerous odd situations but one of the most hilarious of all would be the case of a fundamentalist Jew (Muslim or Buddhist for that matter) who turns into a Christian almost over night and does not even have the slightest clue about it.[69]

What really counts for Schillebeeckx at the end of the day is man's capacity to stick to an ideal because this is precisely how he presents Jesus. For him, Jesus was a man who would rather die than betray his ideal. To begin with, his ideal was to present the law as the will of God which was given for the benefit of humanity. This caused trouble amongst authorities which eventually decided to eliminate him for producing unrest throughout the country. Despite the constant threat to his own life, Jesus continued to cling to his ideal so he preached the kingdom of God which was based on practising God's law for the good of those around us. He was fully conscious that his death was not far off if he continued like this but he did it nonetheless for the full benefit of all men and women.[70] He went on with his message of love to the point that he even warned his disciples of his impending death. He was eventually executed but the fact that he died is not the most important thing we should know about his death. What we should really know about Jesus's death is that it was

---

68. See, for details, Wood, *Spiritual Exegesis*, 111.

69. This is odd because Schillebeeckx rejects the idea of anonymous or implicit Christianity as imperialistic: "In a pluralistic encounter of divergent cultures and religions there is above all the problem of the reconciliation of belief in the uniqueness and universality of Jesus Christ with a positive evaluation of other world religions, without Christianity being able to regard itself in a superior, let alone 'imperialistic,' way as the one true religion which excludes all other religions (and then in fact also often annihilates them), or includes them by annexing them (Buddhists, Hindus, Muslims, and others are then called implicit or anonymous Christians without being asked and without their desiring this title." See Schillebeeckx, *Church. The Human Story of God*, 102.

70. Osborne, *Christian Sacraments in a Postmodern World*, 87.

the climax of a specific and special life. He died and is dead to this day but we should not be bothered by this historical aspect; on the contrary, we should consider the theological and even political implications of his death.[71] Why Jesus's death had theological implications is quite simple: he preached and lived out a life based on God's law as reflecting God's will for the benefit of men and women; but why was Jesus's death political? Because it was the political authorities that killed him in order to put an end to the social and political upheaval in Palestine and, definitely not the least important, he identified himself with those who suffered because of the political elite, especially the poor and those who were ignored for various other reasons. Jesus's message was more or less a plea for political liberation because he fought against evil and suffering caused or at least perpetuated by those in charge of politics:[72]

> We may not isolate the death of Jesus from the context of his career, his message and his life's work; otherwise we are turning its redemptive significance into a myth, sometimes even into a sadistic and bloody myth. As soon as we fail to take account of Jesus's message and the career which led to his death, we obscure the Christian tenor of the saving significance of this death. The death of Jesus is the historical expression of the unconditional nature of his proclamation and career, in the face of which the significance of the fatal consequences of his own life completely paled into insignificance. Jesus's death was a suffering through and for others as the unconditional validity of a praxis of doing good and opposing evil and suffering.[73]

Jesus is important because he preached salvation for men and women but this salvation should not be taken as salvation from sin but rather as liberation[74] from evil and suffering.[75] Schillebeeckx insists on the idea of liberation because Jesus himself used the imagery of a liberating God who shared his love with people in order to make this world a better place for everybody. This is why Jesus always turned to those who were in deep

---

71. McDermott, *Word Become Flesh*, 88.

72. Cf. also Irwin, "Liberation Theology," 675.

73. Schillebeeckx, *Church*, 120.

74. For details about salvation and liberation in Schillebeeckx, see Simon, "Salvation and Liberation," 494.

75. For details, see Keenan, "The Meaning of Suffering?," 85–86.

suffering.[76] Such a presentation of Jesus who fought and eventually gave his life to show people that love and protection of those who were suffering were indeed the essentials of life reveals Schillebeeckx's transition from the traditional doctrine of sin to the modern conviction that sin can be translated as evil and suffering.[77] Thus, for Schillebeeckx, the problem of mankind is not its innate sinful condition which places every human being in opposition to an ontologically real God but the evil which causes suffering and estrangement among human beings.[78] In order to fight this reality and make a real difference in the world, Jesus decided to live out his love for his neighbors to the point of a very deep personal identification with them:

> Jesus's message of and about God was so integrated into his active dealings with his fellow men and women, which liberated them and established communication, that his proclamation and his way of life interpret one another, while together changing and renewing people, liberating them for their fellow men and women in love and solidarity, just as after his liberating encounter with Jesus Zacchaeus the tax collector lets the poor share in his possessions. In turning to both the rich tax collector and the outcast and to vulnerable children, the sick or the possessed, the crippled and the poor, Jesus immediately demonstrates what he is talking about; and in so doing he anticipates eschatological salvation, the kingdom of God, here and now.[79]

It is clear then that, for Schillebeeckx, it was important that Jesus got involved in fighting against suffering of any sort. Human life, the only life that can be lived, is crucial because it is unique. Men and women must understand that there is nothing after death, so improving this life the best we can is the most urgent demand we share as human beings. Jesus seems to have understood this difficult task so he decided to pursue his goal even if this meant upsetting political authorities and eventually facing his own death. As for us, we have to do the same. We must use our rationality in order to counter suffering and do the good which is basically the only

---

76. Schillebeeckx, *Church*, 118–19.

77. For details about Schillebeeckx's view of suffering, see also Schaab, *Creative Suffering of the Triune God*, 14.

78. Levering, *Sacrifice and Community*, 20.

79. Schillebeeckx, *The Church*, 119.

Re-Shaping Christology from Jesus to Christ

thing that we leave to future generations.[80] Based on Jesus's example, the perpetuity of good is what makes human life eternal because, according to Schillebeeckx, hell just does not exist as there is no individual life after one's death:

> I believe rationality, human rationality, to be the way in which we think and reflect on human norms and values. I think that our rationality is under the critique of the history of suffering of the entire humanity. No religion can explain suffering or, even more, nobody can explain innocent suffering. Why do I believe in God if there is so much suffering in the world? Jesus had the message of the kingdom of God, which is that the good, not the evil, will be dominant in the world. Evil can be destroyed only eschatologically. Only goodness is eternal and transcendent to the death of human beings. This is the basis for the belief in the eternity of human life. There is no hell in which we are punished to suffer eternally. Evil is gone when eternal life outlives it. Certainty of belief—not rational certainty—must be accompanied by hope and love. You can have expectations without faith, but belief in eternal life must be accompanied by faith. You cannot prove that there will be any sort of reality after death. Surrending to the mystery of God is the hope of eternal life and salvation.[81]

Jesus did this and so must we, so in order that the world be transformed for the benefit of every human being. Thus, Jesus is important because he lived and died as an example which is worth following.[82] In spite of his death, which is permanent like any other human death, his message continues to inspire people as it did in the days immediately following his burial which prompted his followers to present him as the Christ who lives in their midst.[83] Even if his death was a shock and created panic among his followers, they eventually came to terms with the crude reality of Jesus's death and decided to disseminate his teaching by picturing the dead Jesus of an occupied tomb as the living Christ of the church.

---

80. Haight, *An Alternative Vision*, 310.

81. Schillebeeckx, Ramona Simuț, "Reinterpreting Traditional Theology," 279. See also Corneliu C. Simuț, *A Critical Study*, 176.

82. Rausch, *Who Is Jesus?*, 105.

83. Cf. Godzieba, Boeve and Saracino, "Resurrection-Interruption-Transformation," 777ff.

THE CHRIST OF THE CHURCH AND THE CHRIST OF FAITH

If Jesus is dead—and he is dead indeed in Schillebeeckx—then Christ must be somebody else, somebody different from Jesus. This is not the case in traditional theology, where the juxtaposition of the two names, Jesus and Christ, designates the one and the same person, Jesus Christ, the eternal and preexistent Son of God, who became incarnate, lived and died for our salvation, then raised from the dead, and ascended to heaven in order to stay at the right hand of God the Father so that he could intercede for us. The image of Christ as portrayed in Schillebeeckx is totally different. It is true that Christ has significance only as connected to Jesus, his ministry and death, but Christ is totally different from Jesus for at least two reasons. First, Jesus was a man, a historical character who lived and died in Palestine, so he was part of human history as a human being who had an actual existence in the midst of men and women.[84] Second, Jesus died, so regardless of his paramount importance of his live and death on behalf of his fellow men and women, and despite the fact that he personified God, he was just another mere human being.[85] So, in order to distinguish him from other individuals who lived and died the same way, namely for the benefit of other people, Jesus needs a sort of an extension beyond his actual historical existence.

Thus, in Schillebeeckx's thought, Christ is the logical—not the theological—consequence of the theory which promotes the eternal death of the historical Jesus. In other words, Christ is a theoretical invention devised by Jesus's disciples in order to confer validity to their preaching about Jesus. As Jesus was dead, the need to preach his life and death as well as his teachings was supplemented by the "literary character" of Christ, who is "alive" in the church.[86] His existence is not ontologically real; Christ is real only in the consciousness of the church and for those who do what Jesus had done during his lifetime. The sacrifice of Jesus would have been and would be almost meaningless without the image of the risen Christ. Others have died before and after him for the same reason, namely to help his neighbors, so why should people believe in Jesus, and not in other similar individuals? The answer is the idea of Christ, the

---

84. For a different perspective, which attempts to align Schillebeeckx's thought to traditional theology, see Redford, *What is Catholicism?*, 156.

85. Hill, *Jesus, the Christ*, 187.

86. See also Fackre, *The Christian Story*, vol. 2, 88.

Re-Shaping Christology from Jesus to Christ

Messiah, which has been handed down from generation to generation in the Jewish people as a symbol of God's grace, love, and kindness to humanity.[87] So Jesus, who lived and died in order to show God's love and grace, is the perfect embodiment of the idea of Christ; but as Jesus himself can no longer stay with his disciples because he died, his ideas and ideals survived in the believing community under the concept of Christ which can easily transcend time and be meaningful to every new generation of human beings.[88] Thus, Jesus died as a human being, but his ideals and teachings were resurrected under the image of Christ, which took them over and disseminated them throughout the world as well as through history. Christ does not cancel what Jesus had done and does not obliterate his life and death; it only takes them further and makes them known by conferring validity to them. In other words, the dead Jesus cannot exist and be relevant to future generations of people without the "living" Christ who can permanently actualize and perfect Jesus's life and death.[89] To quote Schillebeeckx:

> Death and resurrection are the determinative climax of the grace of God in Jesus Christ. Only after Jesus, dying, has firmly held God's hand and in turn has known himself to be sustained in this impenetrable situation, is he confirmed by God . . . an exclusive divine act on the part of the Father gives "perfective" constitutive significance to the reality of Jesus's sacrifice. This in no way removes the element of Jesus's own love to the point of death, indeed it even presupposes it, as it is this that is confirmed and sealed by God in the resurrection or glorification of Jesus. Jesus's resurrection is thus a free and sovereign action on the part of God, even if it manifests itself as already beginning *in* Jesus's personal communion with God into which he has incorporated his suffering and dying. From God's perspective, this very communion is already a manifestation of *grace* to Jesus, a grace which simply reveals its inner dynamic in his exaltation or resurrection and is brought to a final consummation.[90]

Thus, Christ is definitely not Jesus; it is just an image meant to complete and perfect the life and sacrifice of Jesus. Schillebeeckx is fully

---

87. Morrill, *Anamnesis as Dangerous Memory*, 96.
88. Zee, *Christ, Baptism and the Lord's Supper*, 182.
89. Wanamaker, *The Epistles to the Thessalonians*, 87.
90. Schillebeeckx, *Christ*, 467.

committed to reinterpreting Christian tradition and especially traditional Christian doctrines and one of the doctrines which needs radical reinterpretation is the divinity of Jesus Christ.[91] The reason for this is because the formula of the divinity of Christ connects Jesus to Christ in such a powerful manner that the two become one single divine-human character.[92] In Schillebeeckx, however, there is no room for transcendental ontology, so divinity must be reinterpreted so that Jesus is kept dead in a tomb, while Christ is preached as being actively alive in the church throughout time and history. Present experiences and the need to offer relevant explanations for today's challenges are again the foundation for the reinterpretation of the church's traditional doctrine of Jesus Christ:

> The church should not be so angry as if living as a Christian were only believing in orthodoxy or in right doctrine. Trusting God through the mediation of Christ is the essence. Doctrines are not permanent. Old doctrines are not relevant anymore. We are not Greeks, but rather Europeans, so—for example—the doctrine of the two natures of Christ, the hypostatic union, is not relevant any longer. Christ was a human person, but he had a unique relationship with God. I have said many times that in our times, in the 21st century, holding that Jesus Christ had both a human nature and a divine nature is like saying that he was a mermaid. Christ was a human being, he was finite as we are. Jesus Christ is a human being with a personal and unique relationship with God—we must realize this. I am not against the formula of the divinity of Jesus, but we must translate it in order to have meaning for us today.[93]

When Schillebeeckx says "Christ was a human person" he actually means "Jesus was a human person" but he uses the name Christ in order to transpose the permanent relevance of the image of Christ on the limited effectiveness of the life and death of the historical Jesus. Nothing else matters but the necessity that today's people should understand what Jesus did and in order to explain this we need the image of Christ. For his "ideal" to make Jesus meaningful to contemporary people, Schillebeeckx is more than willing to reinterpret both Scripture and tradition, so that Jesus is utterly separated from Christ even if Christ confirms, strengthens,

---

91. Cf. Coffey, "The Theandric Nature of Christ," 405.
92. Kennedy, *Schillebeeckx*, 7.
93. Schillebeeckx, Ramona Simuţ, "Reinterpreting Traditional Theology," 280. See also Corneliu C. Simuţ, *A Critical Study*, 170.

Re-Shaping Christology from Jesus to Christ

and even perfects Jesus's life and death. When we hear about Christ we actually hear the story of Jesus in and through the church.[94]

Why does Schillebeeckx prefer Christ without Jesus? Because Jesus was a Jew and his actions in ancient Palestine would be both irrelevant and sometimes offensive to contemporary people, who might feel oppressed by Jesus's Jewishness. Christ, however, embodies Jesus's ideals—not necessarily his historical actions—in such a way that all religions and all people can identify themselves with him. Schillebeeckx is excessively careful not to discriminate among religions, even if—at the same time—he attempts, quite unsuccessfully, to fight what he calls "religious indifferentism" that promotes the equality of all religions.[95] In other words, we should not discriminate among religions but Christianity—with its image of Christ—is somehow different (we must not use the word "superior") from any other religion of the world.[96] It seems more than evident that he does not manage to reconcile the exclusiveness of Christianity and the necessity of not discriminating between religions; his intention to keep this impossible balance is just another attempt to stay in line with the traditional language of classical Christianity.

So, who is Christ? Christ is the literary figure of the New Testament which corresponds to the historical character called Jesus of Nazareth. It is evident that, in Schillebeeckx, there is a break between the Jesus of Nazareth as a historical character and the Christ of the New Testament as a literary figure. As far as Schillebeeckx is concerned this break exists in the New Testament itself and was revealed by the historical-critical method[97] which—having escaped the authoritarian monopoly of the church—teaches us to read the Bible as any other literature thus liberating us from old dogmas in order to have the freedom to interpret Scripture according to our present needs and expectations.[98] One of the greatest achievements of the historical-critical method[99] is—in Schillebeeckx's view—the detachment of the historical Jesus from his New Testament

---

94. See also Fahlbusch and Bromiley, eds., *The Encyclopedia of Christianity*, 469.

95. Schillebeeckx's position is thus "dialogic," an idea coined by Dennis Doyle. See, for details, Doyle, *The Church Emerging from Vatican II*, 272.

96. Schillebeeckx, *Church*, 102.

97. See also Loewe, "From the Humanity of Christ," 314; Hinze, "Reclaiming Rhetoric," 481 n. 32.

98. Swidler, *Yeshua: A Model for Moderns*, 30.

99. Ormerod, "Quarrels with the Method of Correlation," 707.

"honorific" titles (Messiah or Christ, Son of God, Lord)[100] because this allowed us to understand that Jesus was a mere historical figure who, after his death but also despite his death, was confessed to be the Christ of the church or, as Schillebeeckx likes to put it, as the Christ of the church's faith.[101] It is obvious that Schillebeeckx tries his best to keep the historical Jesus and the Christ of faith together even if the two are quite different characters taking into account the fact that the first is dead and the second is a "living" literary character, who is alive only in the New Testament and in the confession of the church. Here is one of Schillebeeckx's attempts to keep the two as close as possible:

> The identity of the "historical man Jesus" with the "Christ of faith" or the "Christ of the church" is a basic affirmation of the New Testament. There are no exclusive alternatives. Certainly we have begun to see more clearly that at the same time they form a relationship in tension without which Christianity is not Christianity and the gospel is not the gospel. For Christians there is no Jesus outside the confession of Christ in the church, just as there is no church confession without the liberating appearance of the historical Jesus of Nazareth for humankind.[102]

What Schillebeeckx says here is that there is no ontological identification between the Jesus of history and the Christ of faith, but only a "relationship in tension."[103] It is as if a certain writer wrote a novel about himself which is ninety percent historically and autobiographically accurate and ten percent fantastic in nature. We would all know that the writer talks about himself but at the same time we would realize that, in his book, the writer is not only a historical figure but also a literary character, mainly due to the fantastic elements of his creation. The same approach should be taken in connection with Jesus. He was a real historical character who lived and died in Palestine. His disciples decided to write about him so they produced literary works (the New Testament more or less) which present the dead Jesus as the living Christ who rose from the dead and ascended to the Father in heaven. Thus, according to Schillebeeckx, we all know that the Christ of the New Testament is actually the Jesus of Nazareth but at the same time, the fantastic elements

100. Hick, "Literal and Metaphorical Christologies," 153.
101. Schillebeeckx, *Church*, 105–7.
102. Schillebeeckx, *Church*, 104.
103. See also Marsh, *Process, Praxis and Transcendence*, 150.

of the New Testament (resurrection, ascension but also preexistence and incarnation) transform Christ more into a literary character than a historical figure, even if the "relationship in tension" between the two is evident. So the relationship between the Jesus of history and the Christ of faith is given by the historicity of Jesus while the tension by the fantastic (transcendent) elements of the literary works of the New Testament.

The New Testament though is the result of the faith of the community which believed in the works of Jesus, so it was Jesus's career that brought the church into existence.[104] Schillebeeckx dismisses once again any traditionally transcendent elements with reference to the constitution of the church even if he does mention the role of the Holy Spirit in building the church community. The Spirit, however, should be understood in human terms as the "spirit" of Jesus, namely his impact which powerfully acted upon the community that decided to preach and promote his career. The church is not—as in traditional theology—the community which preaches salvation from sin but the community which promotes the way of Jesus or his career in order to make it universally valid for all humanity in spite its original Jewish character. Jesus preached the kingdom of God (which is essentially the love of God) to the Jews and he did it exclusively for the Jews without any intention to spread this message beyond Israel.[105] His disciples, however, approached his message eschatologically and began to preach about Jesus's career beyond the limits of historical Israel. It is clear that, in Schillebeeckx, eschatology does not refer to the end of days as in traditional theology but only to the future. Thus, Jesus's disciples understood that the message of Jesus has universal connotations which transcend the present moment, so they started to promote Jesus's career by making reference to the idea of Christ in order to turn Jesus's Jewish message into a universally valid proclamation:[106]

> It is certain that Jesus was one hundred percent behind his message and meant this message to be accepted by men and women in faith. Jesus's conviction that there is a essential link between the coming of the kingdom of God which he proclaimed and the praxis of the kingdom of God and the consequent faith conviction of his followers that the mission of Jesus has a definitive,

104. Bergin, *O Propheticum Lavacrum*, 208.

105. Jesus only wanted to give them a future. See van der Ven, Dreyer and Pieterse, *Is There a God of Human Rights?*, 204.

106. See also Wiley, *Thinking of Christ*, 95.

eschatological and universal significance (as is clearly confessed by the New Testament) necessitates a continuation of Jesus's earthly mission by his disciples beyond the limited time of his earthly life—if time has any ordinary continuation after the death of Jesus (which is unmistakably the case). It is as simple as that. The mission of the apostles and the mission of the post-apostolic church are thus necessary on the basis of the eschatological and definitive character of the whole of Jesus's appearance and career and the whole meaning of his life, founded in Jesus and recognized by Christians. The unique, "one-off" mission of Jesus among the Jews remains untouched by this, because the content of the church's mission remains Jesus's proclamation of the kingdom of God and Jesus's own Jewish career.[107]

This clearly shows that the essential element of the church's proclamation is Jesus's career. So people are called to believe in Jesus's career as a means to proclaim and practise love for the benefit of humanity. The world is not called to repent from sin in order to have eternal life as in traditional theology but only to believe and practise the love of Jesus, who is proclaimed by the church as Christ in order to have universal significance to the entire world irrespective of the historical setting. In this case though, the love of Jesus can be preached by virtually everybody. The church, therefore, comes very close to a full identification with the world.[108] Given Schillebeeckx's undeterred conviction that God acts in the world in such a way that he totally identifies himself to the world, the world itself receives a "distinctively theological significance."[109] This means that the world should be seen as included in Christ because God is so absolutely near to the world that the word identifies itself with God. If this is the case, then the world can easily identify with the church. The identification between the church and the world is not one hundred percent identical but they are both manifestations of Christianity. Thus, for Schillebeeckx, the world is implicit Christianity while the church is explicit Christianity:

> This world, with its profane distinctiveness, is borne into the theologal sphere of the life of grace by man, whose anthropology can ultimately only be fully understood in the light of Christ. This means, in other words, that "the world" is, in the contemporary

---

107. Schillebeeckx, *Church*, 155.

108. This means that salvation can be achieved in the world. See Heyer, *Prophetic and Public*, 50.

109. Schillebeeckx, *World and Church*, 100.

Re-Shaping Christology from Jesus to Christ

saving situation of the incarnation, *implicit Christianity*—a distinctive, non-sacral, but sanctified expression of man's living community with the living God—while the church, as the institution of salvation with her communal confession of faith, her worship and her sacraments, is the "set aside", sacral expression of this implicit Christianity.[110]

To be sure, the world and the church are nothing but two complementary forms of experience of one and the same Christianity. In other words, there is faith in both: the world has implicit faith in Jesus's career (actually in the universality of love)[111] and the church has explicit faith[112] in the same.[113] In Schillebeeckx, this whole theory about the complementariness of the world and the church is based on his drastic reinterpretation of the concept of grace.[114] Thus, grace is no longer God's benevolence to humanity as in traditional theology but God's total identification with the world in the image of Christ based on Jesus's career as means to promote and implement universal love.[115] So the world is the church and the church is the world; even if the two have different ways of manifestation, they nevertheless share the same faith in the universality of love as set before our eyes by the universality of the Christ which originally stems from Jesus's life and death. Why is Christ useful? To promote the idea of universal love, as seen in Jesus's career, in order to meet our present expectations. So, in a way, Christ is a mere psychological prop for our feelings because we know how to behave only through our feelings.[116]

---

110. Schillebeeckx, *World and Church*, 101.

111. For a comprehensive discussion about the integrative faith of the world, see Lewis and Demarest, *Integrative Theology*, 54.

112. Details about the explicit faith of the church can be found in Hughson, "Theology," 110.

113. Schillebeeckx, *World and Church*, 102.

114. McManus, *Unbroken Communion*, 208.

115. Fichter, *Wives of Catholic Clergy*, 137.

116. See, for instance, Schillebeeckx's view of ethics: "There is no Christian ethics—I must say this; there is only human ethics, but we have to seek what is human and humane. To be a human being is the basis of all ethics, but when you are a believer with faith in God, this relationship with God is reflected in the community of the church. We have to take this ethics into our personal relationship with God. Belief, faith, hope, love, charity are our theological and ethical virtues. They are personal and communitary virtues. These are the immediate basis of our humanity. For a believer, however, this humanity, which is the basis of all ethics, is a gift of God. The deepest perception of ethics is God through the mediation of our feeling and through the reflection of what ethics really is.

If we are disoriented and do not know what to do with our lives, we need only look to Christ in order to understand and live out his love for other human beings. This should be enough to quench or at least calm our existential fears and help us live psychologically balanced for our own benefit as well as for the benefit of others.

In the end, we have to decide for ourselves whether Schillebeeckx's Christ is the Christ of the church or the Christ of the world. It seems though that, in his attempt to stretch the limits of the church in order to encompass the world, Schillebeeckx created an image of the church which, despite being full of people, is actually devoid of true Christians, at least in the traditional sense of the word. So here is Schillebeeckx's theological equation: Jesus lived and died for his fellow people, his disciples decided to promote his love-based career to the world and whoever believes in the universality of love as seen in Christ or in Jesus's career is a true Christian; thus, the concept of true Christianity is pushed towards the world, which leaves traditional churches empty because there is no need for people to become explicitly Christian as long as they are and can remain implicitly so. In other words, they can be at peace with themselves and others based on the soothing psychological and existential impact of human love anchored in the image of Christ and his resurrection.

I am in favor of autonomous ethics, but God is ultimately the foundation of ethics. It is only through our feelings that we are able to know what ethics is in reality. We know the will of God through our perceptions." Schillebeeckx, Ramona Simuţ, "Reinterpreting Traditional Theology," 278–79. See also Corneliu C. Simuţ, *A Critical Study*, 173.

5

Re-Assessing the Doctrine of Resurrection

The idea of resurrection in the theology of Edward Schillebeeckx is applied to Jesus but always in connection with his life and death. Schilleebeeckx is very concerned with the historicity of Jesus'ss life and death as well as the social and political implications of his entire career. Jesus was aware of the powerful impact of his work, so he realized his life would shortly be curtailed because of his agitating activity. As a result, he began to talk about his death—which he thought of as imminent—but also about his resurrection. Schillebeeckx performs a drastic re-assessment of the traditional doctrine of resurrection because, in his theology, Jesus remained dead after his execution on the cross. Nevertheless, the idea of resurrection as associated with his life and death should be redefined in order to make his earthly career significant to his disciples and to the entire world. Jesus did not come to life after his death; he "came to life" in the consciousness of the church and the world because of the universal values of his ministry. Thus, his resurrection is not physical—it is not even spiritual—it is only psychological. The same interpretative pattern should be applied to the resurrection of believers, who should not expect a resurrection of their physical bodies—i.e., dead corpses—but rather a revitalization of humanity's global consciousness with view of solving conflictual human problems.

THE RESURRECTION AND JESUS

In Schillebeeckx, Jesus's death was not followed by a physical resurrection as proclaimed by traditional Christian theology.[1] In other words, he did not come back to life from the tomb in which his corpse was placed. When he died, Jesus stayed dead for more than three days; he stayed dead

---

1. Macquarrie, *Jesus Christ in Modern Thought*, 311–12.

for good.² As far as Schillebeeckx is concerned, death is a universal human reality, and it is equally and indiscriminately applied to every human being, including Jesus, who was indeed a mere human being.³ This is why Schillebeeckx is extremely concerned to establish first the historical character of Jesus's death and second the over-encompassing human character of his life which ended—like any other human life—in death.⁴ Jesus's death was shameful and Schillebeeckx has no second thoughts about it.⁵ Jesus died on a cross, which was the Romans' most shameful way of executing a criminal; so, there is no doubt about the fact that Jesus not only died—which places him in line with every single human being—but died a shameful death. This also implies that Jesus's death was unjust and undeserved.⁶ Moreover, as it was a shameful and unjust death, Jesus's death is essentially a thoroughly unfortunate event which should not be ascribed "spiritualized" qualities. In other words, Jesus's death should be not given positive connotations which might suggest that it had any sort of good influence on humanity. Schillebeeckx even suggests that Jesus's shameful death should not be understood incorrectly in light of the resurrection faith. This is obviously a hint at traditional theology which says that Jesus died for our redemption from sin, which is the corruption of human nature and rebellion against God. If understood like that, Jesus's death had a positive influence on the state of the entire mankind give the fact that every human being who believed in him could be given salvation from sin. Thus, in traditional theology, Jesus's death has positive overtones because it saves humanity from its most inescapable state, which is sin. Schillebeeckx, though, does not accept such a positive interpretation of Jesus's death. Jesus died a shameful death, which he did not deserve; he died a totally unjust death and his death is permanent.⁷ He died and stayed dead. The state of death is irrevocable and there is no positive aspect which can be attached to it. Schillebeeckx is aware that the resurrection faith is essentially positive because, in traditional theology, it not only confirms the positive character of Jesus's death but also promotes it into a beyond-

2. Kennedy, *Schillebeeckx*, 115.

3. Ramona Simuț, "Reinterpreting Traditional Theology," 276–77. See also Corneliu C. Simuț, *A Critical Study*, 175.

4. See also McBrien, *Catholicism*, 505.

5. Rego, *Suffering and Salvation*, 304.

6. Schillebeeckx, *Christ. The Christian Experience in the World*, 175.

7. Schillebeeckx, *The Church with a Human Face*, 31–32.

the-grave experience. To be sure, on the one hand, in Schillebeeckx Jesus's death is shameful and unjust and so entirely negative,[8] while on the other hand, there is this resurrection faith which is fundamentally positive.[9] It should be noticed though that Jesus's death and the resurrection faith are two totally different historical realities. Jesus's death is substantially connected to the person of the historical Jesus who died and stayed dead like any other human being, while resurrection faith is powerfully tied to the community of Jesus's followers who believed Jesus came back to life even if he did not. In other words, what Schillebeeckx proposes here is the fundamental difference between Jesus's death and the subsequent belief of the church in his resurrection.

In Schillebeeckx, there are two reasons for such a sheer distinction: first, the historical character of both Jesus's death and the church's belief in his resurrection—as two distinct historical events they cannot and should not be confused; and second, the realization of man's tragedy in death, which is also applicable to Jesus and cannot be given any positive meaning in itself.[10] As an event that marks man's individual experience, death is tragic and remains tragic forever so that there is nothing in the word which could make it positive in any way. As far as Schillebeeckx is concerned, this means that death should not be spiritualized, and this should be especially true with respect to Jesus's death. His death was not atoning or redemptive; his death was shameful, unjust, and tragic. To believe that Jesus's death could be somehow understood in positive terms is—at least for Schillebeeckx—to promote an empty ideology which is devoid of critical reflection.[11] This observation is vital because it displays Schillebeeckx's theological methodology: theology should be understood critically, which is to say that we should read theology in light of our contemporary thought. Thus, if contemporary thought informs us that death is tragic and there is nothing outstanding about it, then this interpretation should be applied to the whole of Christian theology, including Jesus's death. It is as if Schillebeeckx wished that Jesus had suffered an ordinary, common death; much to his dismay, however, Jesus's death was not ordi-

---

8. Edwards, *What Are They Saying about Salvation?*, 72.
9. Mertens, *Not the Cross but the Crucified*, 122.
10. Rego, *Suffering and Salvation*, 304.
11. See also Bosco, *Graham Greene's Catholic Imagination*, 175 n. 44.

nary.[12] Jesus was not permitted to die like any other human being; he was executed and forced to end his life on a cross like a dangerous murderer.[13] Schillebeeckx observes that this particular way of dying was in utter contradiction with Jesus's life, which only adds to the tragedy of Jesus's death. Jesus's death as a historical event has no significance beyond it; it is only a tragic, shameful, and unjust reality that should not happen to anyone. Unfortunately, it has happened to others besides Jesus, and this is another confirmation that his own death is no different from the deaths of those who died like him on a cross. If their lives had no significance for the world, then it is clear—at least to Schillebeeckx—that there is no reason why we should understand Jesus's death differently. Thus, like many others before and after him, Jesus was executed and died on a cross in spite of his extraordinary life.[14] For Schillebeeckx, the contradiction between Jesus's life and his death is *the* confirmation of the tragedy of his death as a historical event: a meaningless, horrible, and ignominious execution which put an end to a selfless life:[15]

> Any meaningful statement about the resurrection of Jesus must be of such a kind that Jesus's shameful death is not trivialized in the light of the resurrection faith. Jesus's death is historically beyond question a defenceless event. To talk of Jesus's atoning death, or of the redemptive value of his death, can become sheer ideology without critical reflection. Paul says that the cross is not a sign of honour but a curse..., an offence and a shame. The resurrection of Jesus does not do away with that. In Jesus's death, in and of itself, i.e. in terms of what human beings did to him, there is only negativity. In this case, this is not an ordinary death, nor an instance of the universal human problem of death as a dialectic of death and life, ... but of a shameful execution which is quite out of proportion to the actual career of Jesus—indeed is in fragrant contradiction to it. Thousands have been crucified, yet nevertheless their crucifixions have not been thought to have universal significance, nor have they been called atoning deaths. So the importance cannot lie in Jesus's death as such. Purely as the death of Jesus, this dying cannot

---

12. See also Hick, *The Metaphor of God Incarnate*, 26.
13. Kennedy, *Schillebeeckx*, 4.
14. Abdul-Masih, *Edward Schillebeeckx and Hans Frei*, 118–19.
15. O'Boyle, *Towards a Contemporary Wisdom Theology*, 251 n. 121.

have any redemptive or liberating force; on the contrary, death is the enemy of life.[16]

Schillebeeckx is fully aware that Jesus's death cannot be left as a mere historical event because, in itself, death is the end of any future possibility. Thus, death should be countered by an equally powerful event but, in the real world, there is no such thing. Nothing in this world can fight death to the point that it brings back life because Schillebeeckx is convinced that the reality of death is virtually the end of the reality of life. With respect to individual persons, death is always subsequent to life, not the other way around. So, if there is no earthly reality which can fight death in the sense that life—physical life—is restored to the same individual who died, the only remaining option is an idea, namely the idea of resurrection. Schillebeeckx does not actually say that resurrection is an idea but he does speak about "resurrection faith."[17] As faith is not a physical reality but a non-physical conviction, it is not too much to infer that—for Schillebeeckx—resurrection is an idea. Resurrection faith should never be mistaken for the resurrection event but it is quite clear that there is no such thing as a resurrection event in historical reality.[18] Historical reality only witnesses resurrection faith which is subsequent to the historical event of Jesus's death. Resurrection faith, however, must not be left totally subsequent to Jesus's death. Such a possibility would suggest that Jesus was an incurable optimist and a totally idealistic person because he preached against social and political injustice while he still hoped for a better future both for himself and humanity. It would also suggest that history proved Jesus wrong because he was executed while not even conceiving of such a possibility.[19] Thus, if Jesus had lived hoping for the best without being aware that he would later have to face his own death, he would have been an idealistic fool. To be sure, if this had been the case, the subsequent idea of his resurrection preached by his followers would have been equally senseless because if Jesus himself hoped for a better world and lamentably failed because he was put to death, why should his followers and why should we have resurrection faith? It would be indeed preposterous and Schillebeeckx knows this very well.

16. Schillebeeckx, *Church. The Human Story of God*, 127.
17. McManus, *Unbroken Communion*, 105.
18. van Beeck, *God Encountered*, 191.
19. See also Bowden, *Edward Schillebeeckx*, 63.

Therefore, in order not to leave resurrection faith utterly disconnected from and subsequent to Jesus's death, Schillebeeckx places the idea of resurrection faith within the span of Jesus's life.[20] Such a movement would no longer leave the impression that Jesus was an idealistic prophet who wanted to change the world in a totally unrealistic way, namely without being aware of the consequences of his disturbing message. In other words, Jesus was definitely not idealistic in his attempt to change the then society; on the contrary, he knew for a fact that his unsettling words could well push him towards his own death. Thus, resurrection faith is not the faith of Jesus's followers which sprang up after his death but is essentially the core of his own message. The idea of resurrection faith confers validity to his message, but also to his life and even to his death. If Jesus was aware of the possibility of facing his death because of his message—and Schillebeeckx is sure he was—then it means that he was absolutely realistic about his message as well as the prospective reformation of society based on the idea of God's love.[21] He knew nothing was easy and everything comes with a price; in his case, the price could be death, which was eventually the case. In this way, the idea of resurrection faith has a meaning but this particular meaning should not be sought in spiritualized interpretations which allude to the possibility of physical life after death. On the contrary, for Schillebeeckx, the essential meaning of resurrection faith should be looked for in the very life of Jesus.[22] So resurrection is meaningful if we understand Jesus's life and if his life includes the idea of death and resurrection, then even his shameful, unjust, and tragic death may have a meaning of its own.[23] As Jesus preached against the social and political injustice of his days, it is clear for Schillebeeckx that the meaning of Jesus's life and death has to do with the daily practice of fighting evil. Of course, Jesus connected the idea of opposing evil to God's absolute power but what we should retain from this is the possibility that every human being should confront evil. Jesus knew this was not easy. It was not easy for him and it will never be easy for anyone. Fighting evil—social or political or anything else—is very difficult and it presents the possibility of one's own death. Nevertheless, his conviction that this

---

20. McManus, *Unbroken Communion*, 105.
21. Schillebeeckx, *The Church with a Human Face*, 23.
22. McMahon, *Jesus, Our Salvation*, 89–90.
23. Schillebeeckx, *God is New Each Moment*, 32.

Re-Assessing the Doctrine of Resurrection

was the right thing to do despite the possibility of losing his life because of this ideal is actually his belief in his own resurrection; of course, it is not his own physical return to life but the return of his message among his disciples who would preach it throughout the world in order to make it a better place for humanity.[24]

In Schillebeeckx, Jesus did not believe in his own physical resurrection but in the resurrection of his ideal with view to a constant attempt to change the world for the better.[25] As a matter of fact, this is the hope which conquers death; the hope that changing the world is a permanent possibility which should be lived out by every individual. As far as Schillebeeckx is concerned, death cannot be overcome physically but only in hope, so resurrection is not a real-physical event but only a real-eschatological hope. Death is part of this world and this means that anything else pertaining to human existence—including the idea of resurrection—should be part of this world. Resurrection has nothing to do with a beyond-the-world reality or with the reality of an ontologically real and transcendent God, as in traditional theology. Resurrection is real only as an idea which is, in fact, the result of Jesus's awareness that his message could trigger his own death.[26] For Schillebeeckx, Jesus did not hope for a resurrection which would have brought him to physical life again because this would have been impossible; he only hoped that his message would be resurrected among his followers who would take over his ideal to change the world. The idea of resurrection has to be connected to Jesus's ministry and life in order for them to be meaningful:[27]

> If the career of Jesus does not show any anticipatory mark of the resurrection, his death is sheer failure and in that case resurrection faith is simply the fruit of human longing . . . Without effective anticipations of the resurrection in the earthly life of Jesus, Easter is ideology. The only subject of the statement of faith "He is risen" is the historical Jesus of Nazareth who believed in the promise by giving it form in his message and above all in his way of life. Jesus's faith in the promise as the source of an original praxis is a historical anticipation of the significance of the resurrection and thus of God's overwhelming power over evil. In his career Jesus is an

---

24. McManus, *Unbroken Communion*, 105.
25. See also Berkhof, *Christian Faith*, 317.
26. Macquarrie, *Jesus Christ in Modern Thought*, 311.
27. McMahon, *Jesus, Our Salvation*, 94.

"already," still of course within the horizon of death, but now that of a death which has already been overcome in hope. The power of God was already at work in the life of Jesus and his death shares in that. Only on this presupposition is belief in the resurrection not an ideology! If only Jesus's death is a historical anticipation of his resurrection (this applies above all for Bultmann and to some degree also already for the apostle Paul), this resurrection is unavoidably the negation of a history.[28]

This text is important for at least two aspects. First, Jesus's existence should be understood within what Schillebeeckx terms "the horizon of death," meaning human life which ends in death, wherein death is the final element of man's life.[29] Thus, death is not only the terminal point of man's life but also its hermeneutical key, in the sense that death may or may not confer meaning to one's life.[30] It is significant that Schillebeeckx introduces the idea of hope within his assessment of death because human hope is the only aspect of humanity which can transcend death. Schillebeeckx's theological language is very close to that of traditional theology; its meaning, however, is utterly different. If in traditional theology hope is personal before death and remains personal after death because resurrection is physically real and it means coming back to life in physical/ontological terms, in Schillebeeckx, hope is personal during man's life but it does not remain personal because resurrection is not physically real. In other words, if resurrection does not mean coming back to life in physical/ontological terms, the idea of hope—once personal during the individual's existence—transcends death only if absorbed within the general idea of the humanity's general hope to find something meaningful in death.[31] Thus, Jesus's life is meaningful because he nurtured the concrete hope of changing the world by offering his own life as an example but also because his once personal hope became the hope of his followers who took it over and spread it all over the world by offering their lives as examples of how to fight evil and do good.[32]

Second, Schillebeeckx's observation is important because he seems very preoccupied with the notion of ideology which is quite clearly as-

---

28. Schillebeeckx, *Church*, 127.
29. Rego, *Suffering and Salvation*, 305.
30. See also Fackre, *Christology in Context*, 200.
31. Migliore, *Faith Seeking Understanding*, 351.
32. Abdul-Masih, *Edward Schillebeeckx and Hans Frei*, 159.

sociated with traditional Christianity. Traditional Christianity is ideology, according to Schillebeeckx, because it supposedly turns the idea of resurrection into a negation of history.[33] In other words, traditional theology promotes the idea of Jesus's physical/bodily resurrection which helped Jesus continue his pre-death existence into an after-death life; both, however, are seen as earthly types of human—though redeemed—existence. Schillebeeckx concurs with the idea that Jesus is the Christ if Jesus is seen as dead and Christ is the proclamation of Jesus after his death.[34] He is not willing to accept though that Jesus is the Christ who came back to life after he was dead for three days. Such a view, promoted by traditional theology, is a negation of history because the belief in the possibility of life after death annuls the factual reality of the universal and terminal character of death. Our daily experience tells us that people do not come to life after death, and Jesus is no exception. To hold that he is such an exception is to neutralize the reality of everyday life and thus to negate history itself.

Thus, in Schillebeeckx, death is eternal but it can be more than a mere tragic event which ends one's existence.[35] In Jesus's case, death—though eternal—became meaningful due to his life. Without the practical and loving example of his life, Jesus's death would have remained meaningless in itself (as it is indeed if considered on its own, as the end of Jesus's life). The utmost negativity of Jesus's death is taken away by the overflowing positivity of his life that was marked by the hope that the world can be changed in favor of those who suffer daily oppression.[36] In Schillebeeckx, oppression takes many forms—it can be natural, social, existential or even political—so Jesus's life is a proof that these forms of oppression can and should be fought. Furthermore, based on the practical example of his life, even his death bears the same meaningful connotation because he lost his life in an attempt to stop oppression and offer a good service to humanity.[37] Evidently, he did not succeed in actually stopping oppression but he definitely hoped for the best and acted as such, so his death was overcome by his hope which eventually began to influence his followers. At this point, Schillebeeckx reintroduces the idea of resurrection which

---

33. See also Perkins, *Peter, Apostle for the Whole Church*, 7.
34. Schillebeeckx, *The Church with a Human Face*, 26–27.
35. See also La Due, *The Trinity Guide to Eschatology*, 7.
36. Bergin, *O Propheticum Lavacrum*, 250.
37. Schillebeeckx, *The Church with a Human Face*, 24.

he defines as being historically anticipated by Jesus's life. Thus, it seems quite clear that resurrection becomes synonymous to hope because he does not believe in the physical resurrection of Jesus's dead body but in the revitalization of his hope for a better world within the community of his followers.[38] To make things even clearer: the type of resurrection wherein Schillebeeckx believes is categorically not the resurrection of a dead body, and certainly not the coming back to life of Jesus's corpse; it is the resurrection of an idea, the resurrection of the idea that hope in changing the world transcends individual death.[39] Jesus could not stand evil, so he fought against it in a practical way. He died because of this but his hope for a better world lived on—or, in Schillebeeckx's terms—came back to life in the belief and practice of Jesus's followers.

Schillebeeckx painstakingly tries to remain within the lines of traditional theology, so he does not refrain from using the word resurrection or the idea that resurrection should be associated to the concept of a superior power which is capable of countering evil. It is clear in traditional theology that Jesus's death—followed by his actual, physical, and bodily resurrection of his dead body—defeated evil once and for all, which actually made our salvation from sin a real possibility. Schillebeeckx retains the basic idea of the conquering of sin—he prefers the word evil—by Jesus's death but his death is permanent and is not *the* actual victory over evil.[40] Nevertheless, Jesus's death is victorious because he lived up to his ideal and fought sin despite the constant threat of death. There is also a second reason why Jesus's death was victorious, namely because his hope of changing the world and his practical example were transmitted to the community of his followers who acted accordingly irrespective of his death on the cross:[41]

> We cannot detach the defencelessness of Jesus on the cross from the free power and the positivity which revealed itself in his actual career of solidarity with oppressed men and women on the basis of an absolute trust in God. God is concerned with the happiness of men and women who live under the threat of nature, social oppression and self-alienation. Jesus is so opposed to this that his concern for his own survival fades away and even plays no part.

---

38. Caputo, *More Radical Hermeneutics*, 223.
39. Yeo, *Rhetorical Interaction*, 30.
40. Rego, *Suffering and Salvation*, 310.
41. Borgman, *Edward Schillebeeckx*, 172–73.

Oppression may not be; the right of the strongest may not apply in the life of the human community. Oppression is injustice and a scandal. So Jesus refuses to regard evil as being on the same footing as good and acts accordingly. Jesus's career itself is therefore praxis of the kingdom of God, a historical anticipation of the resurrection and his death is part of this career. So we can speak of his death as a defenceless superior power, disarming evil. Moreover, it was already the insight of the first Christians that even the earthly life of Jesus has to show positive anticipations of the resurrection if faith in the resurrection is not to be ideological; and that insight is acutely expressed in the story in which the Synoptic Gospels speak of a transfiguration of Jesus during his earthly life.[42]

It would have been most interesting to see how Schillebeeckx understands the idea of Jesus's transfiguration but unfortunately the explanation was not offered.[43] One thing, however, is clear: transfiguration must not be interpreted in ontological terms or in the sense that a higher, divine power from beyond the world transformed Jesus's face in such a way that it began to shed a physical light. In accordance to Schillebeeckx's general theology, Jesus's transfiguration appears to be the realization of the fact that his dramatic message may cause him to face his own death as well as the understanding that his ideal may be realistically taken over and implemented by his followers in view of changing society. Schillebeeckx seems to entertain the idea that he became liberated from any possible human fears when he realized that, following his death, his ideal would be "resurrected" and carried on by this disciples. This is why the idea of resurrection is closely tied to the notion of liberation[44] but it is not liberation from sin, perceived as trespass against a living, personal, and real God, but liberation from disappointment. In other words, the resurrection is not soteriological but only psychological or existential.[45] We actually understand our human fears and we come to terms with our own death; once we accept this dual reality there is nothing ahead of us which can hinder us from living out our ideal; moreover, there is nothing which can stop us from bequeathing this ideal to the next generation. Finally, there is nothing which can prevent the next generation from implementing this ideal

---

42. Schillebeeckx, *Church*, 127–28. For further insights into the idea of defenselessness, see Haught, "Evolution and God's Humility," 12.

43. See also Scirghi, *An Examination*, 139–40.

44. Bowden, *Edward Schillebeeckx*, 124.

45. See Bloesch, *The Last Things*, 116.

in its own context. To be sure, in Schillebeeckx the idea of resurrection is a means to affirm the universal character of human ideals as well as the universality of man's desire to fight evil.[46] If this is true, then the resurrection is not necessarily a personal reality but a universal reality which takes personal forms in individual, personal lives.

According to Schillebeeckx, Jesus lived and died displaying an unshakable trust in God's saving presence which was constant although not always visibly manifest. As in Schillebeeckx God is not the traditional God which has an ontologically real and Trinitarian existence beyond the reality of the created world/universe, but only the temporal reality of our own earthly future the idea of resurrection needs to be seen in this new light. Jesus did not trust the God of traditional Christianity with whom he shared the same divine substance; he trusted only the possibility of seeing his ideals brought back to life in the practical existence of his followers. Schillebeeckx talks about God's saving presence which Jesus trusted; what he trusted in fact was the contemplation of a future that could be the witness of his ideals and hope for a better world. Belief in such a future possibility was liberating for Jesus and, if we are to believe Schillebeeckx, the same should happen to us. We all have to get rid of our fear of death, of having our lives ended without meaning attached to them; if we want to escape this fear, then we have to believe in resurrection, the resurrection of our good ideals in the lives of those who will live in the future. We have to fight evil, we have to do justice, we have to strive for the best, we have to search for the benefit of our fellow men and women;[47] Jesus understood this and his disciples understood it. This is the essence of Christianity according to Schillebeeckx: the necessity to do good and fight evil, with view to a future world which is worth living in. Life ends and this is absurd; our lives end and this is equally absurd. Nevertheless, we must not allow despair to defeat us; we must do whatever we can to transform the world following Jesus's example.[48] If we do so, our lives will be meaningful, and when death comes we will not have lived in vain. Although death awaits us, we are powerful if we do our best to improve the world but we have to be careful never to use this power wrongly:

---

46. Hilkert, *Naming Grace*, 36.
47. Schillebeeckx, *God Is New Each Moment*, 113.
48. Hill, *Jesus, the Christ*, 187.

Re-Assessing the Doctrine of Resurrection

The psalm which Jesus prays on the cross and which begins with the words "My God, my God, why have you forsaken me?" ends in a prayer of thanksgiving for God's abiding, albeit silent, saving presence. God was not powerless when Jesus hung on the cross, but he was defenceless and vulnerable as Jesus was vulnerable. The basic experience of the first disciples after Good Friday was that evil, the cross, cannot have the last word; Jesus's career is right and is the last word, which is sealed in his resurrection. Although the cross was on the one hand the sealing of the superior power of human beings over God, in the dying Jesus God is present and indeed present as pure positivity, as he was with the living Jesus. In that case, suffering and death remain absurd and even in Jesus's case may not be mystified; but they do not have the last word because the liberating God was absolutely close to Jesus on the cross, just as he was throughout Jesus's career. But that was a presence without power or compulsion . . . God's presence was near in power, but without the misuse of power.[49]

It is interesting to notice Schillebeeckx's notion of God's vulnerability, also applied to Jesus.[50] God was vulnerable and Jesus was vulnerable, writes Schillebeeckx, and he is right according to his own definition of God as the future of man and of Jesus as a mere human being.[51] When he writes that God was vulnerable although still powerful, he actually means that our future was uncertain because nobody knew for a fact what would happen to those who believed in Jesus. Things were pretty clear with Jesus; he would die within hours, so his fate was sealed. The future seemed gloomy but it turned out that his disciples decided to fight against evil by taking over Jesus's ideal. So they decided to resurrect Jesus. At the same time, the future was powerful because the possibility of having a better future based on Jesus's teachings was at least a theoretical possibility. Happily, this possibility turned out to be true when the vulnerability of the future was removed by the disciples' decision to preach Jesus's ideal to the world in order to teach people how to be saved as well as resurrected within the confinement of the present world. It is evident that, in Schillebeeckx, salvation and resurrection are entirely existential

---

49. Schillebeeckx, *Church*, 128.
50. McManus, *Unbroken Community*, 66.
51. For details about God's vulnerability in Schillebeeckx, see also Haught, *Responses*, 114.

and social.[52] Our so-called resurrection is definitely not the resurrection of our dead bodies but the resurrection of our ideals. In other words, our "resurrection" will never affect us but those who outlive us if they choose to implement our ideals in society. We will remain dead forever—this is clear beyond doubt in Schillebeeckx—but we have the chance of being resurrected when our ideals are taken over by future generations and used to change the face of the world for the better.[53]

OUR RESURRECTION: EFFICIENCY IN CHANGING THE WORLD

It should be quite clear by now that the traditional notion of resurrection in Christian theology—which asserts the bodily, physical, and spiritual return to life of a dead body—is dramatically reassessed in Schillebeeckx. Jesus died and stayed dead, and the same applies to us. If in traditional Christianity Jesus's resurrection is the hope for and the foundation of our resurrection,[54] in Schillebeeckx the basic rule remains the same with the notorious exception that the very "content" of the resurrection is utterly changed. Resurrection cannot be interpreted in terms of the past, when belief in a bodily, physical return to life of a dead corpse was conceivable; it has to be reinterpreted in terms of the present situation, expectations, and beliefs as the conviction that human life has meaning and, if lived properly, that meaningfulness can be "resurrected" in the future.[55] The same is true when it comes to the relationship between Jesus's career and its subsequent, future understanding by his disciples.

It is at this point that Schillebeeckx introduces the idea of the church, which is a community of men and women who believe in the spiritual presence of Jesus in the church. According to Schillebeeckx, they seemed to have come to terms and eventually fully accepted the disturbing fact that Jesus was dead and would never come back to life again; definitely not as a human person in a human body. He was dead, and this situation was not going to change.[56] They did, however, realize that Jesus's teachings were full of meaning for their lives and for the lives of others. This is when

---

52. Ford, ed., *The Modern Theologians*, 104.
53. See also Haight, *The Future of Christology*, 109.
54. Schillebeeckx, *God Is New Each Moment*, 32.
55. See also Schillebeeckx, *The Concept of Truth*, 137.
56. Tupper, "Theology, Christology and Eschatology," 121.

Re-Assessing the Doctrine of Resurrection

they decided to resume their "relationship" with Jesus—now dead—whom they preached as the "living" Christ of their small community.[57] Of course Jesus was dead and Christ was non-existent as a person; nevertheless, they were so convinced by the reality of Jesus's teachings as well as their capacity to confer meaning to other people's lives that they did not differentiate between the dead Jesus of history and the "resurrected" Christ of their community. As far as Schillebeeckx is concerned, they soon realized that Jesus's teachings, which they began to preach again amongst their fellow nationals, were having a high degree of effectiveness in the sense that lives were changed and more people expressed their wish to be part of their community. Thus, they noticed that preaching about Jesus's resurrection was a good thing to do because their message—obviously based on Jesus's teachings—was effective in changing the world.[58] It is evident then that the idea of resurrection in Schillebeeckx as applied to Jesus needs to be interpreted in terms of its effectiveness in the church. The dead Jesus was now "brought back to life" in the consciousness of the church because his message was effective. Jesus is resurrected, he is "alive" under the name of Christ, precisely because his teachings proved their efficiency in the church and then in the world. For Schillebeeckx, every event that followed Jesus's death and marked the life of the church from Jesus's "resurrection" to the life of the church as driven by the spirit of Jesus should be understood in terms of the effectiveness of Jesus's message. Therefore, he argues that the idea of Jesus's resurrection

> remains an abstraction which we cannot locate properly in theology if we leave aside the living, *pneumatic* presence of the glorified Jesus in his church. Through and in this Christian belief in the resurrection of Jesus, the crucified but risen Jesus remains effective in our history through his followers. Jesus's resurrection, his sending of the Spirit, the origin of the Christian community of God as the church of Christ which lives from the Spirit, the new Testament witness to all this and thus resurrection faith, define one another reciprocally, though they cannot be identified with one another.[59]

It should be highlighted here that Schillebeeckx really strives to remain within the limits of traditional Christianity at least in terms of

---

57. See Abdul-Masih, *Edward Schillebeeckx and Hans Frei*, 157.
58. McManus, *Unbroken Communion*, 34.
59. Schillebeeckx, *Church*, 130.

the theological language he uses; nevertheless, even if his theological language is fairly traditional in many instances he just cannot refrain from adding to it what he believes it is its correct interpretation or rather reinterpretation. To give just one example, in traditional theology the validity of Jesus's resurrection is given by his post-resurrection appearances among his disciples and other people.[60] Schillebeeckx is fully aware of this, so in discussing his theory of Jesus's resurrection he also makes reference to Jesus's subsequent appearances. However, it is a commonplace by now—and Schillebeeckx does not lose sight of this—that his drastic reinterpretation of the traditional concept of revelation as applied to Jesus keeps Jesus in the tomb, so the resurrection cannot be presented as the coming back to life of a dead body but as the effectiveness of Jesus's teaching among his disciples because this is how they related to God through him.[61] This is why Schillebeeckx decides to make further use of the idea of effectiveness not only in connection with his redefinition of Jesus's resurrection but also with reference to his reassessment of the confirmation of Jesus's resurrection. In other words, if in traditional theology Jesus's resurrection is indeed the coming back to physical life of his dead body, a fact which was confirmed by his equally physical—as well as simultaneously spiritual—appearances among his disciples who could see and touch him in a physical way, the same argument must be kept in redefining the resurrection and its confirmation. Thus, Schillebeeckx introduces the idea of the future effectiveness of Jesus's message among his disciples to explain his resurrection while the same idea of effectiveness is also used for the reassessment of Jesus's appearances which confirm his resurrection. This means that, when we say Jesus was resurrected, it means he continued to be effective in the midst of his disciples through his message; this fact was confirmed by Jesus's appearances which should not be understood in physical terms but in connection with the idea of effectiveness. Jesus appeared among his disciples in the sense that he was present in the church in an effective way.[62] He could not have been present physically or spiritually; he was present there effectively. Schillebeeckx does not elaborate this idea but it would be logical to say that Jesus's effective presence among his disciples should be understood as the effective presence of his message,

60. La Due, *The Trinity Guide to Eschatology*, 7.

61. This is also true of the incarnation. See McGrath, *The Christian Theology Reader*, 588.

62. Guerriere, *Phenomenology*, 157–58.

not of his person who was physically dead when his disciples began to sense the effectiveness of his teachings[63]: "We can say that the "church of Christ" which came into being on the basis of the resurrection of Jesus is what is meant most deeply in the New Testament by the appearances of Jesus: in the assembled believing community of the church the crucified but risen Jesus appears, i.e., is effectively present."[64]

The immediate consequence of Schillebeeckx's reinterpretation of the traditional idea of resurrection as essentially physical (but also spiritual) is the fact that there is no such thing as eternal life. Jesus's message is liberating, as Schillebeeckx hastens to underline, but is does not offer any liberation from death in terms of a physical resurrection; it only gives believers liberation from their own fears so that they are able to return to true life, a life which is free of any crisis. Schillebeeckx does not say what sort of crisis he has in mind but it is quite clear that the crisis is mere existential or psychological.[65] Why existential or psychological crisis, and not any other sort of human crisis? Because the goal of Schillebeeckx's theology is the establishment of a better life for humanity here and now, in the terrestrial reality of our history. Jesus is no longer seen as the traditional redeemer from sin in view of humanity's welfare in a future, extra-historical reality with an ontologically real God; Jesus is a mere liberator of individual minds who helps us come to terms with our existence on earth. According to Schillebeeckx, he helps us understand that there is no after life; the only life we have is here, and the only change we have to make things right is also here, on earth and within the limits of history. There is no eternal life as in traditional theology; life is by no means eternal, it is finite and there is no hope for a better life in a future which is not historical. The future of humanity is essentially historical, and Schillebeeckx does not seem to have second thoughts about it.[66] He distances himself again from traditional theology which, in his understanding, promotes a God that oppresses people in history while promising them a better future in a beyond-the-world reality which does not exist. Schillebeeckx is convinced that the God of traditional Christianity does not only oppress people but he also humiliates men and women by misleading them

---

63. See also Schillebeeckx, *Christ, the Sacrament of the Encounter with God*, 178.
64. Schillbeeckx, *Church*, 130.
65. See also McManus, *Unbroken Communion*, 169.
66. Kennedy, *Schillebeeckx*, 44.

to believe in a physical/spiritual resurrection of their dead bodies in a future which is not of this world.[67] Here is what Schillebeeckx has to say about the subject:

> Where the church lives by Jesus Christ, lives by praying and liberating men and women in the footsteps of Jesus, belief in the resurrection does not undergo any crisis. On the other hand, I feel very strongly that it is better that there should be no belief in eternal life than that a God should be presented who diminishes people in the here and now, keeps them down and humiliates them politically with an eye to a better hereafter.[68]

So there is no resurrection and no eternal life in Schillebeeckx's theology, at least not within the lines set by traditional theology. There is no resurrection for Jesus and there is no eternal life for Jesus in terms of a physical return to life which enables him to live physically for ever. If this is the case, then it is clear that there is no resurrection for us and there is no eternal life for us in terms of a physical reanimation of our dead bodies which allows us to continue our existence in an ontologically transcendent future. Schillebeeckx cannot accept the traditional understanding of resurrection because he cannot accept that there is a higher authority for humanity than its own rationality. According to him, we have to reflect on our norms and values based on our own rationality, not on ideas which are imposed on us. There is nothing binding to us in this world, so we are free to use our intellect in order to redefine everything. If there is anything binding to us at all, then Schillebeeckx would definitely list two things: human rationality and human suffering.[69] Human rationality is binding because it is the only reality which helps us cope with ourselves and our expectations. If we do not understand something, we should not go in the past in order to get an answer; what we should do is stay in the present and search the present based on our own grasp of the present. The way we understand the present is given by what and how we use our reason. For Schillebeeckx, the future is always better than the past, so the way we think now is permanently a future reality as compared to the past. The past is bad not because of its value but because of its lack of relevance for today's world, which is always a future reality compared to what lies

---

67. Rego, *Suffering and Salvation*, 233.
68. Schillebeeckx, *Church*, 130.
69. Schillebeeckx, *God Is New Each Moment*, 109.

behind us. This is why Schillebeeckx urges us to use our reason to discern things even if this leads to drastic reinterpretations of traditional doctrines. The reality of suffering is always present in the world and we have to fight against it.[70] Our rationality is permanent in the world and so is suffering; this is why we have to use our reason to solve the problem of suffering.[71] Why should we then believe in God at all? Because the idea of God is linked to the idea of good and the message of theology—traditional or not—is that good will defeat evil.[72] This seems to be essence of Schillebeeckx's theology: the fact that good is here to stay for ever while evil is terminated.

He likes this idea so much that he reinterprets the entire traditional theology in order to make it relevant to the people of the present. Schillebeeckx though is not foolish: he knows evil cannot be destroyed just like that; this is why he connects the reality of today's evil and suffering to the notion of the evil's eschatological destruction. Evil cannot be destroyed now; but it can be fought against now—hope means action.[73] Evil will be destroyed in the future; we do not know when but as it cannot be finished now our only hope is that it will be destroyed in the future. For as long as we have the hope that evil will be destroyed in the future, the life of humanity will permanently be an existence worth living. When he reaches this point of the argument, Schillebeeckx introduces the idea of eternal life. Human life is eternal as long as men and women share the hope that evil will be destroyed in the future. Schillebeeckx does not say whether the destruction of evil is partial or total; he definitely hopes it will be total but there are no guarantees for such a belief. At the end of the day, it does not really matter for him whether evil will be destroyed for good; what counts is the fact that humanity will have eternal life for as long as its representatives decide to counter evil and suffering whenever they have the chance to engage in battle.[74]

It is clear that Schillebeeckx hates the reality as well as the idea of suffering and he hates it so intensely that he reassesses the traditional

---

70. Bowden, *Edward Schillebeeckx*, 94.
71. McBrien, *Catholicism*, 1143.
72. McManus, *Unbroken Communion*, 164.
73. Stone, *Prophetic Realism*, 101.
74. See also Migliore, *Faith Seeking Understanding*, 351.

doctrine of hell.[75] He simply cannot accept the idea of hell, and this is not because it would be totally unreasonable or irrational but because it is associated to the idea of suffering. If evil is defeated in future, then there is no reason for the existence of hell. If we are to believe Schillebeeckx, it seems that even the idea of hell is essentially part of the reality of evil, so if we hate evil we have to reject the idea of hell. So there is no hell but only our own future, and the only duty we have as human beings is to make sure this future will be worth living. The ideas of a physical resurrection and of eternal life should be obsolete by now in Schillebeeckx's argument; this, however, should not bother us. If, by any chance, we cannot give up the idea of salvation and eternal life, then we must reinterpret these traditional doctrines in terms of our present rationality. We have to surrender to God in faith, hope, and love because this is the only way we can believe in the eternity of our life. We are eternal if our life and values are bequeathed to those who come after us. In other words, we have to surrender to our own future if we want to be eternal. We have to believe that the future will be better than the present, evil will be destroyed, and humanity will have the chance to continue its existence eternally.[76]

If there is no eternal life and no resurrection in the traditional terms of a physical return to life of a dead body, nothing remains open to us except for our present reality which dictates how we should understand the world.[77] We are limited though, so Schillebeeckx explains that reality is a mystery to all of us. We have to turn to ourselves, to our experiences and sensibility in order to understand reality, which is at the end of the day our own reality. Reality is a *datum* but we have to interpret and reinterpret it in such a way that makes it relevant to our present experience.[78] This means being constantly open to the future of our reality or, in Schillebeeckx's words, "we have to be eschatologically transparent." Openness to the future guarantees openness to the present reality and the understanding of the present reality by means of reason makes our existence and experience worthwhile. Our own reason teaches us that we need the idea of God as the ultimate mystery in order for our lives to be meaningful.[79] We

75. For details, see Borgman, *Edward Schillebeeckx*, 248.
76. Ramona Simuţ, "Reinterpreting Traditional Theology," 279. See also Corneliu C. Simuţ, *A Critical Study*, 176.
77. Abdul-Masih, *Edward Schillebeeckx and Hans Frei*, 77.
78. Schillebeeckx, *The Eucharist*, 132.
79. Hilkert and Schreiter, eds., *The Praxis*, 60.

have to trust God and be open to him but it is the same reason that tells us that God is our own future, so we have to be open to that future which is forever terrestrial and temporal. This is why, in Schillebeeckx, the traditional doctrines of a physical/spiritual resurrection and meta-historical eternal life are concepts with no relevance to our present reality. Human existence will always remain earthly, so "unearthly" teachings are a matter of theoretical speculation which presents no value to the expectation of our present life:

> Reality is a mystery for us. We reflect the encounter with the world and history via our experiences and our sensibility. We do not create the world, we rethink the world which encounters us, and this is an act of interpretation. There is an ontological basis for our thinking. We do not create the meaning, we have to interpret the meaning which already exists. We have to be eschatologically transparent. We can approach finite concepts and the meaning of the world only by means of our human minds. We have human concepts about God, but the reality of God is unspeakable to us. God is the ultimate mystery, but parts of that mystery of God become transparent through our way of life and our experience. Christianity is a way of life, it is not theoretical speculation.[80]

It is interesting and almost weird, to notice that despite Schillebeeckx's unceasing endeavor to limit the understanding of God to the sphere of human possibilities and rationality, he nevertheless supports the idea of a reality which is superior to mankind. This is probably the only trace of traditionalism left in his theology following his categorical reinterpretation of Christian doctrines. He does not bother too much to define this superior reality which he connects to the idea of the power of God but it has to be said that he does underline the necessity that humanity should cling to it. What is this superior reality? It is the power of God,[81] namely the power of our own future, and it is at the same time the power of the grace of God, which is just another way of saying that the power of the future is universally valid for every human being. In other words, man is surpassed by the power of a future which lies unknown ahead of him and the fact that man does not know what he should expect from this future is perceived by him as a power which overwhelms him. The future is ahead of us, we do not know what will happen but we can hope for the best;

---

80. Ramona Simuț, "Reinterpreting Traditional Theology," 278.
81. See also Schillebeeckx, *Christ, the Sacrament of the Encounter with God*, 205.

hoping though is not a guarantee that the best is there to happen in accordance with our present expectations. The power of the future is therefore a daily experience because each one of us expects the unfolding of the future in a permanent way.[82] Expecting the future is so present in our lives and yet so decisively unknown that it becomes the definitive experience of humanity and, in this sense, it seems to be superior to us. Confronted with such a powerful experience, our lives seem meaningless because we do not know what to expect. What we can do though in order to confer meaning to our lives is to display resurrection faith, that is a faith in the possibility that our present expectation should be met in future with view to the benefit of the entire humanity.[83] This can be achieved if we believe that Jesus, who has been dead for more than two thousand years now, is spiritually present among us in such a way that we can perceive his spiritual presence as a true resurrection from the dead.[84] In doing so, we experience the superior power of God which makes our lives meaningful for our own present and for the future of those who come after us. Here is how Schillebeeckx defines the experience of what he calls the superior power of God:

> The spiritual presence of Jesus in believers has consequences for Christian life. Just as positive anticipations of the resurrection and thus of the superior power of the grace of God could be seen in Jesus's life (and must be seen, if resurrection faith is not to become an ideology), so the same holds true for Christians. Within the defencelessness of our own lives we must be able to *experience* the superior power of God; otherwise we accept it with a faith which is presented as purely authoritarian.[85]

What is our resurrection then? It is certainly not the return to physical/spiritual life of our dead bodies but a continuous experience of our own present. It is now that we understand our role in shaping our own beliefs; it is now that we realize that our physical life will come to an end so we have to make the most of it and turn it into a meaningful experience. Life is definitely not meaningful unless essentially and thoroughly

---

82. McManus, *Unbroken Communion*, 21.
83. Caputo, *More Radical Hermeneutics*, 223.
84. Bergin, *O Propheticum Lavacrum*, 183.
85. Schillebeeckx, *Church*, 130–31.

human, so we must unceasingly humanize our human existence.[86] What we have to do in order to understand and experience the power of resurrection in our earthly lives is to integrate the entire sphere of human existence into the practical reality of daily life. We have to follow what Schillebeeckx calls the gospel, namely the good news that teaches us to believe and live out God's universal love.[87] We have to look for salvation but in Schillebeeckx salvation is not from trespasses committed against a personal and ontologically real God but against other human beings. We find salvation if we understand the gospel of doing good to others; we find salvation if we understand what we can become as humanized human beings, namely as people resurrected to a new understanding of life. Actually, resurrection in Schillebeeckx is a sort of a coming to one's humanized senses when we understand that we can be better and act accordingly. We can become resurrected if we follow the example of Jesus; in other words, we can fully understand that we can live for and love others if we accept what Jesus did when he was alive. Thus, our resurrection is the humanization of our entire existence with view to the application of Jesus's ministry patterns. To be resurrected is to love others as our fellow human beings[88]; to be resurrected is to do one's best in order to change the world by means of the good news that teaches us the validity of universal love. Resurrection is learning; it is applying our own rationality in order to learn how to become better for the benefit of the entire humanity:

> In light of this Christian view of Jesus's career, death, and resurrection, both "God" and "Jesus" can take on a critical and productive, liberating power for us. The criterion of humanization, proclaimed by Jesus and used by him in practice, beyond all human expectations of the *humanum* which they desire and which is constantly threatened, this desire for the humanity of humankind, for our soundness and wholeness, is something which is close to the heart of God and not a reduction of the gospel. For the gospel is good news not just about Jesus but about the God of Jesus, creator of heaven and earth, the God of all men and women ... The message of Jesus embraces the kingdom of God in all its height and depth, breadth and length, not just the forgiveness of sins and eternal life, though it does comprise that and indeed perhaps does so above all. Jesus proclaimed to the end the absolute, freely effective near-

---

86. Kennedy, *Schillebeeckx*, 137.
87. See also Perry, *Love and Power*, 178.
88. See also Schillebeeckx, *God is New Each Moment*, 46.

ness of the God who creates and brings salvation to human beings in all their dimensions. We Christians learn, stammeringly, to express the content of what God is and the content of what men and women can be, in other words the content of human salvation, from the career of Jesus.[89]

This paragraph is crucial for Schillebeeckx's hermeneutic. A key word in this respect is the *humanum* which seems to be the entire sphere of human relationship or the realm of whatever is specific to humanity.[90] At the end of the day, the *humanum* is humanity, and it is this particular concept that defines Schillebeeckx's theological understanding.[91] Everything—God, Jesus, salvation, humanity, resurrection, theology etc.—must be interpreted in light of the *humanum*.[92] This means that everything—God, Jesus, salvation, humanity, resurrection, theology etc.—must be humanized, so God is human, Jesus is human, salvation is human, humanity is human, resurrection is human, theology is human. Nothing is divine before it is human and nothing is divine without being human. Actually, the idea of divinity itself needs to be humanized; so nothing is truly human unless humanized. Everything we know about God must be reassessed by means of the *humanum*, so that our entire existence is fully and decisively made human.[93] God is us, salvation is us, resurrection is us. There are not two types of existence as defined by the ontology of traditional theology: there is no meta-historical divine existence and historical human existence. Existence is essentially human and everything must be seen in light of human existence. Resurrection is essentially human, so our resurrection is historical. Belief in the resurrection is not hope in being brought back to physical/spiritual life after death but hope in being called to life[94]—actually, to a new understanding of life. In other words, we are being resurrected during our own life because there is no life of our own following our death. Thus, according to Schillebeeckx, resurrection is real but it does not happen after one's death; it happens during one's life.[95]

---

89. Schillebeeckx, *Church*, 131–32.
90. Kennedy, *Schillebeeckx*, 136.
91. Borgman, *Edward Schillebeeckx*, 440.
92. Hilkert and Schreiter, eds., *The Praxis*, 105.
93. Torevell, *Losing the Sacred*, 143.
94. Schillebeeckx, *The Church with a Human Face*, 33.
95. See also Depoortere, *A Different God*, 119–20.

Re-Assessing the Doctrine of Resurrection

If resurrection is to happen at all, it has to occur during our lifetime. In Schillebeeckx, resurrection is salvation and salvation is liberation.[96] We are liberated from sin but sin should also be understood in purely human terms. Thus, sin is every bad thing we do to others, and it is from this sin that we must be liberated. Sin no longer has ontological connotations in Schillebeeckx; sin is ultimately social, cultural, and political. When we are liberated from sin, we are resurrected or called to a new life and to all the possibilities presented by this life.[97] If we want to be liberated and resurrected then we have to fight sin in all its forms in order to promote the good in all its forms.[98] At the end of the day, resurrection is involvement in society with view to terminate its flaws and implement its perennial, universal values for the benefit of the entire human race:

> Christian redemption is indeed liberation from sin. But liberation from sin also has a cultural context. In our time the Christian understanding of sin also includes the recognition of systematic disruptions of communication like sexism, racism, and fascism, anti-Semitism, hostility to and attacks on immigrant workers and the Western cultural and religious sense of superiority. The Christian love which is the basis of community therefore also includes the necessity to recognize the need for deep involvement in present-day work of political, cultural, and social emancipation.[99]

What is resurrection? It is being called and open to the new possibilities of human life in accordance with the example of Jesus. If we want to share in the resurrection, Schillebeeckx tells us that we have to accept the fact that there is no life beyond this life and this awareness coupled with Jesus's practical example should help us understand that we have to improve our life as well as the life of others. To be resurrected means to be free from our own fears and despair.[100] To be resurrected is to accept our lives as they are in light of what they can become based on Jesus's example. When we decide to do what Jesus did during his life, then we are saved from our own despair, we accept ourselves, we are resurrected, and then we begin a new life which is not selfishly oriented towards ourselves but selflessly to others. It is evident that, in Schillebeeckx, it is not

---

96. Fackre, *The Christian Story*, vol. 2, 88.
97. Schillebeeckx, *Church*, 132.
98. Abdul-Masih, *Edward Schillebeeckx and Hans Frei*, 159.
99. Schillebeeckx, *Church*, 132.
100. See also Aldwinckle, *Jesus—a Savior or the Savior?*, 58–9.

only salvation which is existential; the resurrection itself is understood within the same lines, namely it is essentially existential and human.[101] Resurrection is ultimately the practical dissemination and implementation of God's love throughout the world in such way that others benefit from this good news. When we are resurrected we understand ourselves and we understand others. Our lives become meaningful and when death comes, we know we did not live in vain. For Schillebeeckx, resurrection is thoroughly existential as it defines the authenticity of life based on what Jesus did for others before his death but also in his death.[102]

To conclude, if in traditional theology we expect our death in order to share in the resurrection and be physically/spiritually alive with our Triune God, in Schillebeeckx we expect our resurrection in order to meet our own death and stay dead with the rest of humanity who will eventually share the same fate. As a consequence of this reinterpretation of resurrection, eternal life is not for us; eternal life is just for those who outlive us only to share in the same, universal, and implacable death which defines human existence as well as bringing it to its end. For Schillebeeckx there is no escape from the world; death itself is not an escape from the world but the absolute confirmation that we belong to the world from the beginning to the end.

---

101. Viladesau, *The Beauty of the Cross*, 24.
102. McManus, *Unbroken Communion*, 102.

6

Re-Imagining Religious Belonging in Ecclesiology

Religious belonging in traditional Christian ecclesiology is given by two essential aspects. First, the personal belonging of the Christian to the person of Jesus Christ seen as risen from the dead and ascended into heaven. The Christian himself is saved from sin and he now personally belongs to the ontologically real person of Jesus Christ, whose existence after death is perceived as real, bodily, physical, and spiritual. Second, the communitarian belonging of the Christian to the body of Christ or the church, which is considered the community of all those who share in the salvation from sin offered by Jesus Christ and who has been renewed by the indwelling of the Holy Spirit. Edward Schillebeeckx's theology dramatically changes the traditional view of Christian religious belonging, in the sense that Jesus is no longer seen as risen from the dead and ascended to heaven. He is physically dead, while only his disciples' understanding of him as the risen Christ shares the attributes of resurrection and ascension. Thus, personal religious belonging is no longer connected to Jesus Christ but only to Christ, in the sense that man does not have a personal relationship with Jesus Christ but only follows the model of Christ. This necessarily leads to the change of communitarian belonging as well, so one does not necessarily have to be part of the church in order to be a Christian; he can indeed follow in the footsteps of Christ while being part of the world as both world and church are partakers of the same realm of God's grace.

PERSONAL BELONGING

It is a commonplace for every traditional Christian that his existence in the world is ontologically connected to the higher and transcendent existence of God, who saved him from sin through the incarnation, life, death, and resurrection of the pre-existent Logos.[1] To be sure, the pre-existent Logos of God became incarnate under the name of Jesus, he preached salvation from sin and the imminent coming of the kingdom of God; he died for the sins of humanity in order to fulfill the prophecies of Scripture and was raised from the dead by God the Father.[2] Then, he ascended to heaven in order to continue his intercessory work for all those whom he has saved and will save from sin, while he sent the Holy Spirit of God to indwell all Christians as a means of connecting the personal life of each individual Christian to the eternal existence of the Trinitarian God.[3] Therefore, in traditional Christian theology, God is seen as an ontological being whose transcendent reality was revealed to humanity in order that men and women be saved from their sinful existence and be brought personally into the presence of God the Father, the Son, and the Holy Spirit. This is why every traditional Christian perceives his existence as a personal belonging to God which is reflected in a very close relationship with Jesus Christ, as well as the Father and the Holy Spirit.[4]

This traditional approach to Christianity was drastically reinterpreted by Edward Schillebeeckx. One of his earliest attempts to reassess Christianity can be seen in his *God the Future of Man*, where Schillebeeckx discusses Christianity based on his conviction that the message of the Gospel—which is essentially the idea of freedom—needs to be reconsidered in new terms.[5] Thus, the classical concept of *metanoia* is exclusively used in an intellectual way, namely in the sense that we must renew our mind as well as our perception of the world we live in.[6] To be sure, Schillebeeckx's *metanoia* has nothing to do with the renewal of one's life after he/she is delivered from sin by the powerful intervention of the Holy Spirit; what he means by *metanoia* is just a renewed approach to ourselves as human beings as well as to our own history.[7] In other words, *metanoia* is not informed by the traditional idea of salvation from sin but by the contemporary reality of the world. The world, however, undergoes

1. For details about the pre-existent Logos in traditional theology, see Grillmeier and Hainthaler, *Christ in Christian Tradition*, vol. 2, Part 2, 277.

2. O'Collins, *Easter Faith*, 44.

3. See also Dupré and Wiseman, eds., *Light from Light*, 276.

4. Stapert, *My Only Comfort*, 55.

5. Schillebeeckx, *God the Future of Man*.

6. Haight, *The Future of Christology*, 191.

7. Guerriere, *Phenomenology*, 150.

an evident process of secularization, which in Schillebeeckx acquires a very positive dimension.[8] Thus, secularization is not seen as damaging to Christianity, but rather profitable for and helpful to Christians and their church. To be more precise, secularization does not mean giving up the idea of God and the rejection of Christianity; it only means social change which quite normally leads to a fundamental reinterpretation of the idea of God as well as of Christianity.[9] In other words, because Christianity is a world religion and manifests itself in society, it will be inevitably affected by whatever happens within society. Furthermore, Christians must be aware of the fact that society changes and they should change their approach to Christianity and the idea of God in accordance to this process of secularization.[10] Christianity is a religion in the world, it is part of the life of the world, so it is also part of society, which means that, as a religion, Christianity is a significant social aspect of the world.[11] Thus, if the world changes, society changes, and if society changes then religion, in our case Christianity, also changes. It is clear then that Christianity is not informed by the teachings of Scripture as in traditional theology—although they should be used in a new way, i.e., dramatically reinterpreted—but by society and social changes:[12]

> If the phenomenon generally known as secularization is considered apart from all ideology, one is bound in the long run to conclude that this word refers to a very complex event, the basis of which is that man's relationship with the world and his social environment is radically changing . . . This phenomenon is connected with religion only indirectly insofar as the image that we form of God and the way in which we experience religion are at work within the current image that we form of man and the world. There is a correlation between what we say about God and what we say about man. Religion, as a living, human reality in the world, is also a visible social factor and therefore implicated in all the great social changes that occur.[13]

8. Ramona Simuţ, "Reinterpreting Traditional Theology," 282. See also Corneliu C. Simuţ, *A Critical Study*, 172.

9. For the necessity of social change, see Doyle, *The Church Emerging from Vatican II*, 213.

10. Lukken, *Per Visibilia ad Invisibilia*, 52.

11. See also Boeve, "Thinking Sacramental Presence," 12.

12. Burtchaell, *From Synagogue to Church*, 176.

13. Schillebeeckx, *God the Future of Man*, 172.

Thus, secularization is good because it is a normal development of the contemporary society, which is heavily influenced by science and technology.[14] It is essential, at this point, to underline the fact that Schillebeeckx has a paradigmatic approach to history in the sense that human history should be seen in paradigms which are characterized by certain dominant word-views. Although he does not develop or minutely explain his paradigmatic approach to history, Schillebeeckx clearly differentiates between contemporary society, which is driven by science, industrial development, and technological progress, and what he calls pre-scientific and pre-industrial society.[15] Our society is obviously scientific and industrial, so pre-scientific and pre-industrial beliefs must change. The reason is simple, at least for Schillebeeckx: pre-scientific and pre-industrial beliefs were oriented to the past, so they kept humanity from progress because they pushed people to consider authorities from the past. These historically-based beliefs must change and will change because science and technology are fundamentally concerned with and oriented towards the future.[16] Schillebeeckx seems to be very optimistic concerning scientific and technological progress, which in his view promotes the well-being of mankind and opens new realities for men and women. If these new realities are to be met, people should not look back to the past but confidently set their eyes on the future.[17]

This also applies to religion and implicitly to Christianity. Religion is part of society, so it is a social factor. If society in general drops off its pre-scientific and pre-industrial beliefs, so should Christianity. It is clear that Schillebeeckx associates pre-scientific and pre-industrial beliefs with traditional Christianity because they were wrongly based on man's helplessness in the world. In other words, in traditional Christianity, man felt helpless, so he invented the idea of the ontologically real God who could help him. As this God is revealed in the Scriptures and the Scriptures were written in the past, obedience to this God meant a constant orientation to Scriptures and to the past. Thus, man needed this idea of God and Scriptures to supplement his own powers and God was a substitute

---

14. Rego, *Suffering and Salvation*, 55.
15. Rego, *Suffering and Salvation*, 43.
16. Walls, *The Oxford Handbook of Eschatology*, 226.
17. Schillebeeckx, *God the Future of Man*, 172–73.

for whatever man lacked.[18] Today's society, however, is utterly different. Due to technological and scientific progress, man feels more powerful, so he does not need the traditional idea of an ontologically real God and of a church which encompasses all those who believe in such a God. Contemporary society is made up of people who are confident in their own powers because scientific and technological progress has opened new possibilities for them in the future. This is actually secularization, namely the detachment of humanity from its previous pre-scientific and pre-industrial traditional beliefs in order to embrace a scientific, technologically informed, worldview which highlights man's own power.[19] This is how Schillebeeckx describes pre-scientific beliefs which must be given up because they belong to the obsolete past:

> In the past, man and civilization had still not come of age from the scientific and technical point of view and this meant a feeling of helpless-ness with regard to the things to be accomplished in the world; man's power had to be *supplemented* by religion. God, the hope of religious man, had in the past to function as his refuge in those secular spheres in which he had not yet achieved a firm hold on the world and human society. Looking back from our present position, we may say that God served, in those by-gone days, as a substitute for the powers which man himself lacked. Now that man seems to be capable of coping with the world on his own, he no longer appeals to God and the Church to supply for his impotence. This aspect of the modern phenomenon can legitimately be called secularization.[20]

Thus, for Schillebeeckx, the traditional God is nothing more than a mere concept meant to help man in his attempt to master his own fears. Any man who believes in such a God is bound to stay in the past and cut himself off the possibility of progress.[21] Schillebeeckx though seems very unrealistic about man's possibilities of mastering the world by means of his own powers, and his argument can be perceived even as being quite naïve. Without diminishing the crucial role of contemporary science and

---

18. See also Evans, *The Church and the Churches*, 6.
19. Cf. Ross, *Extravagant Affections*, 71–72.
20. Schillebeeckx, *God the Future of Man*, 173–74.
21. The same is applicable to the church, which should permanently renew itself in accordance with contemporary expectations and beliefs. See also Stewart, *Jesus the Holy Fool*, 228.

technology in present day society, it has to be said that man is very far from mastering the world let alone mastering himself. The reality of war as well as the all-present reality of all sorts of abuse can hardly be ignored in today's society. Massive destruction by war as well as individual destruction through personal abuse are both realities which cannot be overlooked and they are constant proof of the fact that man is far from being a master of the world and/or himself. His undeterred belief in the progress of science prompts Schillebeeckx to defend the necessity of radical change in religion and Christianity. If we are to be part of the present world, then we—as Christians—must change our past belief into new convictions which are scientifically informed and spiritually relevant. Schillebeeckx does not dismiss religious experience because this seems to be inherent to humanity but he does urge that it should be utterly oriented towards future as well as open to the scientific society of today's world.[22] To quote Schillebeeckx:

> Religion will always express itself and find its context in the concrete human life and will always form a community that is incarnate in the world. Hence it is always a social factor. In former times it exercised its function within the society of the period, which was relatively stable, directed towards the past and intent on perpetuating the past. But the present radical change has obliged religion to function within a new society that is oriented towards the future. Man's religious experience today is therefore having to assimilate something entirely new—an industrial, urbanized world which, under the guidance of science and technological planning, is intent on creating a better future for mankind.[23]

For Schillebeeckx, religion is driven by science and, if this rule is applied to Christianity, then Christianity itself must accept the industrial and urbanized aspects of modern society.[24] This would not be a problem in itself, but the demand that Christianity must radically change so that it becomes heavily informed by science and technology is too far fetched. Schillebeeckx's confidence in contemporary scientific society is much too emphatic even for the modern man who lives in a technologized society. Any modern man who lives today will soon realize that no matter how advanced, science cannot offer all the answers to the very difficult ques-

22. Scirghi, *An Examination*, 132.
23. Schillebeeckx, *God the Future of Man*, 173.
24. McManus, *Unbroken Communion*, 24.

tion which still trouble human consciousness. Why can we not stop wars? Why can we not stop death? Why do some people abuse other people? Why do some people torture, beat, rape, and kill other people? As it is more than obvious today, contemporary industrial and urbanized society is in no way exempted from these social flaws. Traditional theology does offer an answer and this is the very tragic reality of sin, which is both personal/individual and communal/social but Schillebeeckx is not ready to accept such a claim. Sin should be drastically reinterpreted because there is no ontologically real God which defines and hates sin. Without sin and without God, man is left completely on his own in order to handle and supposedly master his own problems. Thus, there is no sense of individual belonging to God as far as man is concerned. Schillebeeckx, however, is aware that he could be criticized for his overconfident belief in technological progress, so he insists that man should not glorify scientific development but rather attempt to make a future of his own. A revolution needs to occur in religion in the sense that man should no longer trust an ontologically real God; what he should do is tailor his future in accordance with his expectations. This is crucial for Schillebeeckx because it is at this point that he advocates the necessity of a new definition of God.[25]

How should contemporary society see God? Definitely not in terms of the past, namely as an ontologically real God, but in terms of the expectations and beliefs of contemporary society itself, which is fundamentally oriented towards the future.[26] Thus, it is not God who determines society, as in traditional theology, but it is society which determines God and what we should believe about God. Therefore, God should no longer be seen as a substitute for human science. Schillebeeckx is crystal clear about the fact that God does not exist within the lines of traditional theology any more. In other words, generations of Christians have been wrong about God but the time has finally come when modern society—heavily industrialized and scientifically informed—can promote a new idea of God which is utterly detached form the traditional concept of transcendence. God is not transcendent in the sense that he has a subsistent, independent and self-sufficient life of his own beyond any possibly boundary of history. For Schillebeeckx, such a conviction links the idea of transcendence to the past when, in fact, it should be oriented towards

---

25. Kennedy, *Schillebeeckx*, 44.
26. See also Schults, *Reforming the Doctrine of God*, 193.

the future.[27] Industrialized society should seek a God which is relevant and appealing to modern man and so should Christians in order for their confession of God to become credible in the world. Thus, the idea of transcendence as applied to God should no longer be connected to the past in order to convey the existence of an ontologically real God, but to the future in such a way that God himself becomes the future of man.[28] In other words, our own future is our own God, whom we should fervently trust. This means that, when man says he believes in God, he actually says he believes in his own future. To conclude, two things must happen within contemporary society in connection with traditional religion and Christianity: first, to reorient the concept of transcendence from the past to the future, and second, to redefine the idea of God based on this newly acquired perspective on transcendence.[29] Here is what Schillebeeckx has to say concerning the first step, the shift from past to future with reference to transcendence:

> In the older culture, orientated towards the past, whenever we thought or spoke of God's transcendence we used, almost automatically, to project God into the past. Eternity was rather like an unchangeable and petrified or eternalized "past"—"*in the beginning* was God." Man knew very well that God's eternity embraced man's present, past, and future, and that God was only "the first," but also "the last," and therefore the presence whose eternal present transcended our present. The older theology had wonderful things to say about this, things which have in no way lost their value. But in that older civilization in which men's eyes were always turned towards the past, a powerful, mutual attraction was felt between "transcendence" and eternity on the one hand and an eternalized "past" on the other. Now, however, in a culture which is resolutely turned towards the future as something that it means to make, what has in fact come about is that the flexible Christian concept of "transcendence," which is open to more than one meaning, is also affected by this shift.[30]

One must give credit to Schillebeeckx's cunning attempt to defend his shift from the past to the future in connection with the idea of transcendence by trying to "redeem" traditional theology. Thus, he infers that even

---

27. Yeo, *Rhetorical Interaction*, 30.
28. See also Häring, "From Divine Human to Human God," 3.
29. McDermott, "Moral Theology," 148.
30. Schillebeeckx, *God the Future of Man*, 180–81.

Re-Imagining Religious Belonging in Ecclesiology

traditional theology had a glimpse of contemporary truth, which is to say that even past theology and traditional Christians have always felt that the past and the future are intertwined in and by their idea of an ontologically real and transcendent God. Schillebeeckx, however, seems to advocate a total detachment from the past when it comes to transcendence because any connection with the past could hinder us from understanding that our God is actually our own future. Thus, we cannot trust old doctrines but only the new possibilities which arise from our new understanding of scientifically oriented expectations. Transcendence is the future, and it is in this respect only that God is transcendent.[31] To be sure, God is transcendent in the sense that he is our future but not in ontologically real terms; it is not as much that God is our future but that our future is our God because it is only within these lines that the idea of God can be accepted based on our daily experiences. To quote Schillebeeckx:

> "Transcendence" thus tends to acquire a special affinity with what is called, in our temporality, "future." For, if divine transcendence really transcends and embraces, from within, man's past, present, and future, the believer will choose, as soon as man has come to recognize the primacy of the future in temporality, to associate God's transcendence with the future and he will be right in doing this. He will associate God with man's future and since this individual person lives within a community of persons, he will eventually also associate God with the future of mankind as a whole. This, then, is the real seed ground for the new image of God in our new culture—provided, of course, the reality of true faith in the invisible God who is the source of the movement impelling man to "form a concept" of God in the light of his worldly experience has been accepted.[32]

This should be taken as a theological affirmation as well as a theological program. Schillebeeckx is convinced that once this new perspective is acquired by every individual Christian, then a new reinterpretation of traditional theology must necessarily happen. If in traditional theology, God was seen as totally transcendent and different from humanity in all respects, now God is not detached from humanity but is actually part of humanity and its history. God is no longer seen in ontological

---

31. This perspective also incorporates the idea of eternal goodness. See Harrington, *Revelation*, 234.

32. Schillebeeckx, *God the Future of Man*, 181.

terms, so he is not to be accepted as a person but rather as the essence of humanity itself. As today's men and women are scientifically informed, they all know that there is no such thing as an independent existence which we traditionally call God; on the contrary, we are God if we set our eyes on the future. Schillebeeckx does not actually put it this way but he does believe in the fact that the future itself becomes our God if we hold fast to it.[33] Thus, God is an idea which is constantly new, very much like the discoveries of science. In other words, to believe in God is to believe in a constantly new future, a future which is planned, devised, and implemented by humanity based on the idea that we must reinterpret the traditional idea of an ontologically real God in order to translate it into our own future. So, God is our own future, or ourselves as oriented to the future; the promised land is the world which is given to us anew as we realize our new God; and our duty is to recreate it anew based on our fresh understanding of God and transcendence.[34]

Scripture should be understood within the same lines, which means that every affirmation of Scripture should be taken historically and scientifically.[35] Thus, Schillebeeckx does not speak about Jesus Christ, but about Jesus who was confessed by his followers as the Christ.[36] Jesus was not a divine-human person but only a human person who lived and died for a cause. He was a prophet who combined mysticism (allusion to traditional theology) with politics.[37] He believed in the welfare of people and preached the coming of the kingdom of God—which is associated with the idea of universal love[38]—even if he knew this could endanger his life. Despite all threats, Jesus continued to preach God's love and he gave himself as an example to the point of accepting his own death because of his unshakable beliefs. For Schillebeeckx, there is no such thing as the Logos of God, who exists from eternity into eternity, who became incarnate under the name of Jesus, who suffered and died for our salvation from sin but was raised from the dead and proved as Christ by his Father who received him at his right hand following his ascension to heaven. In Schillebeeckx's

33. See also Newlands, *Christ and Human Rights*, 103.
34. Schillebeeckx, *God the Future of Man*, 181–82.
35. Ban, *The Christological Foundation*, 175.
36. Lawler and Shanahan, *Church*, 46.
37. Portier, "Interpretation and Method," 34.
38. Abdul-Masih, *Edward Schillebeeckx and Hans Frei*, 117.

Re-Imagining Religious Belonging in Ecclesiology

thought there is no room for ontological categories understood in terms of traditional transcendence. Jesus was a man, who defied the religious and political establishment of his day by preaching and living out the ideal of universal love which he pursued even unto death.[39] Jesus was a sort of a liberator who taught people that love is more important than poverty and political oppressiveness. His death was utterly unjust but this does not preclude him from clinging to his ideal despite constant threats and, finally, his execution by political (and implicitly religious) authorities:[40]

> In [cleansing the temple] Jesus performed an action which was clearly directed against the priestly rules of the temple, who enriched themselves by the poverty of religious people. Historically, the issue here was less a matter of Jesus's anger over the desecration of the temple as the house of God by the trade practiced there than of Jesus's sudden holy anger because this was the very place where the poor were deprived of their rights and exploited. The "mystical" side here clearly has a political element. This was also an action which affected the immediate masters of the priestly caste, the Romans. This fact . . . of itself clearly indicates that Jesus was not apolitical or unaffected by the Roman oppression; only that he saw this in a different way than the Zealots. At all events, at a certain moment, as a result of these factors, Jesus understood that his career too must include rejection and an ignominious death. In one way or another, in the dark night of faith, but aware of his task, Jesus related his imminent death to his preaching of the kingdom of God. Despite this threat of death, at all events he remained faithful to his message and deliberately said farewell to his followers at a festal meal. After that he was executed, by a Roman crucifixion *sub Pontio Pilato* (there is a good reason for that standing in the Christian creed). By any account, this is also a political factor.[41]

Jesus is thus for Schillebeeckx a sort of a political activist whose powerful influence and decisive personal example produced an immediate as well as lasting impact on his disciples and followers.[42] What Jesus did was,

---

39. Jesus's death within a certain historical context is almost an obsession to Schillebeeckx, who seems to be afraid that if suffering is connected only to Christ it could lead to an abstract idea of suffering. See for details Placher, *Narratives of a Vulnerable God,* 130.

40. Portier, *Tradition and Incarnation,* 327.

41. Schillebeeckx, *The Church with a Human Face,* 23.

42. For an interesting approach on Jesus's impact, especially on small groups, see Icenogle, *Biblical Foundations,* 124.

at the end of the day, to liberate and humanize religion as a proof that it should serve God by serving humanity. Doing everything for the benefit of humanity is eventually the goal of religion and this is exactly what Jesus did in Schillebeeckx's view.[43] Jesus's activity helped us understand God in a new way, namely as a future which presents itself constantly anew, with new possibilities of a better life for every human being. Jesus is the very means whereby this future can be achieved, in the sense that whoever does what Jesus did and sticks to his ideal no matter what, for the benefit of his fellow people contributes to the building of this promising future. Jesus helps us understand that our future is meant to be a future of peace if we do exactly what he did, and this peaceful future is actually our God. Once we understand Jesus's activity in light of this new definition of God, we reach the conclusion that the traditional doctrine of salvation from sin is nothing but our own liberation from the past in order to promote peace for the benefit of all humanity.[44] Thus, salvation is not only liberation but also the renewed and the constantly new possibility of human communication. To be sure, salvation is liberation and communication based on Jesus's example.[45]

However, in order to be relevant for the world, Jesus's disciples and followers decided to preach the dead Jesus as the living Christ, who rose from the dead and ascended to the right hand of the Father as a proof that the past lies behind us while a new and peaceful future awaits us. Belief in Jesus is belief in his actions as well as in his ideal to help humanity as reflected in his presentation as Christ. Jesus was definitely not transcendent as he was a mere man; his disciples though attempted to make him transcendent when they presented him as the living Christ, who came back to life from the dead and then ascended to heaven. Nevertheless, we must approach the disciples' confession of Jesus as the Christ from the standpoint of contemporary science in order to understand that the transcendence of Christ should be understood in human terms.[46] Transcendence is not relevant unless thoroughly human; likewise, salvation is not appealing and understandable unless deprived of its traditional connection with ontological transcendence. When ontological transcendence is given up

---

43. Iraola, *True Confucians, Bold Christians*, 93.
44. Abdul-Masih, *Edward Schillebeeckx and Hans Frei*, 69.
45. Knitter, "Religion and Globality?," 115.
46. Torevell, *Losing the Sacred*, 143.

Re-Imagining Religious Belonging in Ecclesiology

in favor of eschatological transcendence, so that God becomes our future and Christ the example of true humanity, salvation also translates into a human experience which helps us assist other human beings in view of a better future.[47] Schillebeeckx defends the identification between the Jesus of history and the Christ of faith but it has to be stressed that this is only ideological, not ontological as in traditional theology. Jesus is dead but he is indeed a historical character; Christ is alive but not as a human, only as an ideal, an ideal which nonetheless helps humanity understand the constantly new reality of God as our own future and of salvation as improvement of the human condition:[48]

> Therefore the Jesus of Nazareth who is identical with "the Christ of faith" confronts us most profoundly with the question of God, with a God concerned for humanity and no other God. Precisely here, human salvation, salvation from God, becomes visible. For from Jesus's message, his life-style and his death, it became clear to believers that the God of Jesus, the God of Israel, accepts men and women wholly and seeks to renew them in their relationships to themselves and to others in a world fit for humans to live in. The specifically Christian experience of what is called "the transcendent" is the experience of this divine affirmation which needs humanity in order finally to be able to affirm oneself and others and to be free to unfold a better history (*iustificatio*).[49]

Schillebeeckx proposes a new concept of God which, in his view, is not oppressive as in traditional theology because it is better not to believe in God at all than to believe in an oppressive God who limits salvation to those who believe in a better world which is to come in a transcendent beyond-the-world future.[50] Such a belief is definitely not appealing to contemporary humans, Schillebeeckx insists, because it does not connect God to our present world. Everything concerning God and salvation must happen exclusively in this world and for the benefit of the world by a God who is not oppressive because of his ontological transcendence but by a God who is in fact ourselves and our future. In promoting a thoroughly humanized perspective on God and salvation,[51] Schillebeeckx

---

47. Wicks, *Handbook of Spirituality for Ministers*, 75.
48. Doran, *Theology and the Dialectics of History*, 388.
49. Schillebeeckx, *The Church with a Human Face*, 29.
50. Rego, *Suffering and Salvation*, 233.
51. For details about the idea of a humanized God, see Thompson, *The Sacraments*, 75.

preaches a dead Jesus, which is made relevant only if helped by the image of the living Christ. Thus, the traditional idea of the believer's personal belonging to God through Jesus Christ and his firm salvation confirmed by Jesus Christ's bodily/physical resurrection and ascension to heaven is demolished. Man must not put his trust in God as ontologically different from him because this would mean surrender to the past. Man must put his trust in himself and follow the example of Jesus which has been made relevant through the idea of Christ in order to explain to people that if they want to find God they must actually find a better way to build a safer future. We no longer belong to Jesus Christ or God or the Holy Trinity as in traditional theology; we belong to ourselves and the world being firmly convinced that the best way to find salvation is to save ourselves by doing good to others.[52]

COMMUNITARIAN BELONGING

Schillebeeckx's drastic reinterpretation of the traditional doctrines of God and Jesus Christ—so that God is no longer seen as an ontologically real person/Trinity but only as a concept which is identical to our own future and Jesus is a dead person proclaimed as the "living Christ" of faith—calls for an equally radical reassessment of the doctrine of the church.[53] The church is traditionally the community of all those who, having been saved by God the Father from their sins based on the work of Jesus Christ, have been given new life in the Holy Spirit.[54] Believers put their entire trust in God as their savior and sustainer, they all believe in the preaching of the Gospel—namely God's salvation from sin in Jesus Christ—and they all await the physical/bodily return of the risen Jesus Christ in order to put an end to history and take them all into heaven to be with God for ever.[55] They all believe in the physical/bodily resurrection of those who died in Jesus Christ, so that all believers that lived throughout history will eventually be with God in heaven. The church—and this is very important—is utterly different from the world both in belief and morality even if the church lives and carries on its mission in and for the world.[56]

---

52. Schillebeeckx, *The Church with a Human Face*, 34.
53. See also Larbig and Wiedenhofer, eds., *Tradition and Tradition Theories*, 363.
54. Jones, *Embodying Forgiveness*, 131.
55. Schreiner, *Paul*, 455.
56. Pickard, *Liberating Evangelism*, 87.

Re-Imagining Religious Belonging in Ecclesiology

Of course, in Schillebeeckx this traditional interpretation of the church stands virtually no chance whatsoever. If God is no longer to be understood as a person but only as a mere concept which turns out to be our own future, then there is no need for the church to be different from the world. Thus, the church should not be understood and presented in traditional terms as being different from the world but in modern, scientific terms, which push our belief towards a church which is essentially the essence of human relationships.[57] Therefore, the church should not be understood as a clearly delineated community but rather as an inclusive human reality which comprises all the aspects of humanity that exist and manifested in the world. Schillebeeckx is very confident in sociological analyses because, as he himself admits, he built his new reinterpretation of the church on what sociology has to say about the contemporary understanding of the church by some of its members:[58]

> Many believers simply do not know what to do with "the church." Sociological research has revealed that people who were previously practising Christians, but who no longer practise, have retained a certain faith in God as the ground of all being and even some faith in the man Jesus, who showed in and through his life on earth the meaning of God's love for men. It has, however, shown that they can no longer accord any place in their faith to the phenomenon "church." They would only be able to accept the church and then perhaps even do so with enthusiasm, if "church" meant nothing more than the foundation of a community between men, in other words, the true form of fellow-humanity in this world.[59]

Some things need to be highlighted here. First, it is a pity that Schillebeeckx does not actually identify exactly his sociological sources which prompted him to change or support his reinterpretation of the traditional doctrine of the church. It can only be speculated that he had access to some Western sociological investigations—maybe specific to Europe or even to the Low Countries—which presented the fact that some individuals, once preoccupied with the church, later decided not to get involved in the life of the church. "Sociological research" is far too vague a phrase to dismiss an almost two thousand year history of both the church and its doctrine. At the same time, sociology is hardly the best instrument

---

57. Borgman, *Edward Schillebeeckx*, 163.
58. Mueller, *What Are They Saying?*, 73.
59. Schillebeeckx, *World and Church*, 98.

to evaluate the dynamics of the church, let alone its essential constitution and doctrine. Second, the fact that some Christians—or so-called Christians—gave up their commitment to the church in reportedly large numbers in no way means that the church, as it has traditionally existed and as it has traditionally believed, should be dramatically reconsidered based on sociological research. Third, the same fact that some people left the church because they had been discontented with some of its aspects does not presuppose that the church is flawed in any way. It can actually be the other way around, namely those who left the church had some serious problems in terms of personal belief in God and in the constitution of the church. Fourth, it is amazingly convenient for Schillebeeckx to notice that those who left to church still displayed some elements of belief in God and Jesus, evidently seen as a mere man, because this would support his drastic reinterpretation of God as our future and Jesus as a dead historical character who is presented as the "living" Christ of the church. To be sure, in light of Schillebeeckx's re-evaluation of the church, the "living" Christ is not only the Christ of the church but also of all those who have hope in God, seen as their temporal future.[60]

It is more than crystal clear that Schillebeeckx is utterly discontented with the traditional interpretation of the church and of the distinction between the church and the world.[61] This distinction belongs to the past and Schillebeeckx is more concerned with the future because God cannot be found in the past but only in the future.[62] God himself—or should we say God itself—is the future so the past bears no relevance whatsoever either to the idea of God or to the traditional distinction (not separation) between the church and the world. Here is how Schillebeeckx criticizes the traditional understanding of the church as distinct from the world:

> In the past, an anthropologically false and dualistic view of the conferment of grace and redemption frequently led to our regarding this as a matter of God and man's *soul*. This meant that the whole of man's activity in this world—and quantitatively this was ninety-nine percent of the factual activity of the majority of men—lay outside Christianity. If this view were to persist, it would inevitably encourage the estrangement between church and world,

---

60. Schillebeeckx, *God the Future of Man*, 182.
61. See also Kennedy, *Schillebeeckx*, 57.
62. Lakeland, *The Liberation of the Laity*, 140.

especially at a time when the distinctive meaning of the world is being discovered.[63]

This brief but essential critique of traditional theology suggests that Schillebeeckx had a wrong perspective on traditional Christianity in the first place. For instance, traditional Christianity is not exclusively or even mainly concerned with man's soul. It does indeed recognize the fundamental importance of the non-visible essential constitution of the human being, which is called soul, but it simply does not show an exclusive preference for man's soul. On the contrary, traditional theology—which is in fact concerned with man's salvation from sin and death as well as his resurrection and post-resurrection existence with God in heaven—displays a constant interest in the whole of man's being: soul and body.[64] This is because man dies in the body and then is resurrected in the body in the very same way Jesus Christ died in the flesh (body) and was resurrected in the flesh (body). The nature of the believer's resurrected body is evidently different from his historical body, but it is nevertheless a body.[65]

At the same time, traditional theology has never promoted a dualistic view of grace in the sense Schillebeeckx understood it. Although he does not elaborate the issue at this point, he seems to have understood that traditional theology promoted the idea of grace with reference to the church, while the world was left outside the realm of grace.[66] This is, however, false because in traditional theology both the world and the church benefit from God's grace although in different ways: the world receives common grace which sustains physical life in general, while the church receives special grace which sustains the spiritual life of those who are saved from sin. It is true that common grace is not saving while special grace is saving but the reality of God's grace is all-encompassing, so both the world and the church share God's benevolent grace in the traditional understanding of Christianity.[67]

Another point of interest is Schillebeeckx's observation that man's almost entire activity in the world lies outside the church if we are to be-

---

63. Schillebeeckx, *World and Church*, 103.
64. Inge, *A Christian Theology of Place*, 53.
65. Thiselton, *The First Epistle to the Corinthians*, 458.
66. Wood, *Spiritual Exegesis*, 111.
67. Elwell and Comfort, *Tyndale Bible Dictionary*, 551.

lieve traditional theology.[68] This is clearly not true because, in traditional theology, believers are encouraged to live in the world and change the world, so there is no such thing as a Christian existence which is fundamentally severed from the world. Christians are indeed different from the world and the church, as a community of Christians, is different from the world because of God's saving grace; however, the reality of the world is not at all foreign to Christians who not only live in the world but are encouraged, urged, and even commanded to live in the world in order to change it through the preaching of the Gospel of salvation from sin. So, Schillebeeckx is not at all right when he displays his belief in the traditional estrangement between church and world; to be sure, in traditional Christianity, there is only a radical distinction between the church and the world based on God's saving activity but there is no estrangement between the two if the Gospel is to be lived out and disseminated everywhere throughout the entire world.

Schillebeeckx though is unshakeable in his conviction that the church and the world must be identical based on his reassessment of the doctrine of grace, which is distributed indiscriminately over all human beings.[69] This brings him to the idea of anonymous Christianity, namely the fact that all people are Christians based on God's all-encompassing grace even if they do not explicitly believe in Christ.[70] Thus, despite their unbelief or even aversion to Christianity, unbelievers are still to be considered Christians because God's grace is present in their lives. They are not explicit Christians as believers; to be sure: they are only implicit Christians due to God's universal grace but Christians nonetheless. Thus, every human being who displays traces of love, justice, truth, and brotherhood is a Christian whether he knows it or not.[71] This renders the idea as well as the reality of atheism totally useless. In Schillebeeckx's words:

> I find it difficult to imagine that a sincere militant communist atheist possesses not one shred of authentically theist faith, just as Paul believed that the Athenians were "very religious," and told them so (Acts 17:22). I do not believe in the absence of religion from the working class world, although I do believe in its having fallen away

---

68. This is why Schillebeeckx suggests that the church should not be an enclave, but open itself to the world. See also Haight, *Christian Community*, 31.

69. See also Carey and Lienhard, eds., *Biographical Dictionary*, 333.

70. Kennedy, *A Modern Introduction to Theology*, 250.

71. See Zuidberg, *God the Pastor*, 98.

from the church. Wherever there is some sense of justice, truth, and above all genuine brotherhood, there is God too. Anonymous religion can take hidden forms. Wherever, despite complete rejection of the church and even moral degradation, sincerely objective values are accepted, to the point where people are prepared to fight for them, there is a latent but genuinely religious life. God has many names—the fathers of the church even called him "the one with many names." We would indeed be guilty of injustice were we to say that the working classes are without any spark of authentic religious sense, when, on the other hand, we make every effort for genuine religious elements in the pre-Christian pagan world and in fact find them there. In the words of the Acts of the Apostles, "God does not leave himself without witness." His grace seeks out all men.[72]

It seems that, for Schillebeeckx, the essence of Christianity is religious faith, not the faith in Jesus Christ, which actually gave Christianity its name. If this is the case, then Schillebeeckx is right when he expresses his conviction that faith, namely religious faith, is still present in the most atheistic persons or contexts.[73] This is evidently true because he connects religious faith with basic human values such as justice, truth, and brotherhood. As these are to be found in virtually every human being in the smallest of possible "quantities," then Schillebeeckx is absolutely correct in saying that religious faith is present in all human beings.[74] His problem though is that he equates this religious faith with Christianity in its implicit manifestation. It is equally true that he later explains that there is a distinction between implicit Christianity, which is based on religious faith and explicit Christianity, which is anchored in faith in Christ, but to be sure, the two types of Christianity are fundamentally identical because Christ is not a human being—he is only a meta-historical model which can produce a lasting impact in those who accept his teachings. To draw the line, implicit and explicit Christianity are based on the same religious faith which presupposes fundamental human values, with the only difference that, in explicit Christianity, these values are embodied in the idea of Christ.[75] In other words, the very essence and objectivity of Christianity

---

72. Schillebeeckx, *World and Church*, 32.
73. See also Vergote, *Religion, Belief and Unbelief*, 15.
74. Whalen, *The Authentic Doctrine*, 155.
75. For a discussion about implicit and explicit faith, see also Berkouwer, *The Church*, 157.

is not the ontologically real existence of God but the presence of human values in all human beings.[76] Within this particular context, the role of Christ is not to delineate between the church and the world, but rather to unite the church and the world. To be more explicit, as the fundamental human values of justice, truth, and brotherhood are constitutive to the church as well as existing in all people, it means that there is no essential difference between the world and the church; so Christ only helps implicit Christians become explicit Christians by making them aware that Christ embodies all these fundamental human values. In other words, the role of Christ is only to make people conscious of their anonymous religious feeling so that they become explicit confessors of this Christ which is the symbol of the universality of God's grace:[77]

> This anonymous faith in God can be purified in the light of the fact of Christ and perfected so that it becomes an explicit and consistent confession of faith I God ... The terrible floods in the Netherlands in 1953 called forth a very deep sense of the brotherhood and togetherness of man and great generosity throughout the world. This was living proof not only that human sentiment was still noble, but also, at a deeper level, that many people were conscious of an anonymously religious feeling of brotherhood in which men's hands were extended to God's grace. Grace simply cannot be regarded as the private property of practising Christians. There still remains a large tract of missionary territory to be Christianized in the depths of every Christian and the Pentecostal fire of the *church* shoulders in the heart of every "pagan"![78]

So the church is the world and the world is the church. A man who does not explicitly believe in Christ but displays the feeling of brotherhood is automatically a Christian, an implicit Christian but a Christian nevertheless.[79] Schillebeeckx is definitely right in saying that grace is not the private property of practising Christians; this affirmation though does nothing but confirm traditional theology, which acknowledges the universality of God's common grace. According to traditional Christianity, however, the fact that a man enjoys God's common grace thus manifesting fundamental human values does not automatically turn him into a

---

76. See also Valkenberg, *Sharing Lights*, 146.
77. Wiley, *Thinking of Christ*, 98.
78. Schillebeeckx, *World and Church*, 33.
79. Rego, *Suffering and Salvation*, 34.

Christian, as Schillebeeckx speculates. One of the biggest problems of Schillebeeckx's identification between the world and the church is the destruction of the traditional feeling of church belonging. Traditional Christians are strongly anchored in their belief that Jesus Christ, their savior from sin and death, redeemed their lives and gave them the Holy Spirit of God who keeps them together in a community which is totally different from the world even though it lives within the world. This feeling of communitarian belonging is based on their faith in Jesus Christ as every individual believer belongs to him and, at the same time, the community of individual believers belongs to God because every individual believer belongs to the community which shares this faith. For Schillebeeckx, however, there is no personal or communitarian feeling of belonging to God because God is only our temporal future. Jesus is dead and Christ is just another way of saying that what Jesus did is good and beneficial to every human being. In Schillebeeckx, people no longer belong to a saving God; they only belong to themselves because it is themselves that make their future, which is at the same time their own God.[80] There is no "inside the church" and "outside the church" any longer; likewise, there is no Christian and non-Christian. Everybody is a Christian, implicit or explicit, and everybody is part of Christianity, implicit or explicit. This means that everybody is part of the church because the church is, at the end of the day, the world itself. God's grace is nothing but the ever new and universal possibility of making the world a better place with a view to a constantly new and hopefully beneficial future to all humanity.

The absolute identification between the church and the world in Schillebeeckx is also supported by his dismissal of the alleged distinction between the *Ecclesia ad intra* and the *Ecclesia ad extra*, a clear reference to the church and the church-to-be.[81] Schillebeeckx's problem at this point is that, for him, the church is defined by means of the ecclesiastical hierarchy, which could well be a more or less obvious hint to the Vatican.[82] Bearing this in mind, he is right when he says that the church cannot simply be identified with the kingdom of God.[83] What he is saying though is not that the two share the same message but that the kingdom of God

---

80. Walls, *The Oxford Handbook of Eschatology*, 226.
81. Nacke, Köppen and Mönninghoff, eds., *Am Puls der Zeit*, 2.
82. See also Lennan, *Risking the Church*, 164.
83. Kennedy, *Schillebeeckx*, 74.

is more widespread than the church; on the contrary, as far as he is concerned, the church—understood as hierarchy—has one message, while the kingdom of God promotes a different message, the message of the saving presence of God that restores human life.[84] Schillebeeckx insists that the church should pay heed to the world and the world to the church so that a dialogue can be established between the two.[85] In other words, there is truth in the church and there is truth outside the church but it is important that both the church and the world learn from the truth they both profess. It seems then, that the "complete" Christian standing is, for Schillebeeckx, the juxtaposition of the church and the world in such a way that the truth of each should become the experience of every human being. This also modifies the traditional definition of the Gospel, which is classically the Good News of salvation from sin as found in Scripture. In Schillebeeckx, however, the Gospel is the Good News which does not come exclusively from Scripture and the church, but also from the experience of the world.[86] The Gospel as understood by Schillebeeckx teaches us that we should not look back to the past when God was conceived as ontologically real but we should look forward to the future, when God is identified with the future itself, in order constantly to find new ways to improve the world and the quality of life. If traditional theology promotes the idea of a meta-temporal existence with God as a result of salvation from sin, Schillebeeckx is convinced that this is no longer the case in our scientific society. Man is saved in a transcendent, absolute, and eschatological way if and when humanity believes that its God, meaning, and future—actually its earthly future—will find a way to create a type of life and society for which it would be worth living.[87] In other words, salvation is nothing but an existential realization that humanity will eventually find the meaning of life and implement it within human society. This confirms once again the identification between the world and the church because the connection between the two, the "living" Christ, is not only the Lord of the church but also the Lord of the world. At the end of the day, the church stands no other chance than to identify itself with the world in a

---

84. See Nyce, "Faithful and Pluralistic," 214.
85. Gibbs, *The Word in the Third World*, 53.
86. Borgman, *Edward Schillebeeckx*, 166.
87. See also Huck, *A Sourcebook about Liturgy*, 165.

partnership which promotes a better and more meaningful human life.[88] These are Schillebeeckx's words:

> A church in monologue with herself is not a partner. If she does not listen to the world, she will disregard as much human knowledge, influenced by anonymous grace, as there are people outside her institutional boundaries or outside her hierarchy. If, on the other hand, she does listen, attentively but critically (because she is guided by the revelation of the word) to the attempts that the "world" is making to throw light on the truth, she will not hear strange sounds coming from outside, but will recognize the voice of her own Lord, who is not only the head of the church, his body, but is also Lord of the "world". She will hear the Good News which is always normative for her and which comes to us not only from Scripture, but also and equally from every human existential experience which is, in one way or another, always confronted by the grace of the living God.[89]

Schillebeeckx seems to realize that, in the best possible case, namely if the church eventually decides to listen to the world and the world to the church,[90] the communication between the two will only be a human exercise which is very unlikely to discover ultimate truth and create a "perfect" society. So, he places this expectation of a meaningful society beyond the temporal boundary of the present into an equally temporal future when mankind will eventually or rather hopefully discover the ultimate meaning of its humanity:[91]

> In man's struggle for a better world, the church has first of all to discover the deepest intention (probably not subject to reflection) which goes beyond what is strictly confined to this world. Ultimately, there is no sense in fighting for a better world without implicit faith in an absolute saving consummation of the individual human person, even if an ideology has no room for this formal assertion. It is precisely because there is an absolute, transcendent, eschatological expectation of salvation for man that commitment to the planning of temporal society and to a world that is more worthy of man is ultimately meaningful.[92]

88. Boeve, "Experience according to Edward Schillebeeckx," 199–200.
89. Schillebeeckx, *World and Church*, 104–5.
90. Alberigo, Komonchak and O'Connell, eds., *History of Vatican II*, vol. 4, 278.
91. Kennedy, *Schillebeeckx*, 136.
92. Schillebeeckx, *World and Church*, 105.

There is always a second possibility, which Schillebeeckx seems to reject, i.e., the very possible scenario of a world which will never be able to live up to the standards of the church because they are totally different. Such a possibility will only confirm the tenets of traditional theology, which promotes the idea that the individual who lives in the world will find salvation and meaning for his life only if he comes to the church, not the other way around. On top of it, there is also a third possibility—and this would be disastrous for Schillebeeckx—that the church and the world will eventually cooperate as partners in order to find a meaningful society but they will never be able to implement this society; that is to say that it is very possible that, even if the church and the world eventually join forces as suggested by Schillebeeckx, they will never be able to achieve the much desired meaningful society.

Schillebeeckx is aware that these possibilities are theoretically valid and even probable given the current state of human affairs. The world does not look like the best place to be for human beings but there is no other place available to us. So, the only remaining possibility is to change the world in such a way that it becomes the much desired place for meaningful life.[93] He also understands that, if the Gospel—regardless of its religious/theological content—is essentially social because the church is the world and the world is the church but also because salvation is to be found in terrestrial reality (most probably in the future), it is possible that the Gospel will be hindered as a result of natural factors.[94] For instance, even if Schillebeeckx himself does not offer any concrete example, it is possible that the Gospel (which promotes the improvement of man's life to the point of finding the ultimate meaning of humanity) might be preached in an economically impoverished country. The people of this country though will not believe this Gospel because of the hardships they experience in their own lives. Such a possibility could be the end of such a Gospel but Schillebeeckx does not lose confidence, so he suggests the introduction of reforms with a view to the dramatic change of the social structures of that country.[95] Thus, he believes, the people will no longer be affected by tough natural conditions, so they will be more willing to listen and accept the message of this Gospel. He goes as far as to suggest that

93. See also Perry, *Love and Power*, 81.

94. These natural factors could cause suffering but this is the context of the Gospel, see McManus, *Unbroken Community*, 40.

95. Borgman, *Edward Schillebeeckx*, 115.

the church's ministers should get involved in politics in order to hasten the implementation of social reforms for a better reception of the Gospel in economically challenged countries:

> The whole of man's planning of the world has, however, another dimension as well. Religion, the free acceptance of God's grace and of its specifically ecclesial forms, is also included, as a free human act, in history with its personal, social, psychic, and even somatic conditioning. As a result, so-called natural factors are able to exert a positive or a negative influence on man's hearing of the Good News. Terrestrial situations may therefore be seen from a pastoral point of view. Thus, it is possible that the church may really be preaching in the wilderness, because man's freedom is caught up in all kinds of social structures which make it impossible for men to be sufficiently free to listen to the Good News and to receive its grace sincerely. From the pastoral point of view, then, it may be almost as urgently necessary to introduce agrarian reforms and to revise the structures of social relationship in certain countries as to preach the Good News. And I see no reason why even a bishop should not lend his support to such social reforms in a pastoral situation of this kind, without directly entering the field of social politics. To make it possible for men truly to listen as human beings to the Good News is, after all, part of the mission of all the believing members of the church.[96]

With these new insights, Schillebeeckx's theology seems nearly mechanical, in the sense that if anything does not work, we fix it and then it should work. This is possible, at least at a theoretical level, because the identification between the church and the world lowers the traditional and ontologically real God to the level of humanity, so God is no longer in us and for us but he actually is us; God is our reality in the sense that we are divine reality.[97] We do not belong to a God who lives beyond history but we belong to the God which is history, namely we belong to ourselves. There is no better and future meta-historical dwelling place for us, as in traditional theology; our dwelling place will be our own world for ever, so our only chance is to make it better. But in order to make it better because we shall stay here for ever or to the end—to its end or to our end—unrealistic and meta-historical concepts such as God, salvation, Jesus Christ, eschatology, and transcendence must be reinterpreted in such a way that

---

96. Schillebeeckx, *World and Church*, 109–10.
97. Cf. Whalen, *The Authentic Doctrine*, 66.

they are detached from their beyond-the-world aspects: God becomes our future or simply ourselves in future, Jesus Christ splits into a dead Jesus and a "living" Christ—a mere literary character of the Bible, eschatology becomes terrestrial hope in future and transcendence turns into the simple idea of temporal future. The future of mankind will be for ever and inextricably connected to the world and this earth, and this is why God himself must be redefined in terms which are fundamentally human. For Schillebeeckx, it is this very and totally human God that we must belong to and, as this God is relevant and meaningful only to and within the world, is it equally evident that we must come to terms with our belonging to this world.[98] Nevertheless, in order to belong to this world in the fullest possible way, we have to accept all human expectations because, as human beings that are called to devise their own earthly future, we must learn to accept each other as well as each other's convictions. Thus, Schillebeeckx alters even the very traditional idea of God's glory which is no longer the praise attributed to a meta-historical and ontologically real God but the measure of earthly success achieved by humanity in its quest to create a better future on this planet for every member of the human race; to quote Schillebeeckx: "God's glory—living man."[99] To be sure, the measure of man's terrestrial success will eventually become his capacity to create a new and future earthly society,[100] which will be able to instill a general and meaningful feeling of personal as well as communitarian belonging to the values and actual life of that much-desired society:[101]

> The modest but nonetheless splendidly practical result of this process of humanization within life in union with God will be that we build up the world in such a way that, in it, men can live a life that is both truly *worthy of man* and at the same time *Christian* and in this way more easily accomplish the will of God.[102]

It is clear then that Schillebeeckx re-imagines the traditional personal and communitarian belonging to Jesus Christ and the church as community of believers in Jesus Christ by proposing a radical reassessment of his

---

98. See also Radcliffe, *What is the Point of Being a Christian?*, 167.

99. Schillebeeckx, *World and Church*, 110–14.

100. For details about the idea of success in building a new society, see Satterlee, *Ambrose of Milan's Method*, 315.

101. Kennedy, *Schillebeeckx*, 44.

102. Schillebeeckx, *World and Church*, 114.

definition of God as well as the relationship between the church and the world. His project consists of the humanization of traditional Christian theology which basically means the giving up of meta-historical and ontologically-real elements. Thus, God becomes our own terrestrial and earthly future, Jesus Christ is seen only as a historical figure (doubled in Scripture by the literary image of the "living" Christ) and the church is identified with the world. Christians no longer belong to the traditional Trinitarian God and his church but to their own world which—together with non-Christians—they hope to transform in a constantly new and meaningful way for the benefit of every human being.

7

Re-Tracing the Boundaries between the Church and the World

IN SCHILLEBEECKX THE TRADITIONAL concept of the church as fundamentally different from the world is no longer relevant for contemporary society. Modern man is the product of social secularization, a process which has affected the entire reality of man's present existence. Secularism has promoted the ultimate validity of human reason as a means to reevaluate man's existence in the world but also his relationship with himself. In light of this secularized rationality, Schillebeeckx promotes the necessity to analyze the relationship between the church and the world once again in a way which makes the idea of the church relevant and meaningful to modern society. His solution consists of giving up the traditional idea of the church which clearly and sharply delineates it from the world in favor of a secularized perspective which re-traces the boundaries between the church and the world. For Schillebeeckx though, re-tracing these boundaries means blurring them, so that the church and the world are no longer conflicting communities but rather complementary or even identical realities.

THE CHURCH, THE WORLD, AND SALVATION

Schillebeeckx's treatment of the church reflects his general, specifically rationalized and existentialist, perspective on Christian theology which professes the abandonment of ontologically transcendent categories. Nothing should be seen as ontologically real in Christianity: neither God and Jesus Christ, nor salvation and resurrection. Everything is human and humanized as well as humanizing: God is our future, Jesus is a mere man, salvation is our involvement in society and resurrection is our decision to act secularly for the transformation of the world.[1] In this particular context, the church cannot escape Schillebeeckx's theological radicalism.[2] Thus, the traditional teaching of the church which is defined ontologically as powerfully anchored in the transcendent metaphysical and meta-historical being of God needs to be given up. The church should no longer be seen in terms which indicate belief in ontological realities. The church exists in the world, therefore it needs to be defined by means of human categories.[3] Moreover, as an entity which is part of the world, the church must realize the fact that there has to be cooperation between her and the world.[4] As the process of secularization has leveled all meta-historical and metaphysical realities to the actuality of history—both the actuality of the present moment and the future—the church cannot be presented in such a way that people could perceive it as different from the world.[5] The church has been traditionally defined as a community, a different community but a community nonetheless; the world itself is a community; a larger community but a community nonetheless. Thus, the secularized rationality of the present tells us that the church and the world have one important aspect in common, namely the idea of community: the church is a community and the world is a community.[6] Therefore, as they are both communities, one should ask whether there are any significant differences between the two communities.

Schillebeeckx has no doubt about the fact that the church is no different from the world; at the least, the church is not significantly different from the world.[7] He is equally convinced that, due to the process of secularization, the world itself tends to expand over the church because the secularized values of today's society do now allow for the existence of ontologically transcendent realities.[8] So if the world decides that ontologically transcendent realities do not actually exist, the church is left without its traditional perspective on itself. Thus, the church must redefine itself

1. Hilkert and Schreiter, eds., *The Praxis*, 56.
2. For what it appears to be a wrong understanding of Schillebeeckx's radicalism, see Icenogle, *Biblical Foundations*, 364.
3. See also Newlands, *Christ and Human Rights*, 103.
4. Baum, ed., *The Twentieth Century*, 243.
5. Wood, *Spiritual Exegesis*, 124.
6. Kennedy, *Schillebeeckx*, 72.
7. See Mueller, *What Are They Saying?*, 57–60.
8. Abdul-Masih, *Edward Schillebeeckx and Hans Frei*, 141.

as well as its mission in such a way that the secularized values of the world are not contradicted. The church has the message of salvation but this message should also be reinterpreted in human terms.[9] The church must take this message of salvation and make it relevant to the world even if this means that she has to redefine itself in a radical way. In Schillebeeckx, the church itself is forced to see itself in a new light given by the world's secularized rationality. Thus, the church will have to take the message of salvation to the world and integrate it within the current reality of the world. The church and salvation will therefore become part of the world because both the church and the world must be seen in exclusively human categories. The church professes salvation in Christ but this should not convey the idea of man's redemption from sin—understood as offense against an ontologically transcendent God—but rather the idea of solidarity based on the example of Christ.[10] The church must be utterly concerned with solidarity and therefore with love. The love of the church for the world must be so intense that nothing can stand between her and the world. Based on the principle of universal love embodied by Christ, the church should seek to identify itself, as well as its message, with the world. The church should exist for the world because, as far as Schillebeeckx is concerned, there is no actual difference between them anyway. There is no distance between the church and mankind because they are both communities which proclaim the message of love for the benefit of every human being.[11] Secularization does not allow for anything which diminishes the value of the individual human being or the human race in general, so both the church and the world should promote a message of hope, solidarity, and love. The secularized church has no room for the traditional idea of the church's separation from the world; the church and the world cannot be separated as long as they are both human communities. Thus, if they are both human communities, and they are, and if they share the same message of hope, solidarity, and love, then the only rational conclusion—at least for Schillebeeckx—is that the church is actually identical to the world. Schillebeeckx realizes that this treatment of the church can be way too radical for some, so he is willing to concede that one could speak of frontiers between the church and the

---

9. Kennedy, *Schillebeeckx*, 11.
10. See also Depoortere, *A Different God*, 57.
11. Hill, *Jesus, the Christ*, 187.

world; these frontiers, however, "are to some extent fluid."[12] At a closer look though it will become evident that in Schillebeeckx's mind the frontiers between the church and the world are altogether fluid, which is in fact a proof of his intention to deconstruct traditional ecclesiology to the point of the church's total identification with the world.[13]

Schillebeeckx's approach to the church is anthropological and begins from what he calls the "biological foundation" of humanity. Mankind is the totality of human persons who all share the fact that they are biologically human.[14] This unique feature of humanity, namely its biological essence, does not constitute the unity of mankind though; Schillebeeckx searches for some sort of higher standard for human unity and this is definitely not biology. In fact, according to Schillebeeckx, the unity of humanity consists of values and it is values that bring people together into a community of persons. Thus, Schillebeeckx reaches the conclusion that human unity is based on human values which need to be expressed in terms of "vocation" and "destiny". These two fundamental human aspects are clearly beyond the mere biological constitution of human beings in the sense that they are not necessarily generated by biology. Man's vocation and destiny are therefore not a specific given reality but rather a task which lies ahead of each human being.[15] This does not mean that Schillebeeckx attempts to connect humanity to a reality which transcends its physical reality, so it is categorically not a return to the values of traditional Christianity. Schillebeeckx only wants to clarify that humanity cannot build any concept of human unity on the basis of biological considerations; unity among men and women must be sought therefore in something which transcends the mere biological level of our existence but remains nonetheless specific to the physical reality of the world.[16] This is why Schillebeeckx proposes the idea of human value as the foundation for the unity of humanity. The idea of human value defines a meta-biological reality but this is clearly not an indication of any possible connection with meta-history or metaphysics. Although meta-biological, human

---

12. Schillebeeckx, *World and Church*, 115.
13. See also Hodgson, *Jesus, Word and Presence*, 285.
14. McManus, *Unbroken Communion*, 58.
15. Schillebeeckx, *World and Church*, 115.
16. Schillebeeckx, *The Eucharist*, 116.

values are fundamentally historical and physical in the sense that they are not meta-historical and metaphysical.

Schillebeeckx, however, warns that human values do not automatically make up human unity; unity among men and women is a task that must be achieved based on human values.[17] At this point, Schillebeeckx resorts to the traditional idea of God's grace, which is evidently reinterpreted to fit his thoroughly anthropological perspective on theology. Human unity is achievable when people respond to the grace of God. If unity is perceived as man's response to the grace of God, then it means that unity itself is a gift of God. Unity is a gift of God because it represents God's "absolute communication of himself" to humanity.[18] It is now that Schillebeeckx introduces another traditional element in his discourse, namely the idea of revelation. God revealed himself to humanity as man's most important value and it is this supreme value that bestows humanity the quality of being called the people of God. Schillebeeckx then explains that the grace of God was given to all men and women, so it is the whole of humanity that can be called the people of God. Based on God's grace, humanity in general is essentially a community which can be called the people of God. This particular community based on God's grace is the "immanent" image of humanity's transcendent community with God. Schillebeeckx then insists that this community with God is actually the unity of humanity which is "willed by God." As it is God's desire that men and women should be united in a community of supreme values based on God's grace, then this community of humanity—which is actually the very unity of humanity—is both the people of God and the community of "sanctified men."[19]

This entire discourse may seem very traditional at first glance. Terms like God's revelation, God's grace, community of God, people of God, and community of saints are indeed traditional ideas which pertain to the classical heritage of the Christian church. In Schillebeeckx, however, all these most traditional phrases are radically reinterpreted so that they acquire a totally new and different meaning in at least three aspects.

First, we must notice that while in traditional theology all these terms are applied to the Christian church, which is clearly separated and differ-

---

17. See also Borgman, *Edward Schillebeeckx*, 73.
18. Maloney, *The Cosmic Christ*, 11.
19. Schillebeeckx, *World and Church*, 116.

ent from the world, in Schillebeeckx they are used to describe the world, not the church. The church therefore is automatically identified with the world. At this point of Schillebeeckx's discourse, there is virtually no difference between the world and the church because all the traditional features of the church as the community of God, the people of God, and the community of sanctified persons are meant to describe the world. Thus, the fluidity of the frontiers between the church and the world, mentioned by Schillebeeckx himself at the beginning of his argument, seems to be total to the point that there is virtually no border between the church and the world.[20]

Second, we have to understand that every traditional theological term is automatically changed in Schillebeeckx because of his thoroughly anthropological approach to theology. Everything needs to be revalued from the perspective of humanity: the idea of God, the church, God's grace etc. It has become evident that in Schillebeeckx God is not the metaphysical and meta-historical being that bestows his benevolence to humanity. As far as Schillebeeckx is concerned, God is just an idea or, as he himself writes, God is a human value. It is the supreme value of humanity but still a human value, not a being or even less so a personal being. God is a value and, as a value, is essentially immanent in the sense that it belongs to humanity. It is not humanity which belongs to God as in traditional theology; in Schillebeeckx, God belongs to humanity because it is a mere human value. God's grace therefore is not the benevolent attitude of a supreme personal being who lives beyond our history but merely man's sense that his supreme value, which he calls God, opens to him a wide range of possibilities for the future in order to accomplish the task of human unity.[21] As human unity is not a datum but a task, it is clear that it is to be accomplished in the future. If this is the case, than God's grace is just another way of saying that our supreme value, namely God, allows us and helps us to achieve human unity in future.[22] Actually, human unity cannot be achieved without this supreme value which, at the end of the day, is nothing more than our present awareness of the future. In Schillebeeckx, God is synonymous with the future because it represents all the possibilities—infinite in number—that can be achieved theoretically

---

20. See also Borgman, *Edward Schillebeeckx*, 337.
21. Borgman, *Edward Schillebeeckx*, 163.
22. For details about the realization of unity in future, see Stoker, *Is the Quest*, 238.

in the future. So when Schillebeeckx says that human unity is actually the community of humanity as a gift of God, we should understand that human unity is based on man's supreme value, namely God, which tells us that this unity is to be achieved in future.[23] Likewise, God's absolute communication of himself to humanity is not the revelation of a supreme metaphysical and meta-historical being but rather the understanding that our supreme value will eventually lead to unity among men and women in future. This is why Schillebeeckx says that humanity and the world, not the church, can and should be called the people of God,[24] which means that humanity and the world, not the church, can and should be called the people of future because God, their supreme value, conveys the idea that human unity can only be achieved in future. Schillebeeckx also presents the fact that the world, not the church, is to be called the communion of the saints.[25] This definition also needs a special interpretation. In traditional theology, the concept of saint was used to explain the fact that the Christian believer, the person who believed in God as a supreme metaphysical and meta-historical being, was totally different from the world in two ways: positionally, which means that the believer was set apart from the world by God for a different kind of life compared to the life of the world and morally, which indicates that the believer practically applied God's decision to set him apart from the world, so he now lived a different life compared to the life of the church. This key traditional distinction between the church and the world is blown away in Schillebeeckx who is convinced that the world, not the church, should be considered the community of the saints. The saint though, as presented by Schillebeeckx, is not the person who is set apart from the world by God as in traditional theology; Schillebeeckx's saint is any human person who believes in the supreme value of mankind as well as in the possibility that this supreme value should help humanity achieve unity in the future.

Third, Schillebeeckx's dichotomy between immanence and transcendence should not be understood in terms of history versus meta-history or physics versus metaphysics as in traditional theology; on the contrary, immanence and transcendence must be kept within the realm of history

---

23. Borgman, *Edward Schillebeeckx*, 177.

24. Abdul-Masih, *Edward Schillebeeckx and Hans Frei*, 97.

25. In order to achieve his goal, Schillebeeckx re-interprets traditional Catholic Mariology. See, for details, Breck, *Scripture in Tradition*, 231.

Re-Tracing the Boundaries between the Church and the World

and physics.[26] Immanence is clearly a human reality even in traditional theology but transcendence—which is fundamentally metaphysical and meta-historical in traditional theology—in Schillebeeckx becomes a purely human reality. Thus, while immanence reflects the historical reality of man's life, transcendence is man's capacity to believe in and act in accordance with his supreme value.[27] This is why in Schillebeeckx the idea of transcendence is not meta-historical but rather meta-biological within the realm of human history. According to Schillebeeckx, the world should understand itself as a transcendent community which reflects the immanent reality of its own historical existence; the world or humanity is transcendent only as a community that is able to believe in meta-biological values such as the idea of God which does not elevate us above or beyond history but only helps us cope with our own future.

Schillebeeckx's use of traditional terms for his presentation of the relationship between the church and the world does not stop here. We must not forget though that whenever he speaks of community he means the world, not the church, because the world is identical to the church and the other way around. The idea of community applies to both, so in Schillebeeckx the church is virtually just another word for the world. As for the world, its quality of being a community is a gift which humanity receives for free. In other words, the world is indeed a community based on human values that are inherent or innate in every human being.[28] We do not have to do anything in order to acquire our human values or the supreme value which is represented by the idea of God. Everything pertaining to the world is human; our values are human and even our supreme value, namely God, is fundamentally human.[29] All the values including the supreme value of God are inherent in all of us; we were all born with these values that must be applied practically in order to transform the world for the better. The idea of the world's transformation, which in Schillebeeckx is humanity's social mandate, is inferred by Schillebeeckx's use of another two traditional terms: the idea of sovereignty and the idea of freedom as applied to God's act.[30] In Schillebeeckx, however, God is

---

26. See also Abdul-Masih, *Edward Schillebeeckx and Hans Frei*, 78.
27. Kennedy, *Schillebeeckx*, 44–45.
28. See Haight, *An Alternative Vision*, 224.
29. Hilkert and Schreiter, eds., *The Praxis*, 56.
30. See also Haight, *The Future of Christology*, 112.

not a supreme metaphysically transcendent person; it is only our future, so God's act should be interpreted in terms of man's capacity to live out its future in a sovereign and free way. From this perspective, namely from the perspective of the future, humanity is called in Schillebeeckx to live our in accordance with its supreme values for the beneficial transformation of the world.[31]

The transformation of the world is a continuous task of man, so it somehow becomes identical to the ideal of human unity which is also a task to be fulfilled in future.[32] In order to convey the idea of the world's transformation based on man's supreme values, Schillebeeckx uses the traditional term of salvation, which is contrasted with the idea of disaster. Again, it has to be stressed that in Schillebeeckx salvation has nothing to do with man's deliverance from his sinful nature, acts, and deeds but rather with his attempt to live up to his supreme values. If these values are applied in practical life for the benefit of every human being, then it means that we are partakers of salvation; if not, we are doomed and we shall eventually face disaster. Schillebeeckx explains this with reference to the Old and the New Testaments:

> But not only is the fact of this community a gratuitous gift. The way in which it comes about also goes back to a sovereign and free act of God. It is clear from the whole history of salvation in the Old and New Testaments that, however great a part ancient Near Eastern view of life played in this process, God did not intend to realize the unity of mankind around the community-founding value of "abstract" fundamental values. He wished to gather mankind into a holy community of persons on the basis of values that were prototypically incarnate in living persons. Again and again, "one of ourselves" was the means of salvation chosen to constitute the "great gathering" of people from the diaspora, the people of God. The gratuitous way in which God founded a community among men was that of representative mediation—for the sake of one man, freely called by God for this task, salvation (or disaster) was brought to many. The representative function of one man or of a limited group of men (Adam, Noah, Moses, Abraham, the twelve patriarchs, Israel, the King, the Son of Man, the Servant of God,

---

31. Borgman, *Edward Schillebeeckx*, 246.
32. Evans, *The Church and the Churches*, 9.

Jesus) with regard to salvation or disaster is essential in the Old and New Testaments.[33]

This text is another proof of Schillebeeckx's intention to deconstruct traditional theology. He uses traditional concepts which he reinterprets drastically, so that traditional theology is deprived of its ontologically transcendent categories that eventually become mere human values. Thus, the traditional idea of incarnation—which in traditional theology refers only to Jesus as the preexistent Logos of God who becomes man by assuming a human person—is stripped of its ontological overtones in order to become a human value assumed by some people with view to social and political purposes.[34] Thus, in Schillebeeckx, the idea of incarnation does not refer exclusively to Jesus but also to other religious leaders in the Old and the New Testaments. The immediate consequence of this reinterpretation is the fundamental humanity of Jesus who no longer has any divine—ontologically transcendent and real—attributes left. Jesus is not divine, he is just a man; a man who understood that he must incarnate the supreme idea of God in order to help others.[35] In this, Jesus is not superior to any other religious leader; on the contrary, they are all the same: people who wanted to apply practically the supreme values of humanity in order to transform the world for the better. Therefore, salvation should not be understood as man's deliverance from his sins or offences to God, but rather as the immediate consequence of the actions of these men who decided to incarnate the universal values of humanity in order to change the world.[36] If these actions were successful, men and women enjoyed salvation; if they failed, people suffered disaster. This means that in Schillebeeckx, salvation is not the feature of the church and the result of God's metaphysical intervention in history as in traditional theology, but the consequence of the actions of some people which can always and equally result in disaster as well.

In his attempt to define the world as identical to the church, Schillebeeckx cannot avoid the language of traditional theology. He does use the Bible in order to prove his point, so he has to make various references to various traditional terms which he reinterprets in a radically new

---

33. Schillebeeckx, *World and Church*, 116.
34. Wood, *Spiritual Exegesis*, 111.
35. See also Kennedy, *Schillebeeckx*, 7.
36. Rego, *Suffering and Salvation*, 257.

way by virtually canceling their ontologically transcendent connotations. For instance, the concept of election which in traditional theology designates the decision of the metaphysical God to choose specific nations of persons is turned by Schillebeeckx into a human symbol that represents the decision to transform the world into a better place:[37]

> This manner of founding a community by means of mediation implies that election and universal mission grew towards each other in the Bible. Although the process was hesitant and gradual, Israel did begin to experience her election as an example to all peoples—as election in the service of the whole of mankind. In accordance with the Old Testament view, the totality of concrete historical humanity owed its existence to Yahweh's redeeming covenant with Noah after the flood. It is precisely in this connection that a list of all the existing peoples of the world (that is, of the ancient oriental world) was made in Genesis 10. What is more, it was in Abraham that all the nations were blessed... The election of Abraham was at the same time God's affirmation of universal salvation.[38]

Thus, election is no longer the decision of an ontologically real God but the decision of man to serve the world.[39] The equally important traditional term of mediation, which again refers exclusively to the relationship between humanity and the metaphysical God in traditional theology, is in Schillebeeckx a merely human action.[40] Thus, mediation refers to the fact that man's decision to act for the benefit of humanity, namely election, is carried out by means of certain historical actions. Thus, God's covenant with Noah should not be understood in traditional terms as the decision of the metaphysical God to keep humanity safe in the world but rather as the possibility of humanity to follow a course which will eventually keep everybody safe in the world. Likewise, God's election of Abraham, which is clearly an intervention of the metaphysical God in our physical world as proclaimed by traditional theology, is presented by Schillebeeckx as the human image of universal salvation. In other words, if we stick to the universal human values professed by Abraham, humanity will lead a better life in the world.

---

37. This particular understanding of election can also be applied to Jesus. See Schillebeeckx, *God Is New Each Moment*, 49.

38. Schillebeeckx, *World and Church*, 116–17.

39. See also McManus, *Unbroken Communion*, 90.

40. Haight, *The Future of Christology*, 191.

Re-Tracing the Boundaries between the Church and the World

This of course changes everything. Salvation is human, mediation is human and they are both accomplished by means of more than just one person.[41] This is why Schillebeeckx writes that "in bringing his transcendent salvation, God wishes to maintain the structure of common humanity."[42] Schillebeeckx continues to use the language of traditional theology which could be a little misleading as God, who is definitely not a person in Schillebeeckx, benefits from all the advantages of a personified discourse. It is not God who wishes that salvation be carried out in human terms; it is actually some individuals that want to be mediators of the universal human values for the entire world. The names which appear in the Bible are merely literary characters; they may or may not have been historical figures but this is not ultimately significant. What is important indeed has to do with their capacity to convey the idea of prototype, because they all embody as well as represent fundamental universal values that are practically applied in history for the welfare of men and women. Thus, they may not be historical but they are definitely human: Jesus was a man but a special kind of man who personified the image of the Messiah and represented Israel, the Son of God. Therefore, his mediation and election are no longer soteriological actions in the traditional sense but social and ethical acts meant to serve humanity. Jesus, the historical individual who was killed in Palestine, is also presented as the Christ because the image of Christ discloses the community of those who believe in his values. Christ's values are essentially our values, the values of humanity, but because they are so noble and beneficial for the entire world we have to understand that all those who share in them may be called "the church of Christ".[43] The church has nothing to do with people being saved from their sinful life—understood as an offense to a superior metaphysical God—but only with all the people who believe in the universal value of Christ's teaching and personal example. Christ is therefore the unifying principle of humanity; people from around the world who act as Christ did are all brought together by their common belief in the universal value of humanity.[44]

---

41. Rego, *Suffering and Salvation*, 201.
42. Schillebeeckx, *World and Church*, 117.
43. Borgman, *Edward Schillebeeckx*, 363.
44. Schillebeeckx, *World and Church*, 117–18.

In Schillebeeckx, salvation is not the "property," so to speak, of the church but the universal feature of the world.[45] Salvation is of the world, from the world, and for the world.[46] Salvation is not carried by a metaphysical God but by a historical man.[47] Schillebeeckx resorts once again to the image of Jesus who acted within history in order to improve the situation of his fellow human beings. Jesus, though a mere historical person, is representative of all of us.[48] What he did was to take the theoretical idea of the new unity of humanity or the community of mankind and turn it into real action. Thus, in the life of Jesus, the idea of unity as community does not only exist in principle but also in practice. If each one of us follows Jesus's example we shall all be part of a new humanity. Jesus is the symbol of this new humanity but he is not superior to us. He is just a representation of what we can also be if we follow in his footsteps.[49] It is clear that every human being has the capacity to become like Jesus provided he or she does what Jesus did. Jesus gives humanity a new significance which teaches us that we must change the world for the better by means of believing in as well as applying the universal values of humanity for the benefit of the world. The idea of Christ, which is the embodiment of Jesus's life and death as well as of universal human values, may be described as the essence of human history.[50] In this sense, Christ is transcendent but not in the ontological terms of metaphysics and metahistory. Christ is transcendent only as the embodiment of supreme human values. Christ transcends the basic level of human biology and even that of human history. Schillebeeckx thus writes that Christ can be even considered "supratemporal, supraterrestrial, exclusively transcendent"[51] but only as a value which has meaning for human history. In other words, the supratemporality, the supraterrestrial character and the transcendence of Christ do not refer to a reality which lies beyond the actual boundaries of the world; Christ represents values that should be elevated above

---

45. See also Abdul-Masih, *Edward Schillebeeckx and Hans Frei*, 159.

46. Valkenberg, *Sharing Lights*, 145.

47. Kennedy, *Schillebeeckx*, 99–100.

48. Borgman, *Edward Schillebeeckx*, 239.

49. The idea of representation can also be applied to the church, which is pictured as the representation on earth of the heavenly sign of salvation. See, for details, Cochran, "Another Identity Crisis," 12.

50. Schillebeeckx, *World and Church*, 118.

51. Schillebeeckx, *World and Church*, 118–19.

our concrete historicity but they will always be significant only for the world.[52] Thus, Christ is meaningful only within history. This is why, in Schillebeeckx, the supratemporality, the transcendence and the supraterrestrial character of Christ must be understood exclusively in connection with the concrete reality of history:

> The glorified man Jesus Christ is, after all, a historical man who has entered completion. At one real point of human history, that is, in Jesus, this history itself was definitely completed and perpetuated in the mode of consummation into eternity. In his representative function with regard to Israel and thus with regard to the whole of mankind, Jesus is the prototypical figure of *our* history, the element which has already entered into glory. That is why the Lord is the ultimate meaning which is immanent in our history, even though it is in a dimension which is, for us, trans-empirical. Thus all human history, even where this takes place in a so-called profanity, can only be understood in the light of the "eschatological man," Christ Jesus.[53]

It becomes clear that the church is the world which finds salvation, namely a way for a better future, by resorting to the universal human values embodied by Christ based on the example of Jesus.[54] Jesus is a man but Christ is the image of all men and women who want to be partakers of this salvation or the improvement of humanity's own future.[55]

JESUS, THE CHURCH, AND THE WORLD

The history of Jesus and especially the image of Christ are crucial for Schillebeeckx's identification between the church and the world. Christ is a principle which gives meaning to humanity based on Jesus's example. In Schillebeeckx though, the Christ principle should be approached entirely in human terms. There is nothing attached to Christ which goes beyond our history. Christ represents the essence of humanity because the values he embodies are meant to change the world for the better and can be put into daily practice by every human being. Thus, if in traditional theology the image of Christ was welded to the reality of the church as different

---

52. See also Sayés, *El misterio Eucaristico*, 234.
53. Schillebeeckx, *World and Church*, 119.
54. Schillebeeckx, *Christ, the Sacrament of the Encounter with God*, 48.
55. See also Kennedy, *Schillebeeckx*, 59.

from the world, in Schillebeeckx the principle of Christ functions as an existentialist reality which has universal validity for the entire world.[56]

It has to be highlighted at this point that Schillebeeckx realizes his radical reinterpretation of the traditional doctrine of the church. Moreover, he seems to be aware that serious criticism could be raised against his identification between the church and the world. This is why he proposes to identify a certain difference between what has been traditionally described as the church and the remainder of mankind which is presented as the world. Schillebeeckx knows very well that the traditional definition of the church implies a fundamental difference between the church and the world. This theory about the identification between the church and the world does not allow for the idea of difference given that mankind as a whole represents the idea of unity as community. Christ, however, is the principle which embodies universal and supreme human values and, like any other principle, it can be accepted or rejected, it can be applied or counter-applied. Thus, he attempts to insert a difference within the reality of humanity described as communion. A difference must be there but not in terms of general humanity; the difference should be presented solely by means of the idea of acceptance. Mankind is different when it comes to accepting or rejecting the Christ principle.[57] Therefore, those who accept Christ and universal human values must be different from those who do not. The difference between the two categories of humanity is not essential because they are both made up of human beings. They have nevertheless different attitudes to the Christ principle and the universal human values represented by it.

At this point of his argument, Schillebeeckx makes use of the phrase "church of Christ" as a means to designate that part of humanity which embraces the Christ principle and its universal values.[58] Thus, all the people of the world who decide to accept the values embodied by the idea of Christ are part of the church of Christ. Schillebeeckx's "church of Christ" has nothing in common with the traditional church of Christ. While the latter is made up of all the people who are saved by God's metaphysical intervention in our historical reality for our salvation from sin—described as an offense against God, the former is only the community of those

---

56. McManus, *Unbroken Communion*, 88.
57. Viladesau, *Theological Aesthetics*, 67.
58. See Prusak, *The Church Unfinished*, 66–67.

who are willing to accept and apply the principles of Christ as well as its universal values.[59]

Schillebeeckx releases an entire chain of traditional concepts which he uses for his anthropological presentation of the church. Thus, ideas such as justification, acceptance, Gospel, faith, Word of God, baptism, and Trinity are used as a reference to what the church had been throughout history. Of course, for Schillebeeckx these traditional concepts do not bear any ontologically transcendent significance; they are merely a range of words that present the reality of that part of humanity which has chosen to follow the Christ principle and universal human values. Schillebeeckx even talks about the admission into the church or into the community those who accept the idea of Christ but this is definitely not the active admission from traditional theology (when a certain individual is accepted in the church by others). Schillebeeckx's admission must be understood as a passive admission (when a certain individual accepts himself as part of that humanity which promotes and practises the Christ principle and human universal values). To sound even more traditional Schillebeeckx also mentions the very traditional doctrines of Christ's ascension[60] and Christ's second coming[61] but they should not be understood as historical realities which are connected to the meta-historical and metaphysical reality of God's ontologically transcendent existence (traditionally Christ's ascension refers to the bodily departure from earth into heaven, from history into meta-history of the physically and spiritually resurrected Jesus, while Christ's second coming is the departure from heaven to earth, from meta-history to history, of the physically and spiritually resurrected and ascended Jesus).

For Schillebeeckx, Christ's ascension and second coming must be viewed in purely historical terms as historical events that have nothing in common with meta-historical realities. Thus, they seem to represent temporal landmarks which correspond to different temporal realities of the church and of the world. Christ's ascension appears to be the beginning of specific temporal age in the history of humanity, namely the period when a certain part of humanity accepted the Christ principles and their universal human values. Likewise, Christ's second coming seems to be

---

59. Wiley, *Thinking of Christ*, 99.
60. Borgman, *Edward Schillebeeckx*, 44.
61. Bergin, *O Propheticum Lavacrum*, 212.

a reference to the subsequent period in the history of humanity which continues the first period marked by Christ's ascension. Thus, Christ's second coming designates the time when not only a part of humanity but all mankind, all the world, will eventually come to embrace the idea of Christ and the universal values of mankind. These two periods though are utterly historical; they begin in history, they unfold in history and they end in history. The end here is not the final point of human history but rather that period of time when humanity reaches its full redemption or completion as a result of accepting the idea of Christ and the universal values of man.[62] Here is how Schillebeeckx explains these issues:

> Christ has in principle (but really) given mankind a new religious meaning which is immanent, that is, which has been realized within our human history. There is, however, a certain distance between mankind gathered together in principle and the factual, public manifestation of this mankind that has been renewed in Christ. The exponent of this distance and tension is the "church of Christ." Within human history, this new meaning acquires a historically visible, public and concrete community-founding character in the church, thanks to free consent to the grace of justification, acceptance in faith of the Gospel or the Word of God and reception of the church's baptism in the name of the Trinity. Admission to this church makes Christ's triumphant grace a manifest, historically recognizable fact. The consequence of this is that, in the period between Christ ascension and his second coming, there will always be a certain difference and a dialectical tension between the *church* and *mankind* (which has in principle—but really—been redeemed).[63]

It is not clear whether mankind is redeemed or the dialectical tension between the church and mankind is redeemed, but it really does not matter. The result is the same: if mankind is redeemed then it means that there is no difference between the church and the world; if the dialectical tension between the church and mankind is redeemed, then there is virtually no dialectical tension left between the church and mankind so the two types of humanity are in fact one single human community.[64]

---

62. Mertens, *Not the Cross, but the Crucified*, 57.

63. Schillebeeckx, *World and Church*, 119.

64. For details about the relationship between the church and the world, see Wainwright, *Worship with One Accord*, 87.

Re-Tracing the Boundaries between the Church and the World

Schillebeeckx is very interested in the personal history of Jesus because the way he understands Jesus's ministry legitimizes his theory that the boundaries between the church and the world are fluid, in the sense that there is no clear line of demarcation between the church and the world. Thus, Jesus was a man who did not have the slightest intention to found a community which was different from the people of Israel.[65] Or, he did not want to build some sort of a sect that was to separate itself from Israel. In Schillebeeckx's general picture, Jesus was not interested in laying the basis of a human community which was fundamentally different from the rest of humanity. Jesus preached the kingdom of God and the kingdom of God represents the universal values of humanity.[66] Likewise, Jesus stressed the importance of repentance, an idea which he addressed to the whole of Israel, not to a certain community of his own.[67] So, what Jesus wanted to do was to transform the entire nation of Israel based on repentance. His plan was therefore to turn Israel into the new Israel, the community of those who understand what repentance really is. Thus, Schillebeeckx drastically reinterprets the traditional concept of repentance, which is the internal work of the Holy Spirit in the heart and mind of the believer with view to his total transformation by the acceptance of Jesus Christ, in accordance with the secularized rationality of the modern man. Consequently, repentance is no longer a meta-historical and metaphysical work performed by the ontologically real God, the Holy Spirit in particular, but rather a human value, the value whereby humanity understands its need to renew itself. In Schillebeeckx, repentance can be perceived as renewal. As renewal needs to affect humanity in general, the concept of repentance is stripped of its specific religious and theological connotations in favor of a secularized idea of renewal—social, economical, political etc.[68]

To draw the line, Jesus was interested in the renewal of the entire Israel, so he dreamt of seeing every single Jew renewed in accordance with his preaching.[69] When it comes to his preaching, however,

---

65. See also Schillebeeckx, *God Is New Each Moment*, 49.
66. Rego, *Suffering and Salvation*, 255.
67. McManus, *Unbroken Communion*, 7.
68. Schillebeeckx, *World and Church*, 120.
69. Prusak, *The Church Unfinished*, 46.

Schilleebeeckx says that it reflected God's intention.[70] We all know by now that Schillebeeckx does not refer to the intention of a metaphysical God, who lives beyond history and gets himself involved in the lives of people on a personal level. God represents here the future of man and especially the development as well as the completion of universal human values from the perspective of the future. Therefore, God's intention is nothing more than a metaphor for the universality of human values. As applied to Jesus, he preached repentance—or renewal—for all Israel because he wanted all the Jews to renew themselves in accordance with God's intention. If we apply this to our present situation, it means that Jesus preached the necessity of renewal, a renewal that must comprise all humanity based on man's universal values.[71] For Schillebeeckx, Jesus's work and preaching ministry was a parable which declared his interest in the whole nation of Israel and consequently in humanity. During the life of Jesus, Israel was best represented by the twelve Old Testament patriarchs, so as Jesus wanted to renew the people of Israel as well as their humanity as a whole, he chose twelve disciples to "replace" the ancient patriarchs; what he did in fact was to replace the idea of Old Israel with the humanizing reality of the New Israel. In Schilleebeeckx, the New Israel itself seems to stand for the idea of a new humanity.[72] Jesus's original plan to renew Israel and make it a new type of humanity did not work, and Schillebeeckx is very keen to underline this. The people of Israel did not understand that Jesus wanted to renew the whole of Israel; what they understood was that Jesus reportedly wanted to build a new and distinct community within Israel, a community which was to detach itself from the people of Israel. In other words, according to Schillebeeckx, Jesus wanted to renew all the individuals in Jewish society but they misunderstood him, so they believed he wanted to found a sect. When Jesus realized that the people were dissatisfied with his teaching because they had got him entirely wrong, he felt death was approaching. He knew for a fact that he had stirred things way too strongly, so his death was imminent. This is when he suddenly changed tactics. He did not abandon his original idea to renew Israel but he added the tragedy of his impending death to his initial message there-

---

70. Schillebeeckx, *God Is New Each Moment*, 26.
71. Borgman, *Edward Schillebeeckx*, 246.
72. Rego, *Suffering and Salvation*, 206.

fore transforming the reality of his death into a symbol of the fight for ultimate human values.[73]

It appears that for Schillebeeckx Jesus began to talk about the church only within the context of his death. Thus, from Jesus's perspective, the church was a metaphor for the new community of the people of God who will lead transformed lives and will transform other people's lives. His vision though seems to have been restricted exclusively to Israel. Jesus, according to Schillebeeckx, did not think beyond the then boundaries of Israel. The new transformed society would have to be Israel itself but in a new state of consciousness. The entire situation, however, changed after Jesus died. His disciples realized that his message appealed to the human situation in general, not only to the nation of Israel. Thus, they no longer referred to Israel when they talked about the church of Christ; they began to preach the church not as a metaphor for the nation of Israel but as a community which is different not only from Israel but also from the entire world. Thus, the "church of Jesus" was not appealing any longer because Jesus was dead after all; what made sense after Jesus's death was the "church of Christ" because the new image of Christ, as representing what Jesus would have been if he had stayed alive, was the perfect pretext to launch a campaign that was meant to deal with the existential problems of the entire world.[74] So it was the preaching of the disciples that changed Jesus's original message about the transformation of the nation of Israel into what was later to become the church of Christ, an organization with specific ecclesiastical offices and activities which was quite different from what Jesus had had in mind.[75]

For Schillebeeckx though it is not very easy to discuss the complex issues of the relevance of the church of Christ without making frequent appeals to the traditional formulations of the Bible. This is why, in his hands the Bible becomes an instrument which helps his case for the simple reason that he reinterprets everything the way he wants. If the church of Christ preached by the disciples repeatedly taught the idea of a meta-historical and metaphysical future existence of the believers with God in a time beyond the time of our present or future history, then the church of Jesus was based on the simple preaching of the kingdom of God which

---

73. Schillebeeckx, *World and Church*, 120–21.
74. Borgman, *Edward Schillebeeckx*, 134.
75. Ormerod, "A Dialectic Engagement," 815.

was to be accomplished here on earth, during the time of this history. Thus, being saved in the church of Christ meant being accepted into an organization which promised man a better future beyond the temporal future of the world; by comparison and even by contrast, being saved in the church of Jesus means being transformed by the message of the kingdom of God hoping that a better future is at hand during the time of present history. Despite the differences between the church of Jesus and the church of Christ and even if the disciples did not get Jesus's message entirely right, their preaching as well as their church did bear significant resemblances to Jesus's original preaching. Thus, they basically retained the name of Jesus as a fundamental part of their message and of their church. The church of Christ is presented as the body of Christ or the body of the Lord, which is for Schillebeeckx an indication that the disciples did not forget that Jesus was with them and he gave his life for his cause. They built the church of Christ on the firm foundation provided by the image of Peter, presented as the rock on which the church of Christ was built.[76] It has to be said here that Schillebeeckx does reveal his Catholic heritage at this point because, as far as he is concerned, the rock mentioned by Jesus was Peter not Jesus or Jesus's message, as it is in mainline Protestant theology.[77]

As far as the church of Christ is concerned, it still remained an image of the redemption of humanity despite its ecclesiastical structure, ministry and offices.[78] Schillebeeckx is convinced that this is the case because people were accepted into this church based on their belief in Jesus. Jesus was of course dead but they believed he was alive and this is why they decided to worship him as the risen Christ, the Lord of the church.[79] In this particular context, salvation becomes a historical reality which is given by the communion of the church. The community itself and the reality of its existence is in fact salvation.[80] Man is not saved from sin viewed as offence against God but it is the very participation at the life of this community, which is the church of Christ. Schillebeeckx again uses the language of traditional theology in the sense that the communion of the church of Christ is the "Father's absolute communication of himself through the

---

76. Schillebeeckx, *World and Church*, 121.
77. See Gowen, ed., *The Westminster Theological Wordbook of the Bible*, 63.
78. Borgman, *Edward Schillebeeckx*, 173.
79. Schillebeeckx, *World and Church*, 121–22.
80. Bergin, *O Propheticum Lavacrum*, 208.

Re-Tracing the Boundaries between the Church and the World

Son in the Holy Spirit" but this is just another way of saying that the essence of the communion of the church of Christ is based on values that transcend the mere historical reality. These values are therefore universal; they apply to every human being and they are valid for ever as features of the new humanity based on the example of Jesus. The church of Christ is more than just communion; it is salvation because it offers the possibility of being part of the kingdom of God, which is the embodiment of the fundamental values of humanity.[81] We are saved because we are part of the church of Christ but, as the church of Christ is founded on the essential values of humanity, we are saved because we share in these values. Salvation therefore has nothing to do with a transcendent reality which is given to us by a metaphysical God. Salvation is a historical reality which will stay immanent for ever because it is informed by the fundamental values of mankind.[82]

At this point, Schillebeeckx's presentation of the church is based on the sharp distinction between the life of Jesus and what happened afterwards. During the life of Jesus, the idea of salvation had nothing to do with the church. The church itself appeared after Jesus died so it is a postpaschal event if we are to use Schillebeeckx's phrase. Thus, the church is a new reality in comparison to the community which existed during Jesus's lifetime. At the same time, the church is new if compared to the universal reality of the people of God. This means that what really counts for man's salvation is not the church itself or being part of the church but rather being part of the people of God which is not necessarily the church. The church seems to be an image of the people of God in Schillebeeckx, but it is definitely not the people of God as in traditional theology.[83] So in order to be saved we should seek to be part of the people of God; if we are members of the church this is not a problem but we must realize that the church only points to the universal human values embodied by the people of God who must accept and practically apply the kingdom of God as the sum of the values of humanity. Jesus died in order to give validity to these values so they were all confirmed by his death. Jesus died for the whole of humanity; his death is therefore representative as useful

---

81. Schillebeeckx, *Christ, the Sacrament of the Encounter with God*, 48.
82. Schillebeeckx, *World and Church*, 122.
83. Kennedy, *Schillebeeckx*, 72.

for the whole world.[84] He was rejected by the world but he still died for the world. He was discredited by the world but he still chose to die in order to redeem the universal values of the world. People rejected Jesus and put him to death but what he did in turn was to find a way to help them even by his death:

> There is certainly a distance between the mankind that has been redeemed by Christ both in principle and in historical reality and the community of Jesus built on the Rock, the institution of the church or "practicing Christianity." If we are to understand this distinction, we must first consider the connection made in Scripture between Jesus's messianic death or "going away," and the church, which is *only* a post-paschal and therefore a *new reality*—new even in comparison with the universal reality which is the people of God . . . Jesus's death was his rejection by mankind—by the Sanhedrin, Israel's representative, by the pagan world of the Gentiles in the person of Pilate and even by the hierarchy of the future church in the persons of the apostles who ran away and Peter who denied him. In his death, Jesus was really alone, crushed by the "sins of the world," and alone in his surrender to the Father in service to his fellow-men.[85]

The death of Jesus left the world without him. In the empirical reality of everyday life, Jesus was no longer present. As far as Schillebeeckx is concerned, Jesus has never been present again as a person in the life of the world. He died for the world, he offered an example of a life worth living for the world and his existence was a proof that the universal values of humanity are still very much alive even if the world rejected him. So Jesus is dead and the physical connection between himself and the world has never been reestablished. Schillebeeckx is very clear about the fact that death interrupts every relationship between human beings and, as Jesus was a mere human being, he went away for ever the very moment he died.[86] Despite his conviction that death is the terminal point of human existence, a fact confirmed by the reality of the absence of the person who died from the realm of empirical existence, Schillebeeckx still talks about the resurrection of Jesus:

---

84. Wood, *Spiritual Exegesis*, 111.
85. Schillebeeckx, *World and Church*, 122–23.
86. Abdul-Masih, *Edward Schillebeeckx and Hans Frei*, 119–20.

Re-Tracing the Boundaries between the Church and the World

> Death, which brought reconciliation, at the same time caused Christ's empirical absence, in other words, the absence of the source of grace ... the rupture in the covenant of grace was made definitive by Jesus's death—mankind banished from this world the "coming of the kingdom of God" into the world in the person of Christ and thus cast it out of the *communio* of men. Of course, every death implies a physical absence and a breaking off of interhuman relationships with the dead person ... this removal of the man of grace, Christ, was therefore irrevocable. It was, after all, certainly not thanks to us and not even thanks to Christ's humanity as such that Christ, by virtue of his resurrection, once again entered into living relationships with us.[87]

This is definitely odd because as Jesus died it would be normal to understand that he cannot be resurrected in any way. The secularized mind of the modern man will never accept the bodily resurrection of a corpse. Schillebeeckx, however, insists that the idea as well as the reality of resurrection can be applied to Jesus and even in keeping with the idea of a bodily return to life. This is possible only if the idea of resurrection is linked to the reality of the church.[88] In Schillebeeckx, the resurrection of Jesus can be conceived but only if presented by means of the church. In other words, the resurrection of Jesus is the church.[89] Jesus did not come back to life in his physical body; he returned among us through the church, which is described as his body. In empirical terms, Jesus died and remained dead; the church though, which is considered his body, rose to life and began to promote the teachings of Jesus as if he had been returned to us from the dead. Jesus is alive through the church even if his physical death is as permanent as the demise of any other human being. Jesus's resurrection is the church itself and, in Schillebeeckx, this is the only reasonable way to talk about the idea of resurrection as applied to Jesus. In fact, Schillebeeckx himself realizes that the idea of resurrection can be applied exclusively to Jesus. Nobody else's death could have brought salvation to humanity; he was the only one by means of whom salvation was made possible. For Schillebeeckx, this means that in spite of Jesus's actual death, he was the only human being who could convey as well as cement the idea of salvation. Why Jesus, and not somebody else? Because he was

---

87. Schillebeeckx, *World and Church*, 123.
88. See Kennedy, *Schillebeeckx*, 115.
89. Depoortere, *A Different God*, 119.

influential enough to determine a bunch of individuals, his disciples, to preach the same values he had preached before his death in such a powerful way that the church, a new community, was founded as some sort of resurrection that was believed to have been Jesus's return from the dead. To be sure, Jesus did not come back from the dead; the church, described as his body, came to life as if Jesus himself had been raised from the dead. So in Schillebeeckx, the resurrection of Jesus can and should be considered exclusively in terms of the founding of the church:

> It is only when we have once understood the full implication of Jesus's death that we can completely appreciate the fundamental saving significance of the resurrection which, on the basis of the sacrifice offered, made the sending of the Holy Spirit and the foundation of the church possible. It was in the resurrection of Jesus, the grace of the Father, that redemption triumphed. But this triumph implies that salvation is henceforth situated in the Jesus Christ who is now empirically *absent* from us . . . Jesus himself linked this going away with the coming of the Holy Spirit and the building up of the church. He wished to continue to dwell among us as the source of all grace in the church, his body, inhabited by the Holy Spirit. The church, "this body," thus became for us the condition or, more precisely, the incarnate form of our restored association with Christ and our entry into the kingdom of God. Jesus's absence from the *communio*, the community of men, was restored by his resurrection—in the church, his body on earth.[90]

In Schillebeeckx, Jesus's death becomes significant only in connection with the idea of resurrection as applied to the church.[91] This is because the church, which came to life after Jesus's death, proclaims the teachings of Jesus that have the capacity to change the world. It should be noted here that for Schillebeeckx the importance of salvation is given exclusively by the fact that Jesus is dead. In other words, the permanence of Jesus's death confers significance to the idea of salvation as presented by Schillebeeckx. This is true because in Schillebeeckx salvation is man's acceptance as well as practical application of the universal human values for the benefit of the whole of humanity, and humanity cannot understand the real meaning of these values without the idea of genuine sacrifice.[92] Nevertheless,

---

90. Schillebeeckx, *World and Church*, 123–24.
91. Abdul-Masih, *Edward Schillebeeckx and Hans Frei*, 120.
92. Schillebeeckx, *Christ, the Sacrament of the Encounter with God*, 32.

there is no genuine sacrifice without the idea of Christ which embodies these universal human values and, as sacrifice is always done for the benefit of others, Schillebeeckx reaches the conclusion that salvation, which is based on the idea of sacrifice, is human solidarity with Christ.[93] This means that in order to be saved, man must accept the universal values of humanity revealed in the example of Christ and then apply them in a self-sacrificing way for the well being of the world.[94] The church connects us to Christ, so it is by means of the church that we learn the fundamental values of mankind as well as the fact that we have to use them for the benefit of the world. Therefore, in Schillebeeckx, we go to the church in order to learn about the values of the world, which is in total contradiction to traditional theology which proclaims the sheer distinction between the church and the world. In Schillebeeck though, things are the other way around. The church teaches us about the values of the world; the church tells us how to become more involved in the world in such a way that the church itself is no longer a distinct community from the world but the world itself. Of course Schillebeeckx does not say this but he does convey the idea that the church should be understood more and more in the terms of the world. The church does not make sense if presented in a language which separates it from the world. In Schillebeeckx, the Christ of the church sums up all the fundamental values of the world so that the church of Christ becomes the image of what the world should be. But because the values of the church originate ultimately in the world and the world is redeemed by the idea of Christ as a metaphor of universal human values, the world itself becomes the image of what the church should be. The idea of human solidarity is crucial at this point: human solidarity is truly significant for Schillebeeckx only if associated to the idea of Christ which places solidarity within the realm of fundamental human values. When Christ, however, is preached by the church as the embodiment of human solidarity, it means that the church must come close to the world. In Schillebeeckx's thought, the church carries within it the idea of Christ, in other words the church embraces the universal values of humanity as presented by Christ. If this is true and this is the case in Schillebeeckx, the church does not make sense as a community which is different from the world because the church ends up preaching

93. Schillebeeckx, *World and Church*, 124.
94. Bergin, *O Propheticum Lavacrum*, 210.

the values of the world. Consequently, the church comes so close to the world that the fluid frontier between the two is virtually dissipated. To be sure, there is a formal distinction between the church and the world in the sense that the church is based on the idea of Christ; nevertheless, as Christ represents the universal values of the world, the church itself is based on the universal values of the world which leads to the unavoidable conclusion that, in Schillebeeckx's theological system, there is no actual difference between the church and the world.

8

Re-Inventing the World

Because Schillebeeckx's teaching of the church is based on the idea of Christ which encapsulates the universal values of the world, any real distinction between the church and the world becomes superfluous. Thus, any discourse about the church is not an attempt to define the church but rather a re-invention of the world based on traditional Christian concepts which are radically reinterpreted. For instance, Christ is just an idea which confers validity to universal human values so Christ defines the world, not the church. Notions like creation and redemption are reassessed exclusively in human terms which make them truly relevant to the world, not to the church. Human solidarity is given a new meaning in light of the idea of Christ as promoter of fundamental human values, so the true significance of solidarity should be sought in the world, not in the church. The church undergoes a process of secularization which humanizes all its traditionally metaphysical values to the point of making them fully human. This humanized idea of the church can easily be embraced by the world; consequently, the traditional doctrine of the church gradually disappears into a re-invented secularized perspective on the world.

THE WORLD AS CHURCH

This is the first step in Schillebeeckx's attempt to deconstruct the traditional doctrine of the church. The church becomes one with the world because the values they both share are the same in Christ.[1] The image of Christ is the unifying principle which turns the church into the world so that the world could be re-invented as church. The notion of salvation runs through both concepts, world and church, because salvation is

---

1. Newlands, *Christ and Human Rights*, 103.

the practical application of the fundamental human values for the benefit of humanity.[2] There is, however, a relationship between mankind and the church, and this relationship should be understood by means of the phrase "people of God."[3] In Schillebeeckx, the people of God are those who choose to accept and apply the fundamental human values for the benefit of humanity in general, so the people of God can be extended to mankind but also to the church because it was in the church that the notion of people of God received plenary significance in Christ. Schillebeeckx presents Christ as "heavenly," namely transcendent to the basic level of humanity but Christ's transcendence is nonetheless historical as he represents the totality of human values.[4] Christ does everything in the church but as he is the very image of human values acting in the church it means that the world, which is the realm of human values, identifies itself to the church, so the world becomes the church.[5]

For Schillebeeckx, Jesus is immanent in the church even if he is dead. His teachings, life, and death inspired his disciples who later on founded the church. The church did not have Jesus as a living leader because he was already dead; this is why the church preached the resurrection of the dead Jesus as the living Christ which became the most salient aspect of the church.[6] Thus, even if he was dead, Jesus managed to transcend his own dead body as well as his entire life because his impact generated in his disciples the desire to found the church. Following this pattern associated to the dead Jesus who transcended his own life, the idea of Christ transcends the church because the values represented by Christ exist, in a way, above the historical reality of the church. Christ's transcendence is nonetheless historical because his values are essentially human.[7] For Schillebeeckx, the transcendence of Jesus as well as the transcendence of Christ—which is essentially historical in nature—has an intellectual, psychological, and existential content in the sense that the universal human values proclaimed by Christ are active beyond the boundaries of the church, so they are also active in the world. Therefore, as these fun-

---

2. Abdul-Masih, *Edward Schillebeeckx and Hans Frei*, 159.
3. Schillebeeckx, *Christ, the Sacrament of the Encounter with God*, 168.
4. Borgman, *Edward Schillebeeckx*, 214.
5. Schillebeeckx, *World and Church*, 124.
6. Rego, *Suffering and Salvation*, 301.
7. Abdul-Masih, *Edward Schillebeeckx and Hans Frei*, 78.

damental human values represented by Christ work both within and beyond the church into the world, there is no need for us to have a frontier which separates the church from the world.[8] In light of Christ's values, the church becomes the world and the world acts as church.

In this new context of the total identification between the church and the world, the idea of anonymous Christianity—which is in fact revealed humanity—becomes relevant at least in Schillebeeckx's system.[9] If the world is redefined as church and the church is virtually the world, everybody who believes in the universal values of humanity as seen in Christ is an anonymous Christian. This particular sort of anonymous belief in Christ or rather in the universal values of humanity broadens the traditional concept of salvation from the initial idea of redemption from sin, understood as offence against God, to the modern acceptance of liberation from suffering, seen as a consequence of evil.[10] Thus, salvation is no longer the property of the church as in traditional theology but the attribute of the world, a task that must be accepted and applied based on the fundamental values of humanity as presented in Christ. To quote Schillebeeckx:

> What the heavenly Christ does, he does in his totality, that is to say, in and with his body, the church. What the church therefore does as church, the glorified Christ also does together with the Spirit of God, who is also his Spirit. What is *Christian* is therefore also of the church, in an indissoluble, living and organic bond. However much Jesus, the Lord, may transcend his body, the church, his immanence in the church is as extensive as his transcendence above the church, because he is transcendent (above the church) by interiority (in the church). In other words, his transcending of the boundaries of his body, the church, is a gratuitous gift of himself in the church to all men, even those who are (still) outside the church. This at the same time means that the Lord is active in our world even in people who have not yet been historically confronted with the "church of Christ." But it also means that this activity of the Lord is at the same time an activity of his body. Every association with Christ, even though it is anonymous, is therefore *ipso facto* also an association with the church. In this way, the church is also the possibility of salvation for the world of men which has not yet

---

8. See also Meng, "The Political Theology," 178.

9. Kennedy, *A Modern Introduction to Theology*, 250.

10. Rego, *Suffering and Salvation*, 168.

> perceived and experienced her in the distinctive form in which she appears historically.[11]

Schillebeeckx struggles to remain within the boundaries of traditional theology at least with view to the language he uses in describing the church and the world. Thus, there is a theoretical distinction between the world and the church because some people are apparently "(still) outside the church."[12] This phrase is merely a stylistic device because, in Schillebeeckx, nobody is outside the church. Everybody is in the church as much as everybody is in the world. Thus, even if he may allude to a theoretical distinction between the world and the church, there is no such thing in practice.

Then Schillebeeckx argues that the distance between the world and the church decreases significantly because the church is present everywhere in the world even if its distinctive ecclesial organization is not there. Even if at first glance Schillebeeckx's intention seems to be an attempt to enlarge the boundaries of the church so that it encompasses the world, it is actually the other way around. He wants to broaden the frontiers of the world so that it can eventually include the church. It is true that Schillebeeckx begins his re-invention of the world from a drastically reinterpreted definition of the church but his purpose is not to have the church spread throughout the world but the world to engulf the church. This is because the image of Christ is interpreted in such a way that it no longer fits within the church; the image of Christ as the representation of the fundamental values of the world does not seem to belong naturally to the church but to the world.[13] From this perspective, the traditional opposition between the world and the church as well as their categorical distinction is practically erased. The church and the world become two communities which have more things in common than they hold in opposition so any attempt to define them in opposing terms seems highly irrelevant. In Schillebeeckx there is no such thing as the church, in its traditional sense and the world as a non-church reality. At this point, however, Schillebeeckx resorts to the traditional doctrine of sin—even if he does not explicitly say it—in order to explain why the church and the world are not so different after all. So, he argues that the church is not

---

11. Schillebeeckx, *World and Church*, 124–25.
12. Schillebeeckx, *Christ, the Sacrament of the Encounter with God*, 213.
13. Borgman, *Edward Schillebeeckx*, 233.

Re-Inventing the World

different from the world because a whole lot of aspects which belong to the world or to the realities and manifestations of the world are part of the lives of those who live explicitly in the church. Even in traditional theology the only thing that connects the church to the world is the reality of sin but, again, Schillebeeckx does not say explicitly that this is the cause of the identification between the church and the world. He only says that many of the things of the world are to be found in the church.[14] It is not entirely clear whether he says this in a positive or in a negative way; he does use the argument though to show that there are virtually no differences between the world and the church.[15]

Even if Schillebeeckx himself establishes quite clearly that there is no rational ground to differentiate between the church and the world given that Christ is the image of the universal values of humanity, he nevertheless argues that a minimum distinction needs to be maintained between the world and the church, namely between the world as anonymous Christianity and the church as explicit Christianity.[16] The difference is actually insignificant and it is not presented by Schillebeeckx in terms which could induce the idea that the world is different from the church. The world is identical to the church but there is nonetheless a very small difference between the two which is given by the internal structure of the church. As a community the church has a specific way of life and a clearly defined structure, so the word church should not be used in connection with anonymous Christianity, i.e., the world. In other words, the world should not be called church even if it is church and it shares the same values with the church.[17] Both world and church are concerned with salvation because in Schillebeeckx salvation is connected to the idea of Christ which embodies the universal values of humanity as meaningful or saving for those who accept and apply them. Both the world and the church are communities of human communion so they are both preoccupied with salvation.[18] Thus, even if the church is explicitly Christian while the world is implicitly or anonymously Christian, the concept of grace—which is

---

14. Berkouwer, *The Church*, 343.
15. See also Lakeland, *The Liberation of Laity*, 140.
16. Schillebeeckx, *The Mission of the Church*, 76.
17. Schillebeeckx, *World and Church*, 125.
18. See also Levering, *Sacrifice and Community*, 22.

conveyed by salvation in Christ—actually unites the two communities.[19] The church may have appeared as the resurrection of Christ in the world but the idea of grace itself shows that the difference between the church and the world should be kept to a minimum because the realm of the church's existence as well as activity is the world especially based on the principle of human solidarity which is common to both.[20]

It seems that Schillebeeckx's identification between the church and the world—despite the very insignificant though evident difference between them—is based on the idea of historical visibility.[21] We believe things to be true if we see them in the world and if we assess as well as comprehend their existence rationally. It is therefore rational to see that the church and the world are both visible communities which work for the benefit of humanity. As part of the world the church still has some sort of preeminence in explicitly defining man's desire to apply the universal values of humanity for the benefit of all men and women and the church does this by means of the idea of Christ. When the world does the same, namely applies the universal values of humanity even if it does not realize they are encapsulated in the idea of Christ, the world tends to become church.[22] As far as Schillebeeckx is concerned, every human being has at least theoretically the explicit capacity to apply the universal values of humanity in his own life for the benefit of others. Thus, the acceptance and the application of the universal values of humanity are not the sole property of the church but rather a characteristic of the world. When the world does this it shares an anonymous bond with Christ even if it is not aware of this. The bond, however, is visible in history due to the actions of those—both from the church and from the world—who apply the values of humanity in a practical way. This is another confirmation for Schillebeeckx that grace is active inside and outside the church in explicit as well as implicit forms of manifestation. Whether grace is applied inside or outside the church, the result is the same: humanity benefits from actions which are meant to make the life of men and women worth living.[23] Therefore in Schillebeeckx grace is no longer the benevolent attitude and

---

19. Wood, *Spiritual Exegesis*, 111.
20. Schillebeeckx, *World and Church*, 125–26.
21. Kennedy, *Schillebeeckx*, 62.
22. See also Borgman, *Edward Schillebeeckx*, 337.
23. Rego, *Suffering and Salvation*, 158.

action of a meta-historical and metaphysical God who wants the welfare of humanity, but man's own realization that the application of goodness as well as universal human values in general can only be beneficial to everybody.[24]

Schillebeeckx continues his dialectics between the church and the world in an attempt to remain as close as possible to traditional theology. Thus, even if the world and the church are virtually identical in sharing the conviction that the application of universal human values is meaningful to the lives of men and women, the church seems to be a little bit different from the world when it come to practical expression. In other words, it is not enough for the church and the world to know that the application of universal human values is indeed useful and beneficial for humanity; they must also express their knowledge in practical ways. For Schillebeeckx, the church knows and expresses this knowledge by means of its traditional structure and manifestation; this particular reality of the church should function as a model for the world, so that the world becomes church:

> The fact that the deep meaning that is obscurely present in the dynamic life of mankind is not grasped according to its real significance does not mean that the distinction between "mankind," and church is only one of "not knowing explicitly" as opposed to "knowing explicitly." It is, after all, true that man only comes completely to himself in expressing himself. What is experienced anonymously always remains a fragile datum if it cannot authentically *express itself*. (This is more than simply a question of knowledge!) Without the church's form and expression of this most profound core of life in Christ, which were given by God in Christ himself, this experience remains "a light hidden under the bushel," a flickering flame that any draught may extinguish. It is within the sphere of the church proper that God's word of forgiveness is spoken, baptism administered and the Eucharist celebrated, and men believe that nothing can separate us from the Lord and that absolute loneliness is impossible for man since God has been with us and this environment (which is the believers themselves) is vitally necessary if what grace accomplishes anonymously in the lives of men is to be brought to its saving fulfillment. But this special value of the church as a sign and as disclosure requires the church to go back again and again to her evangelical sources and to show

---

24. Schillebeeckx, *World and Church*, 126.

herself in forms in which this authenticity will come forward to meet us clearly and impartially.[25]

This paragraph has a paramount importance for Schillebeeckx's identification between the world and the church because it legitimizes the world as anonymous Christianity.[26] This has to do again with the concept of grace which does not work exclusively in the church but also in the world.[27] Grace itself, according to Schillebeeckx, works in the world anonymously but this also means that, as grace conveys specific Christian insights, it turns the world into anonymous Christianity. Thus, the fact that the world is anonymous Christianity is not merely the natural consequence of defining the church as explicit Christianity; it is actually the work of grace which turns the world into anonymous Christianity therefore legitimizing it by means of a Christian reality, namely grace.[28]

Schillebeeckx is so convinced that the world and the church are virtually identical that he reinterprets the concept of church mission.[29] It has become evident by now that the world strives to become church, and this is definitely one side of the process of salvation, seen as the application of universal human values for the benefit of mankind. The other side of the same process is the mission of the church which wants to become the world in the sense that it somehow welcomes the world's effort to become church. Thus, the world moves in the direction of the church and the church moves in the direction of the world due to the saving effect of grace, which is the human realization that the application of the universal values of humanity is good for mankind. The concept of historical visibility is used once again by Schillebeeckx because these two sides of salvation are visible forms of its effectiveness.[30] The language of traditional theology comes once more—and quite naturally—in Schillebeeckx's argument because the way he reinterprets the concept of *pneuma* confers validity on the extent of salvation.[31] Salvation is the result of grace but it is also the effect of *pneuma*, which cannot be severed from grace. *Pneuma* though,

---

25. Schillebeeckx, *World and Church*, 126–27.
26. See also Lewis and Demarest, *Integrative Theology*, vol. 2–3, 54.
27. Janowiak, *The Holy Preaching*, 45.
28. McManus, *Unbroken Communion*, 14.
29. Utzinger, *Yet Saints*, 273.
30. See also Janowiak, *The Holy Preaching*, 49.
31. Mitchell, *Real Presence*, 34.

as a traditional concept, is not the traditional person of the Holy Spirit of God as ontologically transcendent, metaphysical, and meta-historical. In Schillebeeckx, *pneuma* seems to be a practical manifestation of grace as human awareness of the necessity to apply the fundamental values of humanity.[32] When applied practically, grace—as awareness—turns into the spirit wherein grace becomes manifest. We should not lose sight of the fact that the idea of grace as well as the notion of spirit are very important for Schillebeeckx because they remind us of Jesus—both the historical figure and the eschatological man pictured by the idea of Christ.[33]

The dead Jesus is kept alive by means of the image of Christ which is fundamentally based on grace and spirit. Grace as man's awareness of the necessity to apply the universal values of man and the spirit as the practical manifestation of this awareness maintain the image of the Jesus—despite the fact that he is dead—is very much alive in our minds today. Jesus emptied himself and died for humanity but then he was resurrected through the idea of Christ.[34] Christ ascended to heaven, which in fact means that he as well as the universal human values represented by him were elevated beyond the level of human biological existence to the transcendent—though still historical—level of grace and spirit, symbolizing the awareness and the practical application of the universal values of humanity. For Schillebeeckx though the attitude displayed by Jesus and eternalized in Christ is not the property of one single man, Jesus or anyone else. This attitude is specific to humanity in general; it was also present in Jesus and, due to his long lasting impact on his disciples and the church, it was subsequently personified in Christ but the desire to help others and the willingness to sacrifice one's life for this ideal is, for Schillebeeckx, a general human feature. Therefore, the church cannot claim exclusivity when it comes to Jesus or the values represented by Christ because they are in fact the legacy of the world. This is why the church tends to extend its frontiers towards the world while the world does the same towards the church.[35]

There seems to be no doubt in Schillebeeckx's mind that what was once traditionally the task of the church has now been taken over by the

32. Borgman, *Edward Schillebeeckx*, 59.
33. Schillebeeckx, *World and Church*, 127.
34. Kennedy, *Schillebeeckx*, 115.
35. Schillebeeckx, *World and Church*, 127–28.

world. The church does the work of the world and the world does the work of the church; in other words, they both do the same thing as they promote the same universally valid human values for the benefit of every man and woman.[36] The actions of the church and of the world are historically visible so there is virtually no reason to believe the world is different from the church. The boundaries of the two communities—world and church—that exist within the reality of history are therefore superfluous. The church is different from the world because of its structure and organization but this is only a formal aspect; in reality the two are identical:

> The constant struggle for life in mankind, hoping against all hope, is the anonymous echo of this—there is more in it than simply secularity, even though it is perhaps expressed in a purely secular way. Not only are the frontiers between the church and "mankind" merging in the direction of the church—they are also merging in the direction of "mankind" and the world. The modern process of desacralization and secularization clearly indicates that what was previously regarded as a separate and distinctive activity of the church (dispensing alms to those who were deprived, work of charity and so on) has now become a task undertaken by humanity in general. Many aspects of what in the past appeared as something strictly pertaining to the church have now become a distinctive form of the lives of men in the world. This osmosis from the church to the world can have no termination on earth because the "old" aeon and the "new" continue to exist side by side in the world— the coincidence of the "community of men" with the "community of saints" in clear visibility is therefore only a heavenly event, not something that happens on this earth. The merging of the frontiers between the church and mankind can therefore never do away with the dialectical tension between the two on earth, although this does not imply that this tension cancels out the dynamism of the world's tendency to become church on the one hand and the church's tendency towards sanctifying secularization on the other. It is, moreover, important to stress the fact that this process of secularization is *sanctifying*, in other words, that it stems from the transcendent community with God in Christ.[37]

The church and the world are two complementing realities to the point that the church is the explicit, specifically Christian, embodiment of the

---

36. See also Borgman, *Edward Schillebeeckx*, 361.
37. Schillebeeckx, *World and Church*, 128.

universal values of humanity which are present in the world.[38] The church is not a human organization, namely a human distinctive unit within humanity or a smaller entity within the larger realm of humanity. The church is just another way of expressing the truth and values of the world.[39] Thus, what is implicitly confessed by the world, namely the universal values of man for the benefit of humanity, is explicitly put into practice by the church. Schillebeeckx's optimistic identification between the church and the world is somehow counter-balanced by his more down-to-earth remark that in historical reality the distinction between the church and the world is here to stay. It is as if, in an ideal word, the identification between the church and the world would work perfectly well but in this world, which is not quite perfect, the difference between the world and the church will last forever; not because the church and the world are unable to function perfectly well as one single community but because some people will never be able to comprehend and accept their fundamental identity—this is why they will always think in terms of the church and the world as two distinct realities within the realm of history. Schillebeeckx, however, prefers the ideal situation of the church's total identification with the world so he presents the church as extending itself towards the world and the world as broadening its boundaries towards the church. The result is the juxtaposition of two traditionally opposed realities: the secularity of the world[40] and the sanctity of the church,[41] in the sense that we can now speak of the secularity of the church and the sanctity of the world. As for Schillebeeckx, what cannot work together in traditional theology is fixed to perfect cooperation in his radical thought; this is why the identification between the church and the world is described by means of the phrase "sanctifying secularization" which, in his mind, places the church and the world together.[42] One should notice though that the essence of the phrase "sanctifying secularization" is the idea of secularization, which is the feature of the world and it is this secularization—ultimately the world itself—that acquires the sanctifying influence of the church. At the end of the day, it seems that Schillebeeckx's stress falls on the world and its

---

38. Mueller, *What Are They Saying?*, 60.
39. Wood, *Spiritual Exegesis*, 124.
40. Kennedy, *Schillebeeckx*, 60.
41. Bergin, *O Propheticum Lavacrum*, 188.
42. Borgman, *Edward Schillebeeckx*, 363.

essential feature of secularization. Therefore, "sanctifying secularization" no longer describes the church but rather the world which has finally accepted the universal human values as also preached by the church, while the church itself is an explicit—specifically Christian—manifestation of the world.[43]

"Sanctifying secularization" as the fundamental feature of the world is the result of grace which permeates both the world and the church.[44] The result of grace is, in the language of traditional theology, redemption.[45] For Schillebeeckx, grace represents and actually is the absolute communication of God to man as well as man's community with God.[46] Therefore unlike traditional theology which pictures grace as a one-way movement from God to man, Schillebeeckx suggests that grace is a two-way reality: from God to man and from man to God. This theory deprives the traditional concept of grace of its metaphysical side by humanizing and secularizing the reality of grace as applied to man. Grace is not metaphysical or ontologically real as originating in meta-historically transcendent God; grace is a human reality which transcends only the level of pure biology. In any other aspect, grace is totally human and historical. In Schillebeeckx, grace is Trinitarian but this must also be understood in human terms. God is not a metaphysical and meta-historical person and neither are Christ and the Spirit. God is the infinite openness of our future temporality, Christ is the embodiment of the universality of human values while the Spirit is the application of the awareness of the validity which characterizes the world's universal values. Thus, Schillebeeckx's trinity is human,[47] so grace is human,[48] and salvation is human.[49] To explain salvation, Schillebeeckx uses the dialectics between creation and redemption. Unlike traditional theology where creation and redemption are the result of God's activity, in Schillebeeckx creation and redemption are the effects of man's work. Every man must orient himself towards Christ if he wants to understand what human values are and how they should be applied. Man's orientation

---

43. Schillebeeckx, *World and Church*, 128–29.
44. Wood, *Spiritual Exegesis*, 111.
45. Schillebeeckx, *World and Church*, 129.
46. This is also true for Rahner, see Torevell, *Losing the Sacred*, 142.
47. Wiley, *Thinking of Christ*, 93.
48. Abdul-Masih, *Edward Schillebeeckx and Hans Frei*, 65.
49. Borgman, *Edward Schillebeeckx*, 208.

towards Christ is actually a new awareness of his natural constitution, which is essential for his participation in the church, which is actually his participation in the world. When man understands the necessity that he should follow the universal human values embodied by Christ he is created in Christ, namely he becomes aware that the values promoted by the idea of Christ have universal significance for humanity.[50] The very moment he decides to step outside the reality of his own creation in Christ, man is actually redeemed because he will now apply these universal human values for the benefit of his fellow human beings. Being created and redeemed means being part of the church and consequently of the world. It is very evident that Schillebeeckx enjoys breaking traditional boundaries because he actually levels the fence that once delineated the traditional *extra ecclesiam nulla salus*.[51] If this phrase was traditionally meant to say that salvation is possible only within the frontiers of the church, not of the world because the world is outside the church, in Schillebeeckx the reality of man's salvation by God within the exclusive boundaries of the church becomes the reality of man's creation and redemption by man within the inclusive frontiers of the world. As human beings, we must understand that our salvation resides in ourselves and it happens within history, in other words we are saved when we understand that the universal values of humanity have to be applied for the welfare of the entire world:

> The church bears in herself the principles and the incipient reality of this eschatological peace by virtue of the fact that she, the fruit of Christ's redemption, is in the world as the "body of the Lord" in and through which the glorified Christ accomplishes his worldwide activity in the Spirit. In this way, the church, as the sign for the whole world, is the forerunner of eschatological salvation in our human history. This is the basis of her missionary duty and of the call that she constantly experiences to go back to the evangelical sources of the structures of the church that have developed throughout history, especially at a time like the present, when the image of man and of the world is being radically changed.[52]

Schillebeeckx appeals to this particular kind of explanation because he is convinced that our world has reached an age when people's perspective on the idea of man as well as on the idea of the world has undergone

50. Schillebeeckx, *World and Church*, 129–31.
51. Valkenberg, *Sharing Lights*, 145.
52. Schillebeeckx, *World and Church*, 132–33.

dramatic reinterpretation. Things have changed rapidly and definitively so we need a new framework which should be both rationally intelligible and existentially satisfactory. Old traditional explanations do not and cannot suffice, so we need new insights into the values that were once explained in metaphysically ontological terms. Ontological metaphysics, however, is totally unable to explain and reflect the secularized rationality of the modern man, so the reality of the church—once metaphysically anchored in the ontology of meta-history—needs to be reinterpreted now in order to fit the historicity of our contemporary secularization.[53] In other words, man no longer needs to see his creation and salvation in terms which leave the impression that we can be lured into a metaphysical existence beyond our present and future history; what man needs now is the concrete historicity of his own natural awareness which is given by reinterpreting traditional creation and salvation as essentially performed by man for the benefit of humanity in a church that is no longer the traditional exclusivist community of strict Christians but the secularized inclusivist community of rational human beings, the world itself.

THE CHURCH AS WORLD

In order for the church to be understood as the world, the church needs to be like the world, it needs to act like the world.[54] In Schillebeeckx, if the church does not act like the world, it is no longer meaningful for modern man. This is why Schillebeeckx speaks about the "blurring" of the boundaries between the church and the world—as well as those between grace and nature[55]—so that the world is able to understand the church not as a separate community within the world with metaphysical expectations but as a special community which promotes the validity of universal human values. So there is no contradiction between the world and the church because the two are not antithetic; they are complementary as both are informed by the Spirit of God.[56] The Spirit of God is not the spirit of a metaphysical God but rather the spirit of humanity in general, the spirit which guides humanity from the perspective of its open future. This Spirit that is fundamentally anchored in the conviction that a better humanity

---

53. Haight, *The Future of Christology*, 106.
54. See also Lewis, *Between Cross and Resurrection*, 356.
55. See also Kennedy, *Schillebeeckx*, 135.
56. Borgman, *Edward Schillebeeckx*, 252.

is at hand for everybody guides both the church and the world. The only difference is that in the church the spirit produces an explicit, specifically Christian understanding of reality, while in the world the spirit generates an implicit, specifically human perspective on the same reality. This means that regardless whether we are members of the church or not, we live in the world and the same spirit breathes in us the same natural awareness of our own universal human value. The church has the capacity to extend itself in the world but this does not happen structurally or organizationally. The church extends in the world, due to the spirit of God—which is the spirit of humanity, the spirit of the world—and this happens spiritually.[57] The reality of this situation is historically visible since the church has its own structures while the world does not follow the pattern of the church in this particular instance. The world follows the pattern of the church in the same way that the church extends towards the world only in spirit, namely based on their conviction that the universal values of humanity can be useful and beneficial to men and women.[58]

This dynamic dialectic between the church and the world provides Schillebeeckx with the opportunity to present the church in distinctively social terms. Thus, in the spirit of God or in the spirit of the world's better future, the church must be socially oriented in order to help those who find themselves in various difficult situations.[59] Schillebeeckx's social perspective on the church also acquires economic as well as political overtones as he explains that the church's social preoccupation is in fact an image of the necessity that wealthy countries should assist undeveloped countries.[60] Even though Schillebeeckx insists that politics has nothing to do with his theory, it is almost impossible to conceive that such a tremendously demanding economic assistance could be offered without any political involvement whatsoever. The true motives for human assistance of any kind should be solidarity, a concept that in Schillebeeckx works both for the church and for the world. The essence of the church, but also of the world, is the idea of communion which reveals itself in "the luxury of excessive love"[61] which transforms the individual person into

---

57. This is actually Schillebeeckx's way to reconcile the church and the modern world. See McGonigle and Zagano, *The Dominican Tradition*, 96.

58. Schillebeeckx, *World and Church*, 133.

59. See Houlden, *Jesus in History*, 208.

60. Rego, *Suffering and Salvation*, 174.

61. Hilkert and Schreiter, eds., *The Praxis*, 55.

one's brother.[62] This is an activity which aims at founding a community, namely a community of persons who share the same fundamental human values for the sake of applying them in everyday life. The church itself as a community was founded due to such an example of love but, even if the church has its own distinctive structure and organization, its goal must be to impart love for the benefit of the entire world.[63] The structure of the church, which Schillebeeckx does not criticize in any way, must serve the fundamental purpose of the church by making it possible for human solidarity to be shared with the world based on the example of Christ who embodies all the good and universal values of humanity:[64]

> This anonymous church-founding activity thus goes beyond the frontiers of the church as the sociologically situated, clearly historically visible form of the community of those who confess Christ and take their places in the Eucharistic table-fellowship. It goes so far beyond these frontiers that even this abundance of love, however significantly visible it may be in the saints of the church, is not primarily or only realized *historically* by practising Christians. and yet it is only where love makes fellow-men into brothers that church is genuinely founded. The church-founding activity of love is, in a word, the very essence of the church's being. It was precisely in order to safeguard this essence that Christ founded an office in his church and that he continues to assist this hierarchical office in a special way so as to keep his people in the one community of love and hope, based on the one faith in Christ. Ultimately, however, the church is not so much concerned with this hierarchy as with the church-founding activity of love and the hierarchy has the function of serving this activity, although this function may be in the manner of Christian authority.[65]

To be sure, anywhere in the world where love and solidarity are shown in a brotherly way a church is automatically established.[66] Thus, founding the church is not seen in terms of a community which is the result of the metaphysical intervention of an ontologically real God, so the church is not a community founded by God for men but a community founded by man for humanity. The very basis of the church is essentially social in

---

62. Schillebeeckx, *World and Church*, 134.
63. Doyle, *The Church Emerging from Vatican II*, 213.
64. McManus, *Unbroken Communion*, 125.
65. Schillebeeckx, *World and Church*, 134–35.
66. See also Kennedy, *Schillebeeckx*, 131.

Schillebeeckx and it has to be historically visible so that the application of brotherly love should result in a communion as well as a community. This is the only way for the church to be relevant and meaningful in society and in order to be like that the church must embrace the universal values of humanity. The church is of course free to use its traditional values but we all know that the so-called traditional values of the church are nothing but universal human values that have been concealed in specific theological terms. These terms need to be reinterpreted in such a way that the world today finds them relevant. The terms of traditional theology, however, all point to the universally valid concept of disinterested love.[67] Schillebeeckx's idea of disinterested love must be also unconditional because it must convey the meaningfulness of sacrifice as presented and represented by Christ. In Schillebeeckx, Christ is not a person but a sign that confirms the reality of grace. As for grace, it is not relevant unless shown by means of love, brotherhood, and solidarity.[68] These universal human values are present in the world in more or less concrete forms but whenever and wherever these values are practically applied for the benefit of human beings a church is founded, a community of communion established. The historical visibility of its practical acts is a proof that the world has not run out of its fundamental values.[69] Thus, the church must be constantly engaged in social action because this is the only way, at least for Schillebeeckx, in which the church may become attractive, meaningful and appealing to the secularized minds of modern people. Nevertheless, the church must not apply the fundamental human values just for the sake of historical visibility; human values are at the disposal of the church for the sake of every man and woman living in the world, so the church must put the universal human values of love, brotherhood and solidarity into daily practice based on the equally universal human values of joy and hope.[70]

Schillebeeckx seems to lose sight of the fact that the traditional church does the same but for a totally different reason. The traditional church does in fact display love, solidarity, and brotherhood for the

---

67. Hilkert and Schreiter, eds., *The Praxis*, 126.

68. The idea of brotherhood and sisterhood is crucial here. See also Carmody and Carmody, *Bounded in Christ's Love*, 216.

69. Janowiak, *The Holy Preaching*, 49.

70. Borgman, *Edward Schillebeeckx*, 177.

sake of helping the world and it does this in joy and hope.[71] Unlike Schillebeeckx's church, the traditional church does not assist the world in order to become the world or even in order to be relevant and meaningful for the world. The traditional church does not care too much—if at all—about relevance and meaningfulness because it knows that there are no such things as relevance and meaningfulness in a sinful world. For the traditional church, nothing can be meaningful or relevant in a world that refuses to accept its sinful way of being as opposed to the meta-historical and metaphysical realities of God. Because of sin, everything ends up in death so, if there is any relevance at all in dying (even for the sake of others), then the traditional church would probably be interested in spreading relevance and meaningfulness throughout the world but it is not. The traditional church is concerned with one single thing: to proclaim the salvation of humanity due to the atoning death of Jesus Christ for our sins, which is confirmed by his actual, physical, and spiritual resurrection and ascension to heaven. Thus, the promise of a better meta-historical future is made explicit to humanity but we will have to wait until history comes to an end. It is evident that this message is preposterous for Schillebeeckx as well as the secularized mind of today's men and women. This message though, as preposterous as it may be, continues to make sense at least to some secularized minds. It may not be entirely intelligible to everybody but some still find it relevant and meaningful for them. This makes Schillebeeckx's theory if not utopian at least questionable. One may ask why Schillebeeckx's message seems to be utopian and questionable. For instance, one answer is simply because the authority which informs his theory about the identification of the church with the world is thoroughly human.[72] Why should we believe other human beings in an age when we are more than free to believe what we want? Why should we believe the message of the traditional church in the first place? At least for the simple reason that its authority is not human or not exclusively human. The existence of a metaphysical God in traditional theology explains, among other things, why humanity is so wretched if left to its natural devices. In traditional theology, humanity will never be able to understand its own nature because of the tragic reality of sin. Sin alters everything and distorts everything so that even reason is twisted and cannot be trusted for

---

71. McManus, *Unbroken Communion*, 120.
72. Mbogu, *Christology and Religious Pluralism*, 245.

an objective assessment of its own values. Humanity can understand its real condition only from the metaphysical and meta-historical reality of God's ontological transcendence.

For Schillebeeckx, however, this is not an alternative. There is nothing beyond history than our own terrestrial future with its open and infinite range of possibilities.[73] This is our God as well as the secularized man's only source of relevance and meaning.[74] We have to find enough sources within ourselves if we want to perceive life as relevant and meaningful. We should not look for relevance in irrelevant places because they will only substitute our true need for relevance. At this point, Schillebeeckx deconstructs the traditional concept of substitution[75] which is ascribed to Jesus Christ in classical theology. Thus, in traditional Christianity, Jesus Christ is the preexistent Logos of God who became incarnate under the name of Jesus. He lived and died for our salvation from sin and death, was resurrected from the dead by God and then he ascended to heaven having been confirmed as the Christ. Jesus Christ died for us in a substitutive way: he was our substitution. He died in our place so that we may die in him. He was raised from the dead and ascended to heaven so that we might experience resurrection and life with God beyond history. So Jesus Christ did everything in our place as our substitution. Jesus is not physically present among us—though he is spiritually present in us by his Spirit—but his substitutive work makes our life worth living for him as well as for us. For Schillebeeckx though, the idea of substitution is not satisfactory because it seems to convey the idea that the action of substitution has no immediate practical relevance. For instance, if secularized man is told that he must find relevance for his life in Jesus, who is not physically with us, he may be disappointed because Jesus's presence is not historically visible. On the other hand, if the same secularized person is told that he must find relevance for his life in other people, who are physically present with him and can help him, he is no longer disappointed because the people he was told about are historically visible. These people embody the image of Christ, namely the universality of human values, so the secularized person will understand that he can be a means of saving others from a meaningless

---

73. McManus, *Unbroken Communion*, 21.

74. Kennedy, *Schillebeeckx*, 32.

75. For details about substitution in contemporary radical Catholicism, see O'Hanlon, *The Immutability of God*, 31.

life. This is why in Schillebeeckx substitution[76]—which also includes the idea of representation[77] or mediation[78]—does not work at all:

> We should not regard the church's representative function in respect of mankind outside the church as a "representative" function, by which those who do not belong to the church are dispensed from this abundant activity of love and are saved by "substitution," that is, by the abundance of love that is present at least in the church of Christ. Representation and mediation never mean substitution or replacement in a truly Christian perspective—they signify a prototypical reality which communicates because of its abundance, *with the consequence* that others are really enabled to accomplish themselves, by virtue of the grace acquired, what has already taken place before them by the living example of the prototype. In this sense, the church herself lives in the power of the Spirit of Christ for the benefit of the whole mankind. But it is equally true that this operation of Christ's grace in the whole of mankind through the church also has to gain a visible form, especially in the church's missionary activity. This also means that, in the church's historical confrontation with mankind, those who belong explicitly to the church must *de facto* be the prototypes and the living examples of this superabundance of love and this forfeiting of one's own life for the benefit of others.[79]

It is obvious that for Schillebeeckx Jesus Christ is no longer our prototype or the prototype of our humanity because his concept of prototype involves immediate historical visibility. Jesus is dead while Christ is only an image so neither is historically visible. This is why Schillebeeckx gives up Jesus Christ as our prototype in order to reinterpret the idea of prototype as applied to us.[80] We are the prototype of humanity because we are historically visible and our actions can have immediate results. What we do happens in the world so it can be assessed rationally with the result of being considered relevant and meaningful. We have to follow Jesus and live in accordance with the universal values of humanity as embodied

---

76. For other details, see Rego, *Suffering and Salvation*, 277.

77. For details about the idea of representation, see Bergin, *O Propheticum Lavacrum*, 186.

78. Further information about the concept of mediation can be found in Haight, *The Future of Christology*, 191.

79. Schillebeeckx, *World and Church*, 136.

80. In the best of cases, Christ—not Jesus—is the prototype of our lives. See Schillebeeckx, *Christ, the Sacrament of the Encounter with God*, 29.

by Christ but neither Jesus nor Christ can meaningfully work as our prototypes. Any allusion to them as prototypes orients the modern man towards the past therefore depriving him of the immediate relevance of actual historical visibility. The only chance is to find another prototype and the prototype of the modern man is the modern man himself. He may look back to the universal values of man as understood in the past but he must reinterpret them for the present in order to see himself as the prototype of the new rationalized humanity. The modern man is his own prototype, in very much the same way that he is his own authority and relevance. This is another confirmation of Schillebeeckx's thesis that the church becomes the world because the prototype of humanity was switched from Jesus Christ in traditional Christianity to man himself in radical theology. Modern man does not need any influence from outside so he looks within himself for relevance, authority, and meaning. The church is identical to the world because, in Schillebeeckx, the modern man who may or may not be part of the church is guided by his own values in order to change the world which includes the church.[81] Thus the church and the world are seen as communities which, in spite of their different types of organizational structures, they nevertheless share the same prototypical image of man as the source of the fundamental values of humanity. The fundamental values of humanity are inherently universal so whatever applies to the world is also valid for the church and the other way around.

In Schillebeeckx, the church is no longer the traditional church and the world is not the traditional world. The church moves towards the world, and the world moves towards the church.[82] The church has the tendency to become the world by means of a sanctifying secularization while the world has the tendency to become church. Therefore, based solely on this equation, there are no frontiers left between the world and the church at least in the traditional sense of the word. For Schillebeeckx, this would be the ideal situation. The actual situation is however a bit different because the church as an institution[83] on earth does have some clearly delineated frontiers which, in a way, separate it from the world. In Schillebeeckx's argument though these ecclesiastical frontiers are not

---

81. Borgman, *Edward Schillebeeckx*, 363.

82. Schillebeeckx, *Christ, the Sacrament of the Encounter with God*, 213.

83. Schillebeeckx does not like the institutionalization of the church but he accepts it as a sociological reality. See Ormerod, "The Structure," 3ff n. 34.

fundamental.[84] They are indeed important because they individualize the church in a positive way by stressing the church's internal organization as well as offices with view to mission. Even if the church has these distinct frontiers cemented mostly throughout the church's historical evolution, the church itself is not different from the world in its essence which has to do with its concern for the benefit of humanity. The purpose of the church is to help us meet Christ in a personal way. Nevertheless, as Christ is just an image of Jesus's life example the encounter is not necessarily between two persons, but between the human person and the prototypical image of another human person who was willing to sacrifice personally for the sake of applying the fundamental values of humanity so that every human being would be able to enjoy a better life.[85] This encounter with Christ or with the image of the man who encapsulates the fundamentals of humanity must be personal because once we meet Christ, namely once we understand the validity and usefulness of these universal human values we have to apply them practically as well. We have to understand, according to Schillebeeckx, that we all have a religious sense that can be exploited in an explicitly Christian form in the church, and it is at this point that our meeting with Christ is so important.[86] Schillebeeckx explains that our meeting with Christ is important because it is in this particular way that we meet God. This fundamental affirmation needs to be translated in accordance with Schillebeeckx's radical reinterpretation of traditional theology. When he says we meet Christ, it is clear that we are not supposed to meet a person who is transcendentally alive and metaphysically real in the meta-historical reality of his existence. Schillebeeckx's Christ is not the Christ of traditional theology. His Christ is just another way of saying that the historical Jesus displayed the very essence of what it means to be human.[87] All the values of humanity were shown in Jesus who was willing to die for them because he was willing to die for the benefit of his fellow human beings. These human values, fundamental and universal, were captured by the church in the image of Christ which we must meet in a personal way so that we are be able both to understand and apply these universal human values the very way they were applied by Jesus,

---

84. See also Borgman, *Edward Schillebeeckx*, 359.
85. See also Bergin, *O Propheticum Lavacrum*, 182.
86. Schillebeeckx, *Christ, the Sacrament of the Encounter with God*, 219.
87. Kennedy, *Schillebeeckx*, 7.

namely for the welfare of our fellow people in the spirit of brotherhood.[88] When we do this, it means that we meet God. Again, the God we meet in Schillebeeckx is not the God of traditional theology. It is not the God who exists beyond our history in a reality which is ontologically transcendental and metaphysical. Schillebeeckx's God is the real possibility of having the universal human values embodied by Christ open before us in a future of endless possibilities.[89] This is actually Schillebeeckx's God: the reality of our future which presents us with unlimited capacities to apply the universal values of humanity for the benefit of every human person:

> A tendency to *become church* is clearly discernible in the whole of mankind and . . . there is also a similar process taking place in the church, a tendency *towards sanctifying secularization*. Although certain frontiers remain inviolable—those which are formed by the word, the sacrament and the office, all of which are *serving* functions—the frontiers between church and mankind are becoming blurred. The form of Christianity that is completely capable of being integrated in our lives is objectively offered to us in our explicit encounter with Christ and his church. This church ought consequently to be a home that is genuinely fit for human habitation and is also the church's task to make herself so in different ways at different periods of history. The full religious sense has an explicitly Christian form which is experienced within the church.[90]

In general Schillebeeckx's theology is very clear and precise, but every now and then his thought becomes a bit confusing. This is primarily because of his continuous struggle to remain within the limits of traditional theology in terms of language even if his main theological line is drastically reinterpreted in the direction of theological radicalism and deconstructivism. For instance, despite Schillebeeckx's very clear exposition of his perspective on God and Christ as non-personal realities which affect us personally, he still believes that the biological reality of humanity is doubled by a meta-biological—which is nevertheless historical—reality that comprises the traditional concept of prayer and communion with God. If Schillebeeckx's understanding of the notion of communion with God has already been deciphered as the personal apprehension of our

---

88. McManus, *Unbroken Communion*, 155.
89. Rego, *Suffering and Salvation*, 64.
90. Schillebeeckx, *World and Church*, 136–37.

openness to the realities of future, his concept of prayer seems to be connected to the idea of silence.[91] In traditional theology prayer meant—in most cases—words spoken to God while in Schillebeeckx's thought prayer is predominantly silence. For him, silence is a way of speaking which makes the dialogue possible. Of course, Schillebeeckx cannot ignore or reinterpret the traditional reality of prayer which places the believer in a close connection with God. This is why, even in Schillebeeckx, the idea of prayer as silence binds us to God. We have to pray to God because God is God. Now, this affirmation sounds thoroughly traditional and it seems to evade any radical interpretation but, as God is not the God of traditional theology in Schillebeeckx, even the most traditional affirmation has a radically different meaning. So, what does it mean for Schillebeeckx that we have to pray to God because God is God? A possible interpretation is this: as prayer means silence, we have to keep a silent attitude when we come closer to the reality of our own future. Why silent? Because silence seems to enhance man's power of reflection when it comes to evaluate, understand and accept the paramount importance as well as the existential relevance of universal human values as embodied by the idea of God.[92] Silence appears to be some kind of fruitful inactivity whereby we personally appropriate the universal values of humanity for ourselves, which is then followed by the equally fruitful activity whereby we apply the universal values of humanity for the benefit of our fellow human beings. It is crucial to notice though that in Schillebeeckx the idea of silence before God—which replaces the traditional reality of prayer before God—is a fundamental human characteristic.[93] If in traditional theology prayer is predominantly the spiritual activity of believers, namely of those who are part of the church not of the world, in Schillebeeckx silence—which translates as prayer—is a feature of all the people living in the world. Silence should make us aware that we cannot come closer to God unless we come closer to our fellow humans. Thus, getting closer to other people in order to make their life better is in fact coming closer to God. As far as Schillebeeckx is concerned, the realization of this truth must be done in silence:[94]

91. Rego, *Suffering and Salvation*, 309.
92. See also Schillebeeckx, *God Is New Each Moment*, 18.
93. McManus, *Unbroken Communion*, 102.
94. This also happened to Jesus, who had to face God's silence as he trusted him to death. See Hilkert, *Naming Grace*, 115.

> Precisely because of this, Christianity—however involved it may be with or everyday cares and tasks and the whole of our activity in the world, in and through which we grow in intimacy with God—also has a sacral sphere that is separate from the history and civilization of this world, a sphere in which we pray and are simply together with God in Christ. At the purely anthropological level, silence is an aspect of speaking or of social intercourse. At this level, silence has no real meaning in itself, but is merely a function of human solidarity and social intercourse. It is necessary in order to make contact between human beings human and to keep it human. Its purpose is to humanize inter-human contact. Silence personalizes speaking—without it, dialogue would be impossible. In a revealed religion, however, silence with God has a *value in itself* and not simply as a function of our intercourse with our fellow men—precisely because God is *God*. To fail to appreciate the believer's simple, "inactive" being together with God as the beloved is to ignore the very essence of Christianity. It is, of course, true that the whole of our being in this world of people and things permeates this being together with God and does so essentially and not simply as distraction in prayer. We are only able to tell God that we love him or at least that we wish to love him more with words, concepts and images that are taken from our human world. What is more, this being together with God is not individualism, since our prayer is insincere—it is not prayer—if we pray "*Our* Father ..." and forget the kingdom of God and our fellow-man.[95]

At times, Schillebeeckx's radical discourse is so full of traditional concepts that it leaves the impression that he would truly love to believe traditional theology with its God, its Christ, its life but he simply cannot do it. It is as if he would really like to believe in a world which is beyond this world in the most traditional metaphysical sense but he cannot. This is why he is stuck with this world, our world, the world of our history which has no other future than its own unfolding in space and time, our space and time. Likewise, this explains why Schillebeeckx—though a Christian theologian by virtue of his preoccupation with Christian theology—is more a religious philosopher than a Christian thinker. The confirmation of this assessment is given by Schillebeeckx's acute sense of humanism; everything in his theology is humanized or humanizing, from his concept of God to our response to God in silent prayer.[96] We have to work

---

95. Schillebeeckx, *World and Church*, 137–38.
96. Borgman, *Edward Schillebeeckx*, 246.

together with God, Schillebeeckx urges us, for the benefit of humanity but his urging message is nothing but philosophical advice that we should work together with ourselves and with other human beings, for the welfare of humanity, for our own good, present and future. Therefore, his discourse cannot stay confined within the boundaries of Christian theology because his ideas are religious rather than specifically Christian. What causes his discourse to be considered Christian is his frequent use of traditional Christian theology which he systematically deconstructs in order to make it more religious, more human and even more humane. His dialectic between God and man is nothing but man's understanding of himself from the "higher" perspective of universal human values, so it is man that understands man from a human perspective. Our love of God which, Schillebeeckx underlines, cannot be separated from our love of man is in fact love for man and his universal human values. When we say that we love God we actually love ourselves because God is only a symbol for our human and humane values which are universally valid, useful and meaningful for every person on earth.[97]

Schillebeeckx's noble intention to bring the church into the world so that the church becomes more active socially has in fact brought the world into the church with disastrous consequences for the church and its traditional theology. Traditional Christianity has been reduced by Schillebeeckx to the level of a socially active religion which humanizes its own theology in order to be relevant and meaningful to the secularized mind of the modern man.[98] Schillebeeckx does not deny that some Christians continue to find traditional theology relevant and meaningful but he almost takes for granted the fact that the majority of Christians—he probably means people—will find relevance and meaning in what he calls "secular holiness,"[99] namely in religious forms which are not necessarily Christian or traditionally Christian.[100] The concept of secular holiness blows away any factual boundary between the church and the world with the result of having not so much the world become the church but the church become the world. At the end of the day, in Schillebeeckx, the church dilutes itself into the all-encompassing reality of the world; therefore the future of the

97. Schillebeeckx, *World and Church*, 138.

98. A major concern for Schillebeeckx in this respect is the Eucharist, see Whalen, *The Authentic Doctrine*, xii.

99. This can also be found in Rahner, see Bergin, *O Propheticum Lavacrum*, 71.

100. Schillebeeckx, *World and Church*, 138–39.

church is the world and the future of the world is the world itself. Thus, traditional Christianity is reduced to being an explicit manifestation of the universal values of humanity which find their complete relevance and meaning in the humanized as well as humane historicity of the world. In very much the same way, traditional Christian experience is nothing but a human experience which in the secular profanity of the world becomes the expression of man's belief in the universal values of humanity.

A Concluding Synthesis
Edward Schillebeeckx's Theological Radicalism as Philosophical Non-Realism

EDWARD SCHILLEBEECKX'S THOUGHT IS an open attack on traditional Christianity and its values. Schillebeeckx prefers to say that his work is in fact a reinterpretation of traditional theology based on revelation with special reference to the necessity that radicalism should be associated with this process of reinterpretation. Therefore, the reinterpretation of traditional theology must not just be another way of expressing the old doctrines of past Christianity but a radical process which drastically changes the very content of traditional theology. Schillebeeckx's theological radicalism proposes the reevaluation of the concept of God in light of contemporary society and its secularized rationalization. This means that modern man can only think in terms of his reason and his reason can only understand the things of this world. Thus, because human reason is essentially of this world, it cannot search into any other world. This results in a theological perspective which is based exclusively on the realities of this world. If traditional Christianity was anchored in realities which went well beyond this world mainly because of its perspective on God—seen as supernatural, meta-historical, and ontologically real—the people of today's secularized society can think of God only in terms of a natural, historical, and ontologically non-real concept. In other words, Schillebeeckx radically reinterprets the idea of God which in this thought loses its supernatural, meta-historical, and ontological categories. In Schillebeeckx, God is no longer part of the realm of metaphysics but a concept which has to be understood within the realm of physics.

Schillebeeckx's theological radicalism is similar to what has been termed philosophical non-realism, an equally radical reassessment of Christian theology and religion in general promoted in the last few decades by the English theologian and philosopher Don Cupitt. Though initially a traditionalist as well as a minister of the Church of England—a status which he has managed to preserve even to this day—Cupitt gradually changed his original belief in Christianity's supernatural and metahistorical existence of God into a conviction which could be described as a non-realist perspective on religion. Thus, Cupitt reached the conclusion that God does not have a real and objective existence beyond the reality of our history; God is only a concept which is utterly dependent on human language and culture. For Cupitt God has a real existence only as a concept; God is real only if we accept him as a powerful symbol. Therefore, God is a metaphor of our human values, a mere projection of our inner feelings. As a matter of fact, the only real existence of the things pertaining to religion is religion itself; God does not exist beyond the practical, strictly historical, manifestation of religion. Christianity is a religion and it should be treated like any other religion but regardless of whether we discuss the God of Christianity or the God of any other religion, the existence of God is exclusively non-supernatural and non-metaphysical. God is a concept which helps us understand our own human reality and it should be approach by means of language and culture. This means that, as a concept, God has a meaning for humanity and we must find this meaning. Cupitt's non-realism rejects any form of supernaturalism in favor of a thoroughly existential approach to the concept of God. God is real only in so far as he has a meaning for us.[1]

Cupitt is convinced that this new perspective on God as a non-real being but rather as a real subjective concept is the result of a long process of secularization, which has reached its peak in our scientific society. Thus, the world gradually ceased to be preoccupied with realities which were believed to exist beyond it, so it chose—slowly but surely—not to look up any longer but down to itself and its values. In other words, the world put aside the barbaric values of traditionalism, which proclaimed an ontologically real and supernatural God, and grew to accept the more feminine values of a high civilization.[2] This was the end of metaphysics[3] and the beginning of a new world, the world of science and reason. If pre-scientific people understood reality in terms of myths, animism, and explanations down from above, the man of modern science decided to

---

1. Cupitt, *Sea of Faith*, 241.
2. Cupitt, *Sea of Faith*, 27–28.
3. Cupitt, *Sea of Faith*, 20.

find the meaning of myths by searching for explanations up from below. Today's men and women do not need the non-real lies of pre-scientific traditionalism; they need the real truths of scientific rationalism.[4] As for religion, it remains only a means to inspire humanity due to its meaningful message for our natural existence:

> As the change of the old world-view to the new takes place, people feel less and less need to refer to the religious realm. It no longer seems so urgently necessary to secure the favor of spirit-beings behind the scenes. We no longer instinctively look for supernatural admonitions on the small reverses of fortune that happen to us every day. Those people who do think they are receiving little messages all the time seem to be superstitious or even mad. The explanatory utility of religious ideas thus fades away. Myth begins to get a bad name and to be equated with untruth. Religion seems to be evacuated of its descriptive content, that is, its capacity to inform us about how things are and how the world works. Few people still think that some one religion gives the only correct account of what there is out there in the universe. The job of describing the universe seems nowadays to be done more adequately by science. So religion comes to be seen as concerned rather with inspiration than explanation. It expresses itself inwardly as piety, outwardly as ethical striving to realize its ideals.[5]

For Cupitt, traditional theology is mythological thinking, and "mythological thinking is not clear thinking." The man who lives in our scientific society must learn to accept the truths of science, not the blurring explanations of religion.[6] As for religion, it still has a place in the life of contemporary people, if they are ready to see it as a source of meaningful insights liberated from realism; therefore, religion—which includes traditional Christianity—"is a way of responding to life, shaping life, giving ultimate meaning and value to life."[7] In other words, there is no real God out there, in a realm which has its own reality and existence beyond our world; the only real God we will ever be able to find is the sum of feelings and values that we can find within ourselves.

It is worth noticing here that Cupitt himself sees his philosophical non-realism in terms of theological radicalism. To be sure, theological

---

4. For a critique of Cupitt, see McGrath, *The Science of God*, 156.

5. Cupitt, *Sea of Faith*, 31.

6. For Cupitt, non-realism offers traditional churches the last chance of a rational future. See Cupitt, *Is Nothing Sacred?*, 48.

7. Cupitt, *Sea of Faith*, 35.

A Concluding Synthesis

radicalism is nothing but modern man's effort to bring down metaphysics as well as what Cupitt believes to be the oppressive dogmatic system of the traditional church. The traditional dogmas are seen as pure ideology which does not help us understand his inner needs; they only tell us how to be concerned with the higher reality of the so-called ontologically real God. This is why we need to rid ourselves of the oppressiveness of traditional dogmas in order to accept the liberating perspective of theological radicalism which opens a new world of unlimited meanings for our inner life. Theological radicalism helps us escape the birth of myths by demythologizing and de-objectivising ideological traditionalism; thus, as people of today's scientific society we will understand that what really counts for us is not the alleged afterlife but the life of the present moment.[8] God is no longer objective in the traditional metaphysical sense of meta-historical transcendence, but non-objective and non-real. We have to understand this, and when we do, we finally display a religious feeling which is in itself universal and encompasses the non-real God as concept. This means that true religious feeling is no longer the property of the traditional Christian church but of all religions of the world. In Cupitt's words, "religious feeling . . . has become democratized" or spread around all the religions of the world. This particular religious feeling tells us that God is merely a poetical and signifying concept which refers to everything and nothing in particular. God is as good as nothing for theological radicalism, and this is also true of philosophical non-realism because God is both everything and nothing; in other words, religion—which speaks of God—is essentially non-cognitive and purely emotive. Religion has to do with the way we understand the concept of God for ourselves, namely with the meaning—or lack of it—we decide to ascribe to the idea of God for our historical lives.[9]

Theological radicalism or philosophical non-realism not only reinterprets traditional Christianity or traditional religions in general by stripping them of supernaturalism and metaphysics, but also turns their values upside down. Thus, if in traditional theology God is the ultimate reality and anything else which intervenes between himself and humanity is an idol, in theological radicalism or philosophical non-realism the idea of realism itself as embodied by the traditional concept and reality of God

---

8. Cupitt, *Mysticism after Modernity*, 104.
9. Cupitt, *Mysticism after Modernity*, 141–43.

is a form of idolatry.[10] For radicals and non-realists, realism is idolatry because it is a fixation of the religious feeling on a particular object, namely God as ontologically real, which reportedly annuls the universality of the religious feeling as well as its all-encompassing validity for humanity in general.[11] For non-realists, the idea of God triggers religious feelings so the word God is a mere casket for a concept which exists in our heads and is able to be meaningful for all religious traditions in accordance with their specific terms for what we call God.[12] Deprived of its supernaturalism and metaphysics the concept of God does not refer to the absolute being but only to an idea which works existentially. The existential relevance of the religious feeling though is a confirmation of the non-realist theory that God is no longer the absolute. There is no absolute in this world so why should be there an absolute beyond it? Nothing absolute is beyond this world because there is nothing at all beyond this world. Historical as it is, this world is and should be understood in terms which are fundamentally anti-absolutist and anti-realist. If nothing is absolute, nothing is fixed, and if nothing is fixed, nothing is certain, and if nothing is certain then it means that everything is fluid; everything flows endlessly as an all-encompassing reality made up of secondary meanings. The human being is left on his own to deal with his own identity and his place in the world. However, as there is no primary identity because the traditional concept of the ontologically real God was denuded of its supernaturalism, we must understand that our identity is a secondary reality. We are what we understand ourselves to be; we are what we are in accordance with the meaning we find for ourselves.[13] Meaning is crucial because it is revealed by language. For Cupitt, language for theological radicalism and philosophical non-realism is what the Bible or the objective revelation in the Word of God represents for the realism of traditional theology. If in traditional theology the Word of God reveals in a very objective way the real existence of an ontologically real and metaphysical God, in theological radicalism language reveals in a very subjective way the meaning of our historically real and physical lives. Nevertheless, unlike the traditional Bible which is considered absolute by traditionalists, language is

---

10. See Habblethwaite, *The Ocean of Truth*, 13–14.
11. Michener, *Engaging Deconstructive Theology*, 11.
12. Cupitt, *Mysticism after Modernity*, 143.
13. Cupitt, *Mysticism after Modernity*, 146.

A Concluding Synthesis

not absolute for non-realists. Language is just a means which helps us understand ourselves, it helps us find our own meaning in life; in Cupitt's words, language "gives us ourselves" by opening before us an infinite range of possibilities or "possible worlds" which can be meaningful for every individual life.[14]

Like Cupitt and his philosophical non-realism, Schillebeeckx begins to lay the foundation of his theological radicalism from the concept of secularization[15]—see chapter 1—which is perceived as a process that brought the use of human reason to a climax in contemporary society.[16] Modern people, namely those who live nowadays in a scientific society, find it difficult to believe in the metaphysical God of the past or the God of a pre-scientific society. Thus, because the answers of traditional theology which confesses the God of the past pre-scientific theology, modern man feels himself compelled to look for a different answer. If the valid, relevant and meaningful answer for our lives cannot be found in the metaphysical God of traditional theology, then Schillebeeckx suggests that we should seek him in our world. In this context, secularization is the rational process whereby people began to look for meaningful answers for their existential questions in their world, not in a world beyond.[17] For Schillebeeckx, traditional theology and its faith in a metaphysical, supernatural, and meta-historical God is outmoded or outdated, irrelevant, and meaningless because modern man cannot rationally understand it since it confesses a God who lives beyond our world. The process of secularization is based on man's reason which assesses everything that exists in this world. Therefore, the rationalized secularization of modern man cannot conceive the existence of supernatural realities because the only realities that he can see, perceive, and understand are part of this world. Rational reflection is crucial for the modern man because the progress of science could not have happened without the increasing use of reason. Schillebeeckx urges us not to be fundamentalists, namely people who do not use their reason well enough so they believe in supernaturalism and metaphysics. We should use rational reflection in order to understand that our lives must find their meaning in this world because, as reason tells us,

---

14. Cupitt, *Mysticism after Modernity*, 138.
15. See, for details, Schillebeeckx, *God the Future of Man*, 53ff.
16. Kennedy, *A Modern Introduction to Theology*, 88.
17. Borgman, *Edward Schillebeeckx*, 436.

there is no other world apart from this. This is why humanity must be concerned with this world, the world of people, and this is what secularization really entails: man's preoccupation with the world in order to find it meaningful for his life. Secularization means discovering the world, this world, not the world of traditional faith which exists below or within the metaphysical world of God. Likewise, secularization means giving up the traditional faith of the past which promotes supernaturalism in favor of a new, modern faith of the present that teaches us how to discover naturalism and the world of our own history. Our world is the world of the future but not of a metaphysical future; our world is the world of our historical and terrestrial future which Schillebeeckx portrays in the optimistic terms as the future of our rational liberation and meaningfulness. When we understand this, we will also understand that our faith should no longer be in non-scientific metaphysics but in scientific approaches to the main concerns of the world such as technology, politics, sociology, social involvement, and psychology. All these approaches show us that we cannot believe in a metaphysical God any longer but in a God which is the product of humanity.

Schillebeeckx's position on secularization resembles very much Cupitt's philosophy. For Cupitt, secularization is the process whereby something, a concept or an idea, is transferred from the realm of the sacred to the secular world.[18] This means that religious concepts in general and Christian doctrines in particular acquire new meanings as well as new functions in the world. Thus, the ideas which lay the foundation of Christian doctrines are no longer the exclusive property of the church but become the legacy of the world.[19] The church does not control doctrines any longer; the world has the right to ascribe its own understanding to the concepts which were traditionally the sole property of the church. In other words, secularization is liberation from the control of the church.[20] Secularization contains in itself the very idea of progress because leaving aside church control and domination of religious concepts is already a step forward with respect to the development of human reason. Another idea which, for Cupitt, belongs to the very essence of secularization is

---

18. Cupitt, *Sea of Faith*, 27.
19. Cupitt, *Sea of Faith*, 28.
20. Hall, "Journeying on the Sea of Faith," 71.

A Concluding Synthesis

tolerance.[21] Therefore, the traditional so-called intolerance of the church, which accepted within its members only those who believed its doctrines, is replaced by the contemporary tolerance of the world that comprises all religious beliefs irrespective of their content. Due to this process of secularization, traditional Christianity—now modernized—comes very close to secular humanism because the reinterpreted values of the church look very much alike the current philosophical concerns of today's humanists. To be sure, man is the centre of reflection—either religious or philosophical—and his life must be meaningful in order to be worth living; this reflection though must be done independently of church control or of any other sort of religious domination. This of course has dramatic repercussions in ethics and morality; the secularized man has his own personal and independent ethics. He chooses to live in accordance with a morality which can be both different from and opposed to traditional church doctrines. Cupitt is convinced that modern man should be ethically autonomous or liberated[22] in the sense that he not only can but also should invent his own personal ethics.[23] This is just another proof that secularization is always a better option than religious traditionalism because the idea of personal choice or option is associated with the idea of progress. Man moves forward by choosing what he thinks is best for him, and this is ultimately the goal of science, technology, economics, and politics, all of which are part of the secular world at least as long as Cupitt is concerned. Religion, however, should not be totally dismissed because it carries with it ideas that bear meaning. Despite the scientific progress of the modern world, the secularized man still experiences a deep sense of loss, a lack of meaning for his life that can only be provided by religious ideas. Religion thus is profitable if approached in a secular way in order to be existentially meaningful for humanity.[24]

In order to be understood properly in light of contemporary scientific secularization, Schillebeeckx believes that God needs to be approached in terms of the world[25]—see chapter 2—because the only valid, ontological, and meaningful reality is the reality of the world. In other words, God has

---

21. Cupitt, *Sea of Faith*, 12.
22. Insole, *The Realist Hope*, 189.
23. Cupitt, *Sea of Faith*, 30.
24. Cupitt, *Sea of Faith*, 76.
25. See, for further details, Schillebeeckx, *God the Future of Man*, 69ff.

to be looked for in the world, not beyond the world as traditional theology teaches us. As secularized people who use their reason in a scientific way, we have to abandon our old image of God as supernatural, metaphysical, and meta-historical in order to adopt a new image of God as natural, physical, and historical. Therefore the God of secularized society is a God who can be found in the world and is totally of the world.[26] God is not personal and transcendent as in traditional theology, but existential and immanent because it is reasonable to accept today that the idea of God, not the person of God as in traditional Christianity, can help us find the proper meaning for our lives.[27] We have to find God in our experience, which is always new and oriented towards future, because experience is permanent while theological concepts and especially those of traditional theology, are transient. Personal experience must be evaluated based on the discoveries of modern science, not against the background of traditional metaphysics. We have to realize that when we attempt to seek God our experience is religious but our religious experience should not be detached from science; as modern people, we should embrace and trust science in order to make our religious experience meaningful and scientific. When we do this, we shall understand that our religious experiences should not be negative as in traditional theology which present us with an angry God who punishes sinners but positive as in modern science that seeks to heal suffering and prevent death. The idea of positive reality is accompanied in Schillebeeckx by the equally important concepts of relevance and meaningfulness.[28] In order to be accepted, ideas need to be positive, relevant, and meaningful otherwise it would be unreasonable to accept them. Schillebeeckx applies this rule to the idea of God, which has to be positive, relevant, and meaningful in order to be accepted, and the only way for us to appropriate the idea of God is to find it and define it in terms of the world.[29] God is not supernatural, ontologically real, metaphysical, and meta-historical because, if he were so, our reason would tell us that we are on the verge of accepting something negative, irrelevant, and meaningless. Therefore, God has to be natural, immanently real, physical, and historical in order to be accepted as positive, relevant, and

---

26. Rego, *Suffering and Salvation*, 259.
27. McManus, *Unbroken Communion*, 160.
28. Borgman, *Edward Schillebeeckx*, 110.
29. Kennedy, *Schillebeeckx*, 32.

meaningful for our human experience in the world. In other words, God has to be an idea which helps us find as well as enhance or natural awareness of our historical existence.[30]

Schillebeeckx's God is not substantially different from Cupitt's. God is non-real for Cupitt, and this means that in terms of the actual existence of reality we cannot speak of God. The God whom we traditionally know as the God of the Bible, the objective, meta-historical, transcendent, and metaphysical being that is supernatural by comparison to our existence in the world is at the end of the day mere delusion. If we are to think of God in meaningful terms we have to accept that God can only be accepted in a rational way. Thus, the God of the Bible needs to be replaced by the God of reason because the God of the Bible is totally hidden from and inaccessible to us. Reason tells us that such a God cannot exist but if we still feel the need to talk about God and believe in God, then we should accept a God which has a non-real existence.[31] This God does not exist as we exist, so he does not have a personal existence or an ontological existence for that matter; this God only exists in our minds as an idea which can prove to be meaningful for our lives.[32] Cupitt speaks of God but it is clear that he likes the idea of faith instead. God is non-real and non-objective, but faith is real and objective; faith is religious feeling and it makes sense, so we have to reinvent faith for our time. We have to choose whether we have an objective God or an authentic faith, a faith in a non-objective God; it is one or the other.[33] As for Cupitt, he would have the non-objective God of reason because this cannot be monopolized;[34] the non-real God is a democratized reality based on a meaningful and rational idea. Thus the idea of God must be approached critically. For Cupitt, critical thinking applied to religion is to be concerned with the nature of faith and only then with the object of faith.[35] God must not be perceived as the object of faith because he does not have an ontologically real existence; God is the very nature of faith so critical religious think-

---

30. Borgman, *Edward Schillebeeckx*, 261.
31. Cupitt, *Sea of Faith*, 54.
32. Cupitt, *Sea of Faith*, 51.
33. This means that we are responsible for our beliefs and we have to choose what to believe. See also Sardar, *Postmodernism and the Other*, 115.
34. Cupitt, *Sea of Faith*, 178.
35. Cupitt, *Sea of Faith*, 258.

ing should be concerned with the nature of the object of faith.[36] So faith informs the idea of God or the type of God, not God informing faith. In other words, we build our own God, our own non-real God; we do not receive faith from an ontologically real God as in traditional theology. The non-real God has an obvious social dimension[37] as it is the product of the members of society. For Cupitt, the non-real God is a God of society but also a God for society because every human being has the possibility to create his own God in such a way that it could meet mankind's existential as well as social needs.

Reading through Schillebeeckx, it is clear that we have to be naturally aware of our humanity[38]—see chapter 3—and leave aside traditional theology which teaches us to be supernaturally aware of who we are.[39] This means that in order to understand our lives properly, we must not define ourselves based on the belief in a supernatural, metaphysical, and meta-historical God but rather on what science tells us about ourselves.[40] For Schillebeeckx, it is important to understand who we are by looking at history; we have to see ourselves as historical beings whose existence is empirical and temporal. Every human being who sees himself or herself as an individual historical existence in the world will realize that humanity has to face the reality of sin, which in Schillebeeckx is suffering and death, not man's existence traditionally defined as an offense against God.[41] Therefore, as human beings who are naturally aware of their historicity we have to accept the reality of suffering and death in a positive, meaningful, and relevant way which will help us engage in a constant fight against them.[42] Waging war against suffering and death is the only way for the secularized rationality of modern man to find a sense of positivity, meaningfulness, and relevance for human existence. Our fight against suffering and death must take practical forms of manifestation in the sense that wealthier nations should help poorer countries socially, politically, and economically. We must fight oppression of any kind, and in order to do

36. McGrath, *Christian Theology*, 180–81.
37. Cupitt, *Sea of Faith*, 267.
38. Schillebeeckx, *World and Church*, 19ff.
39. Borgman, *Edward Schillebeeckx*, 261.
40. McManus, *Unbroken Communion*, 102.
41. Hilkert, *Naming Grace*, 36.
42. Schillebeeckx, *God is New Each Moment*, 113.

this effectively we have to be self-confident. Self-confidence, however, cannot be discovered and fostered unless we are naturally aware of our human capacities. Nobody can or should tell us how to think of ourselves but us. Man is man's highest authority, so the grounds of human authority are firmly historical, not supernatural.[43] At the same time, we have to cultivate a sense of humility in the face of the world's constant challenge by suffering and death; this is why Schillebeeckx suggests that we should embrace humble humanism, namely our natural self-awareness based on the realistic knowledge of the self and of the world.[44] We have to be confident in ourselves and for this we do not need the supernatural God of traditional theology; what we need though is our natural awareness and self-knowledge. Once we are naturally aware of ourselves in accordance with the information provided by modern science, we are ready to advance as human beings so progress lies ahead of us.[45] In Schillebeeckx, however, the idea of progress is not restricted to science and technology, but it is extended to man's rediscovery of himself. When we rediscover ourselves by re-kindling our natural awareness we make a huge step forward in terms of finding the universal values of humanity such as love, justice, and morality. To be aware of these universal human values is to be created anew, so creation must not be understood traditionally as the work of a supernatural God, but existentially as the work of man who understands that he is created as a human being by himself when he comprehends and accepts the universal human values of love, justice, and morality.[46] Likewise, redemption should be accepted within the same lines, we are saved or redeemed when we practically apply these universal human values for the benefit of the entire world following the example of Christ.

There is nothing more important than man in Cupitt's philosophy. Man is seen in totally secular terms so he is the beginning and the end of everything. Man is present in the world (*saeculum*), so the very essence of man is secular.[47] Man is not only a being that is present in the world but he is also the creator of the world. The world itself should be seen as being made by man, which means that the world should be interpreted solely

---

43. Borgman, *Edward Schillebeeckx*, 46.
44. McManus, *Unbroken Communion*, 137.
45. Hilkert and Schreiter, eds., *The Praxis*, 145.
46. Wiley, *Thinking of Christ*, 93.
47. Pinto, "The *More* Which Exceeds Us," 199–200.

from a secularized human perspective.[48] The existence of man in the world is not only secular, but also autonomous and morally independent. This means that man does not have a higher authority that tells him what to do or not to do; there is no need for such a higher authority, traditionally described as the supernatural God of classical Christianity, because man makes his own world as well as his own morals. Man is confined within the limits of the world and he has to manage it. This is why man should be considered an economical being because he transforms the world for his own benefit by scientific progress.[49] Everything revolves around man on earth and nothing is more important than him. He is not affected by the sinful flaws of traditional theology; in Cupitt man is no longer seen as a fallen being but rather as a rising being. Man does not need anybody but himself in order to make his life meaningful.[50] Supernatural powers are non-existent or non-real but man does not need them anyway. He can make his own world the way he chooses and at the same time he can construct his own meaning in the world. Man is aware of himself and lives accordingly. Thus, he develops an autonomous ethical perspective on life which makes him understand that life is important; this natural awareness of the importance of life should be applied both to his life and also to the life of other human beings.[51] Therefore, man works for the benefit of his life and for the benefit of the entire mankind. Man does not have to look up to the supernatural world which does not exist anyway;[52] it is time for man to look down at the world in which he lives. At the same time, man should begin to look at himself and within himself because this is the only realm that can give meaning to his life. For Cupitt man is a being of the present, or a being of a constant present, for whom the actuality of the present moment is crucial.[53] Man should not live in the past because the past belongs to the non-scientific tradition of the church; the present is heavily informed by science, and this situation makes man fully conscious of himself as a being that can build his own world and way

---

48. See also Hebblethwaite, *The Ocean of Truth*, 79.
49. Cupitt, *Sea of Faith*, 30–31.
50. Cupitt, *Sea of Faith*, 64.
51. Cupitt, *Sea of Faith*, 109.
52. Cupitt, *Sea of Faith*, 144.
53. Cupitt, *Sea of Faith*, 186.

A Concluding Synthesis

of life.[54] He needs no model but himself, and in this sense not even the image of Christ can be a model for him.[55]

When it comes to Christ—see chapter 4—we have to understand that Schillebeeckx's Christology reflects his perspective on God, man, and secularization.[56] Thus, as God may no longer be seen as supernatural following the pattern of traditional Christianity but rather as a natural concept which confers validity, relevance, and meaning to humanity,[57] Christ also loses his traditional double nature so he is no longer presented as Jesus Christ, the divine Logos of God who assumed a human form (person). In Schillebeeckx, Jesus is the historical figure who lived and died in Palestine, while Christ is the disciples' presentation of Jesus as being alive in the consciousness of the church. Schillebeeckx's Christology begins with an explanation of the role of experience because it is our present experience that dictates how we should understand Jesus and Christ. We live in the world and we experience the world by means of conversation or language. We find out about Jesus when we read the Bible, but the Bible is written in human language and we have to understand it in order for it to be meaningful to us. The only way to understand the language of Scripture is rational so we have to apply our secularized rationality to the language of Scripture in all respects, including what it tells us about Jesus Christ. At the same time, we must make a correlation between the past and the present with special reference to experience.[58] This means that the experience of the past must be understood in terms of the experience of the present, which means that at the end of the day the experience of the past cannot be different from the experience of the present when it comes to our general human existence. The traditional image of Jesus presented in the Bible which highlights his supernatural experiences of preexistence, incarnation, resurrection, and ascension must be reinterpreted in accordance with our secularized understanding of the present experience which does not believe in supernatural realities. Therefore, Jesus did not have any preexistence, he did not become incarnate, he did not rise from the dead, and of course he did not go to heaven. He was a mere man who

---

54. See also Michener, *Engaging Deconstructive Theology*, 149.
55. Cupitt, *Mysticism after Modernity*, 112.
56. For details, see Schillebeeckx, *Christ*, 64ff.
57. Kennedy, *Schillebeeckx*, 32.
58. Schillebeeckx, *God is New Each Moment*, 62.

was concerned with the welfare of his nation. His concern for his fellow human beings brought him into conflict with religious and political authorities, which eventually succeeded in having him executed. Jesus died a horrible death, totally unjust and unfair, but Jesus had been aware of his fate, so he said he would rise from the dead in order to continue his work.[59] According to Schillebeeckx, we know today that he did not come back to life; he remained dead but his disciples, who were well aware of his death, began nonetheless to present him as the living Christ who brings salvation to humanity. For Schillebeeckx, salvation is believing in all the ideals professed and applied by Jesus, who would rather die than betray his ideal to help his fellow human beings. This should be an inspiration to us today so that we also embrace Jesus's ideal, as presented by means of the image of Christ and apply it for our lives as well as for the lives of others.

In Cupitt, Christ functions as a model but it is not necessarily a model. Christ works better for the religious man who can identify himself with the image of Christ. This is not compulsory, however, for every man because meaning is highly subjective and it is at the same time a personal reality which is made by every individual human being for his own self. Thus, Christ could be a model for the modern man because he is part of a wider range of religious symbols which represent human emancipation and perfection.[60] Religion tells us that we can identify ourselves with these religious symbols in order to make our lives worth living. It is not compulsory to do it, but if we so choose then religious models can be helpful. The Christian religion in particular teaches us that Christ can be a model for us because Christ represents a new humanity. Christ has nothing to do with the traditional God-man of classical Christianity; Christ is a mere religious symbol that informs our social consciousness. The poor and the outcast can identify themselves better with Christ but any other human being can also learn from Christ that we have to be socially involved in helping those in need. Christ should not be understood as a supernatural being who came in our natural world; this understanding should rather be reversed in the sense that man can rise beyond his natural condition. Thus, the traditional doctrine of the divinity of Christ should be interpreted as a teaching about every human being; the divinity represents the possibility of every person to transcend his own limits. In other words,

---

59. Rego, *Suffering and Salvation*, 14.
60. Cupitt, *Sea of Faith*, 119.

A Concluding Synthesis

Christ is the mythical picture of human spirituality.[61] Christ is not a supernatural reality but a natural image which confers meaning to every human being or at least to those who choose to follow his example.[62] For Cupitt, we do not have to believe in a supernatural reality or in the traditional as well as supernatural God in order to believe in Christ; Christ has nothing to do with the supernatural but has everything to do with the natural reality of our existence. Christ represents love so we must not seek him above his world but rather in our hearts. If we aim higher, if we want to be better, if we desire to have a meaningful life, all these human wishes can be represented by the image of Christ.[63] Christ can be whatever we aim at provided the result is meaningful for us.

In Schillebeeckx, the practical application of the image of Christ for existential and social relevance cannot be done without the reinterpretation of the traditional concept of resurrection[64]—see chapter 5—which is the foundation of Christ's image. Schillebeeckx begins his argument about resurrection from an analysis of Jesus's death which was tragic and unjust; he describes his death as an unfortunate event which did not exert any good influence on humanity.[65] Jesus's death was not even an ordinary death like the demise of any human being; Jesus suffered an atrocious death which was designated for the worst criminals. He was humiliated, tortured, and then executed as if he had been a murderer. Jesus's death was an immensely tragic event and was the end of any future possibility for Jesus. For Schillebeeckx, death is final and, in light of our present experience which tells us that people do not come back to life, we have to understand that unlike traditional theology which says Jesus rose from the dead Jesus stayed dead. There is no such thing as a physical resurrection of a dead body; Schillebeeckx is very clear about it and his conviction is applied to Jesus. Jesus died and his death was the end, the ultimate and final end of his ministry. Nevertheless, while he was still alive Jesus foresaw the possibility of his untimely death because he had warned his disciples of it before the tragic event really happened. At the same time, however, he knew his death could be one of the worst kind, and despite

---

61. Cupitt, *Sea of Faith*, 93.
62. Cupitt, *Sea of Faith*, 259.
63. Cupitt, *Sea of Faith*, 260.
64. Schillebeecckx, *Church*, 130ff.
65. Rego, *Suffering and Salvation*, 294.

this possibility, Jesus realized it was worth paying the ultimate price for the work he was doing, since it would lead to the improvement of life of his fellow people. This is why he told his disciples that he would rise from the dead and his work will be continued. According to Schillebeeckx, we know that Jesus did not come back to life; he remained dead like any other human being. His disciples though realized that his ministry was beneficial not only for the people of Israel but for humanity in general, so they resumed the idea of Jesus's resurrection and they began to preach about Jesus by saying that he was the Christ who came back to life from the tomb.[66] We must understand that Jesus did not come back to life, he was not resurrected because this is a sheer impossibility in real life; believing otherwise, namely believing in resurrection is mere ideology.[67] We should believe in the resurrection of Christ, namely in the resurgence of the idea that we must fight for the benefit of every human being which is symbolized by Christ's resurrection. Thus, resurrection is nothing but our awareness that we must be effective in changing the world for the better because we belong to this world for ever.

In Cupitt, resurrection should be understood from the perspective of our culture.[68] As our culture is no longer under the influence of traditional Christianity, we can finally approach the idea of resurrection in terms which have nothing to so with supernatural interpretations. Thus, devoid of its supernatural content, resurrection can no longer be seen in terms of a reality which involves the return of dead bodies to life;[69] resurrection therefore is not a realistic event but rather a spiritual image.[70] If resurrection is not an event which took place in history by means of a supernatural agency, then it means that resurrection should no longer be seen as unrepeatable and unique. As a spiritual reality, resurrection is both repeatable and common to humanity.[71] Resurrection has nothing to do with traditional realism but with rational non-realism.[72] Thus resurrection points to the possibility that every human being should be brought back

---

66. See also Hick, *The Metaphor of God Incarnate*, 20.
67. Rego, *Suffering and Salvation*, 304.
68. Cupitt, *The Way to Happiness: a Theory of Religion*, 6.
69. Hebblethwaite, *The Ocean of Truth*, 5–7.
70. Cupitt, *Radical Theology*, 37.
71. Cupitt, *Radical Theology*, 84.
72. Cupitt, *The Great Questions of Life*, 22–24.

to meaningful life; thus we come back to life by our own decision, not as a result of the intervention of a supernatural power. Resurrection cannot be conceived in Frankensteinian terms; nobody can come back to life after he or she has been declared dead. Nevertheless, we can be spiritually resurrected by our own powers throughout our historical existence. For the secularized mind of the modern man there is no biological resurrection. From a purely biological viewpoint, we are "recycled into the biological life of this world."[73] This is why, if we still cling to the idea of resurrection which is at the end of the day a human concept, resurrection has to make reference to something else, to something spiritual. Thus, in Cupitt, man resurrects himself in the sense that he can find a new meaning in life in the very same way traditional Christians found a new meaning in their lives after the death of Jesus. From this perspective, Christ's resurrection symbolized man's spiritual progress towards a meaningful life which is entirely a spiritual reality. Man has to engage in a personal struggle for a new and better understanding of life and religion. This new understanding of life must be done in accordance with the scientific discoveries of today so even a thoroughly traditional concept like resurrection must be conceived within these lines. Resurrection must be approached in terms of existential meaning, so the idea of resurrection must define man's quest for meaning. We are all resurrected when we find a meaningful purpose for our lives. We must understand that our lives will come to an end, and it is the realization of this human reality that confers meaning and happiness to our existence despite our imminent death.[74] In Cupitt, we are resurrected if we understand that there is no bodily resurrection. We are resurrected if we accept that we have to find meaning for our lives despite their transitory character. This is the right religion which teaches us that there is no God and no bodily resurrection; there is, however, the real possibility of having our transient lives resurrected by finding what is meaningful to them.

The idea of belonging—see chapter 6—is crucial to Schillebeeckx because it changes the pattern of the traditional idea of belonging as contained in traditional theology.[75] Traditional Christianity says that Christians belong to the church, not to the world; they live in the world

---

73. Cupitt, *Life, Life*, 4.
74. Hall, "Journeying on the Sea of Faith," 70.
75. Schillebeeckx, *God the Future of Man*, 172ff.

but they belong to the church because they were ransomed by Christ and they are God's children. Thus, they belong to Christ and the church. Christians belong to Christ personally and to the church communitarily. Therefore, in traditional theology there are two types of belonging: personal, the Christians' belonging to Christ and communitarian, the Christians' belonging to the church. Schillebeeckx reinterprets both so the idea of belonging is anything but traditional. Personal belonging must be understood as our connection with the idea of God, which is seen in terms of modern science and technology.[76] In order to comprehend how this works, we have to come to terms with the fact that religion does not supplement man's scientific power as in the past.[77] Today, science has reached an unprecedented peak so that even religion must be approached scientifically. The God of traditional theology goes through an equally dramatic transformation from a supernatural being to a natural concept which makes life worth living. It is to this modern God—the idea that helps us cope with the meaninglessness of human life—that we belong nowadays and we have to understand this if we want our lives to be meaningful.[78] The acceptance of this new perspective on God which has to define our modern, specifically scientific, personal belonging causes us to get involved in society.[79] This dramatically altered perspective on God and our personal belonging to him helps us fight what was traditionally described as sin but is now understood as suffering and death. The duty of every human being is to fight suffering and death from the perspective of our new image of God and the sense of personal belonging to him. Fighting sin and death is a constant demand that we face both personally and communitarily, so we must be aware that it is only the future that can put an end to these human problems. Our personal sense of belonging to God is actually our awareness that we must fight suffering and death by getting involved socially, politically, economically, etc. This is a proof that our belonging is not exclusively personal but also communitarian. We no longer belong to the church of traditional Christianity; we now belong to the entire world because the newly discovered idea of God is not oppressive as in traditional theology where God only accepted the members

---

76. Kennedy, *Schillebeeckx*, 11.
77. Rego, *Suffering and Salvation*, 44.
78. Kennedy, *A Modern Introduction to Theology*, 89.
79. Schillebeeckx, *God is New Each Moment*, 29.

of the church, but liberating because God now accepts everybody since every human being has to fight suffering and death.[80] Schillebeeckx's dramatic change of the idea of personal and communitarian belonging also transformed the traditional doctrine of the church which comes so close to the world that it virtually identifies itself with it.

As far as Cupitt is concerned, the idea of belonging is not explicitly present in his writings but it can be inferred through his notion of identity.[81] It is obvious from the start that in Cupitt man belongs to humanity because the world of humanity is the only real world that exists and its existence can be verified by reason and science. Thus, there is no need to mention in an explicit way that man belongs to world as the world is the cradle as well as the realm of mankind. It is important, however, that man should realize the fact that he belongs to this world, not to another—supernatural and metaphysical—world. Man cannot fully accept his belonging to the world unless he realizes what his identity consists of. In Cupitt, man seems to come to terms with his true identity as soon as he rids himself of the traditional dogma of the church which dictates certain petrified patterns of morality. In other words, man cannot find who he is or establish his own identity unless he discovers what he really is quite apart from dogmatic impositions from outside his inner reality. Man can get rid of these old doctrines if and when he accepts that God does not have a supernatural existence but he should rather be conceived in terms of natural sciences and concepts. Non-realism can help man escape the dictatorship of traditional church doctrines and their rigid morality. The immediate result is a new identity which man finds in relationship with himself and the world.[82] Identity can also be religiously informed in the sense that a particular religion can confer a feeling of personal and communitarian identity as man belongs to a certain religion that speaks positively about their way of life. In this case, identity is not naturally determined, but emerges as a religious task.[83] We have to discover our identity by accepting certain religious values which must be interpreted in a non-realist manner, namely in a way which avoids supernaturalism. Identity, however, which gives us a certain sense of personal and com-

---

80. Schillebeeckx, *Christ, the Sacrament of the Encounter with God*, 48.
81. Cupitt, *Is Nothing Sacred?*, 85.
82. Cupitt, *Sea of Faith*, 11.
83. Cupitt, *Sea of Faith*, 267.

munitarian religious belonging is not a lasting reality. In our postmodern world Cupitt does not see any absolutes left, so nothing can claim to stay for ever. Identity itself, both as reality and task, is subject to this rule so at the end of the day it can lapse into nothingness. Therefore, as nothing is absolute but rather transient, identity can be seen as being already dead, and if identity is dead the feeling of belonging must be sought elsewhere. The only chance we have left is to find identity in the very essence of our postmodern reality; in other words, we have to find our identity in the midst of a world which does not have any identity. We finally get to sense our own identity as soon as we realize that there is no such thing as a prescribed identity of any sort, social, religious or else. The loss of identity will eventually give us a new sense of identity which should be seen in terms of a personal faith in the meaningfulness of life. We have to understand that in Cupitt traditional theology is turned on its head and everything must be seen in a reversed way. If in traditional theology, our identity was given by our belonging to Christ and the church, now things have to be understood in an opposite way. Identity in Cupitt must be sought anywhere in the world but not in the church.

Though a radical himself, Schillebeeckx is nonetheless a little bit less radical than Cupitt. The church as presented by Schillebeeckx—see chapter 7—is based on his conviction that there are no ontologically real and transcendent categories which define reality.[84] Reality is exclusively historical and immanent; it has to do with the things that exist and happen within the realm of nature. Nothing beyond history can be given ontological constituency because nothing exists beyond the world or the universe as we know it. This has a crucial impact on the traditional doctrine of the church which is presented as being anchored in the metaphysical reality of God. In Schillebeeckx, however, the church cannot be connected to metaphysics because there is no such thing as metaphysics. There is no God beyond this world but only in this world, so what we have called the church needs to define or redefine itself in accordance with the scientific fact that there is no reality beyond what we perceive as reality.[85] If in traditional theology the church and the world were fundamentally different because they did not have many things in common, in Schillebeeckx the situation has been reversed. In traditional theology the

---

84. Schillebeeckx, *World and Church*, 115ff.
85. See also Kennedy, *Schillebeeckx*, 86.

church is different from the world even if it exists in the world because the lives of its members are believed to be connected to the metaphysically transcendent reality of God; but because there is no such God as ontologically real and transcendent, then the church cannot claim that it has a supernatural component any longer.[86] The church is a community, a distinct community but a community nevertheless, and this is exactly what it shares with the world. For Schillebeeckx, both the church and the world are communities, so the church is like the world based on its communitarian composition. The church cannot be conceived as being radically different from the world because they both share the same universal human values of love, justice, solidarity, and hope. The church may be historically distinctive from the world because it has its own organization and offices but the values it fights for are basically the values that the world also tries to apply in everyday life. The church has the mandate to transform the world, and this was the case even in traditional theology, so the church must move towards the world by love. Schillebeeckx's radical reinterpretation of the church as a distinct human community which no longer has any connection with metaphysics does not change the original mandate of the church because the church lives in the world and its entire activity is directed towards the world. Based on the example of Christ, the church has a duty to serve the world, but this is not the exclusive task of the church. Every man and woman is equally responsible for the welfare of the world, so the church and the world have boundaries which are definitely not as firm as explained by traditional theology. For Schillebeeckx, the frontiers between the church and the world are actually very fluid since both the church and the world are concerned to serve humanity by promoting the universal values of justice, love, solidarity, and hope.[87] Therefore, even though the church is distinct from the world due to its structure and offices, there are no actual differences between the church and the world.[88]

Cupitt is not particularly interested in offering a clear definition of the church because he seems to see it as a smaller community within the larger community of mankind. The church is a special community because its members think in religious terms while the rest of humanity thinks in

86. Borgman, *Edward Schillebeeckx*, 133–34.
87. See also Hilkert and Schreiter, eds., *The Praxis*, 140.
88. For more details about the relationship between the church and the world in Schillebeeckx, see Knitter, "Religion and Globality," 116–18.

scientific and mechanical ways. The church has a particular kind of religion which for Cupitt is the traditional theology of classical Christianity. Thus, the religion of the church or the religion of traditional Christianity is full of symbols which reflect the duality of its doctrines as oriented both to supernaturalism and naturalism. The church is a traditional institution which believes in a supernatural God that has a real existence like any other person who lives in history. The essence of this religious realism is the conviction that everything that exists in history originates in the supernatural world and especially in God.[89] Cupitt does not display a vivid interest in the church because he seems to be convinced that if realism succumbs to non-realism the church itself or the idea of the church becomes somehow superfluous—its traditional doctrine at least is definitely superfluous. This is very likely to happen because, for Cupitt, the church is nothing but a human institution or community which has always been deeply rooted in culture.[90] Thus, the very essence of the church's system of belief incorporates religious elements from the Jewish culture but also from the Greek philosophy.[91] In other words, the church has had secular roots from the very beginning and undergoes a complex process of secularization. This is important because the so-called myths of the church—all the doctrines that contain supernatural and unscientific elements—are reinterpreted by means of the modern man's creativity and reason. As these symbols can be interpreted and understood by modern secular people, it is clear that the substance of the church's doctrines is not specifically supernatural or exclusively Christian.[92] The values of the church were common to ancient societies and they are common to our modern societies. The church promotes—in a religious and symbolic form—human values which are common to the whole of mankind so, at least from this perspective, the church is not different from the world. What we have to do today is reinterpret these values and religious symbols by stripping them of the supernatural elements in order for them to make sense to the secularized mind of today's world. If we do not do this, the church will always be at odds with the world because it will have its own ethics as well as intellectual understanding of the world based on its traditional

---

89. Cupitt, *Sea of Faith*, 38–9.
90. Michener, *Engaging Deconstructive Theology*, 143.
91. Cupitt, *Sea of Faith*, 39.
92. Cupitt, *Sea of Faith*, 40.

A Concluding Synthesis

realism. The traditional teaching of the church must be deconstructed so that the church should no longer completely control the communication between God and man.[93] We must understand God in human terms so that our communication with ourselves as well as with others should be made meaningful. The traditional spirituality of the church was predominantly introvert so we have to deconstruct it in order to become extrovert in all respects, but mainly in ethics and morality.[94] This means that the church, once secularized, should accept values which were traditionally forbidden to its members, such as for instance homosexuality, because the Bible—which for Cupitt is full of mythical symbols—can be read in order to support one's lifestyle. Thus, if the church does not have a specific morality as different for that of the world, the boundaries between the church and the world are virtually non-existent.

Schillebeeckx explains at length that the world encompasses the sum of historical realities which include the church—see chapter 8—so the church is the world and the world is the church.[95] For Schillebeeckx, however, things are not so simple. He argues that the world has the tendency to become church while the church has the tendency to become world. The image of Christ is crucial here because it represents the embodiment of universal human values. As the church promotes Christ, it means that the church promotes universal human values; in other words, the church promotes the world. As for the world, it is clear that its concern is the welfare of every human being and as the progress of humanity is based on the dissemination of the universal human values preached by the church, the world has the tendency to become church. This process whereby the world becomes church is called by Schillebeeckx sanctifying secularization because the idea of sanctity is attached to the church while the reality of secularization is the characteristic of the world. Thus, the traditional slogan of the church according to which there is no salvation outside the church has been turned into the modern reality that there is no salvation outside the world. For Schillebeeckx, this is true because both church and world are concerned with humanity and they both work for the benefit of all human beings. Within the context of the world's identification with the church, the idea of salvation is no longer seen as redemption from

---

93. Cupitt, *Mysticism after Modernity*, 16.
94. Cupitt, *Mysticism after Modernity*, 18.
95. Schillebeeckx, *World and Church*, 124.

sin, understood as offence against God, but rather as the practical application of the universal human values embodied by the image of Christ. Schillebeeckx's idea of sanctifying secularization as illustration of the world's tendency to become church is completed by the equally important notion of secular holiness which defines the church's tendency to become the world.[96] To be sure, the world moves in the direction of the church by sanctifying secularization and the church moves in the direction of the world by secular holiness. Sanctifying secularization and secular holiness as applied to the world and to the church respectively confer validity, relevance, and meaning to both. The world is relevant as church and the church is relevant as the world because both the world and the church share the same universal values of humanity which they apply for the benefit of every human being as well as the emancipation of mankind in general. For Schillebeeckx, the ideal situation is given by the future possibility of having the world and the church come together into a liberated world that has found its ultimate meaning in promoting the fundamental and universal values of mankind.

This is also possible for Cupitt. The church has been going through a process of accelerated secularization so it is only a matter of time until the values of the church are decrypted and translated into secular values. The values of the church had a secular side to begin with, but it appears that the church will not be able to survive much longer unless it changes its theological realism into a thoroughly secular perspective on reality. The world is the only reality that exists, so we have to understand it by means of science. No supernatural element should ever disrupt our scientific understanding of the world.[97] The world must be seen as nature and there is nothing beyond it or below it. There is no God beyond this world so the world is not God's creation and the dead who are buried do not continue their existence in the ground. The world continues to exist as nature whether we like it or not while the dead remain dead and buried. The world does not have any connections whatsoever with a supernatural reality; the world exists by itself and all the phenomena of the world are strictly natural so they can be deciphered scientifically.[98] Nothing in the world is in relation to God and everything exists apart from God be-

---

96. Borgman, *Edward Schillebeeckx*, 363.
97. McGrath, *A Scientific Theology: Reality*, 254.
98. Cupitt, *Sea of Faith*, 57.

cause there is no such thing as an ontologically real God. The world is not a theater for the manifestation of God's power; the world is the scene for the manifestation of man's power which is able to create and transform the world. If the world still wants to preserve religion and religious language, then it has to be deconstructed so that supernaturalism is no longer the hermeneutical key of religion. Thus, the world can embrace religion and can even be defined religiously if religion does not talk about an ontologically real God but about doing good things to other people. The world should be characterized by community loyalty and the practice of goodness because the religion of the true world should be always a matter of practice, not a matter of doctrine.[99] The world is the totality of historical reality wherein people are concerned with each other because they know that religious symbolism must be interpreted in a demythologizing way so that we all benefit from the human values promoted by religion. To be sure, Cupitt prefers a world which is post-metaphysical, and fully horizontalized in which everything is immanent and democratic.[100] In such a world, the divine no longer exists as ontologically real, but is dispersed into every single individual person. We may resort to and even return to religion, but religion must be treated as non-realism in order to make sense and be meaningful to us.[101] The world must always remain a world of language and meaning because, for Cupitt, this seems to be the only way to strengthen our faith.

It is obvious then than Schillebeeckx and Cupitt share the non-realist conviction that secularization has left us with a God which cannot be seen in the traditional terms of theistic realism but rather as a non-realist concept which informs our religion. As for religion, it is a cultural phenomenon that can be evaluated linguistically and existentially based on our contemporary secular rationality. This will always turn traditional supernaturalism into non-realist religious concepts which are intended to promote the universal values of humanity for the perpetual welfare of mankind. The people of today's secularized society must come to terms with the reality of the religion's rationalistic deconstruction. For Schillebeeckx, but also for Cupitt, there seems to be no other way for us if we really want to find meaning for our lives. Religion in general and

---

99. Cupitt, *Sea of Faith*, 58.
100. Cupitt, *Mysticism after Modernity*, 91.
101. Cupitt, *Mysticism after Modernity*, 146.

Christianity in particular do not disclose the metaphysical and metahistorical existence of an ontologically real and supernatural God; they only tell us that traditional supernaturalism should be seen as historical naturalism which promotes the fundamental values of humanity as man's way to happiness and meaning.

Selected Bibliography

PRIMARY SOURCES

Schillebeeckx, Edward. *Christ, the Christian Experience in the Modern World*. London: SCM Press, 1990.

———. *The Mission of the Church*. London: Sheed and Ward, 1973.

———. *The Concept of Truth and Theological Renewal*. London: Sheed and Ward, 1968.

———. *Church, the Human Story of God*. London: SCM Press, 1990.

———. *God, the Future of Man*. London: Sheed and Ward, 1968.

———. *The Church with a Human Face: A New and Expanded Theology of Ministry*. New York: Crossroad, 1985.

———. *World and Church*. London: Sheed and Ward, 1971.

———. *God is New Each Moment*, edited by Huub Oosterhuis and Piet Hoogeveen. London: Continuum, 2004.

———. *Christ, the Sacrament of the Encounter with God*. Lanham: Rowman and Littlefield, 1963.

———. *The Eucharist*. London: Continuum, 1968.

SECONDARY SOURCES

Abraham, William J. *The Logic of Renewal*. Grand Rapids: Eerdmans, 2003.

Alberigo, Giuseppe. Joseph A. Komonchak, Matthew J. O'Connell, eds. *History of Vatican II*, vol. 4: Church and Communion, Third Period and Intercession, September 1964–September 1965. Leuven: Orbis/Peeters, 2006.

Aldwinckle, Russell F. *Jesus—a Savior or the Savior? Religious Pluralism in Christian Perspective*. Macon: Mercer University Press, 1982.

Astorga, M., Christina A. "Culture, Religion and Moral Vision: A Theological Discourse on the Filipino People Power Revolution of 1986." *Theological Studies* 67, no. 3 (2006): 567.

Attfield, Robin. *Creation, Evolution and Meaning*. Aldershot: Ashgate Publishing, 2006.

Avis, Paul D. L. *God and the Creative Imagination: Metaphor, Symbol and Myth in Religion and Theology*. London: Routledge, 1999.

Ban, Joseph D. *The Christological Foundation for Contemporary Theological Education*. Macon: Mercer University Press, 1989.

Baum, Gregory, ed. *The Twentieth Century: A Theological Overview*. Maryknoll: Orbis Books, 1999.

Bergin, Liam. *O Propheticum Lavacrum: Baptism as Symbolic Act of Eschatological Salvation*. Roma: Editrice Pontificia Università Gregoriana, 1999.

Selected Bibliography

Berkhof, Hendrikus. *Christian Faith: An Introduction to the Study of the Faith*. Grand Rapids: Eerdmans, 2002.

Berkouwer, G. C. *The Church*. Grand Rapids: Eerdmans, 1976.

Bloesch, Donald G. *The Last Things: Resurrection, Judgment, Glory*. Downers Grove, IL: InterVarsity Press, 2006.

Boeve, L. "Theology and the Interruption of Experience", in *Religious Experience and Contemporary Theological Epistemology*, edited by L. Boeve, Y. de Maeseneer, S. van den Bossche. Leuven: Peeters, 2005.

Boeve, Lieven and Lawrence P. Hemming, eds. *Divinising Experience: Essays in the History of Religious Experience from Origen to Ricoeur*. Leuven: Peeters, 2004.

Boeve, L. and L. Leijssen, eds. *Sacramental Presence in a Postmodern Context*. Leuven: Peeters, 2001.

Boeve, Lieven, Hans Geybels, and Stijn van den Bossche, eds. *Encountering Transcendence: Contributions to a Theology of Christian Religious Experience*. Leuven: Peeters, 2006.

Bonsor, Jack A. "History, Dogma, and Nature: Further Reflections on Postmodernism and Theology." *Theological Studies* 55.2 (1994): 295.

Bordoni, Marcello. "Christology and Truth: Contemporary Christology in Light of the Question of Truth," in *The Uniqueness and Universality of Jesus Christ: In Dialogue with the Religions*, edited by Massimo Seretti. Grand Rapids: Eerdmans, 2004.

Borgman, Erik. *Edward Schillebeeckx: A Theologian in His History*. London: Continuum, 2004.

Bosco, Mark. *Graham Greene's Catholic Imagination*. Oxford: Oxford University Press, 2005.

Bowden, John. *Edward Schillebeeckx: Portrait of a Theologian*. London: SCM Press, 1983.

Breck, John. *Scripture in Tradition: the Bible and Its Interpretation in the Orthodox Church*. Crestwood: St. Vladimir's Seminary Press, 2001.

Breyfogle, Todd. "Religious Mystery and Rational Reflection." *Cross Currents*, Summer 1999, 266.

Brown, David. *The Divine Trinity*. Chicago: Open Court Publishing, 1985.

Burgess, Joseph A. and Jeffrey Gros, eds. *Building Unity: Ecumenical Dialogues with Roman Catholic Participation in the United States*. Mahwah: Paulist Press, 1989.

Burtchaell, James T. *From Synagogue to Church: Public Services and Offices in the Earliest Christian Communities*. Cambridge: Cambridge University Press, 1992.

Byrne, Brendan T. "Christ's Pre-Existence in Pauline Soteriology." *Theological Studies* 58, no. 2 (1997): 308.

Byrne, Peter. *God and Realism*. Aldershot: Ashgate Publishing, 2003.

———. *The Moral Interpretation of Religion*. Grand Rapids: Eerdmans, 1998.

Cahill, Brendan J. *The Renewal of Revelation Theology (1960–1962): The Development and Responses to the Fourth Chapter of the Preparatory Schema De Deposition Fidei*. Roma: Editrice Pontificia Università Gregoriana, 1999.

Cahill, Lisa Sowle. "Marriage: Developments in Catholic Theology and Ethics." *Theological Studies* 64.1 (2003): 78.

Campbell, Anthony F. *The Worshipper of Spirit: A Believable God Today*. Grand Rapids: Eerdmans, 2008.

Caputo, John D. *More Radical Hermeneutics: On Not Knowing Who We Are*. Bloomington: Indiana University Press, 2000.

Carey, Patrick W. and Joseph T. Lienhard, eds. *Biographical Dictionary of Christian Theologians*. Westport: Greenwood Publishing Group, 2000.

Selected Bibliography

Carmody, Denise L. and John T. Carmody. *Bounded in Christ's Love: Being a Member of the Church—An Introduction to Ecclesiology.* Mahwah: Paulist Press, 1986.

Chua Soo Meng, Jude. "The Political Theology of John of Paris OP," in *Doctor Angelicus, volume III, 2003*, edited by Brunero Gherardini, Rudolf M. Schmitz, Wolfgang Waldstein, and David Berger. Norderstedt: BoD, 2006.

Clack, Beverley. "God and Language: A Feminist Perspective on the Meaning of 'God,'" in *The Nature of Religious Language: A Colloquium*, edited by Stanley E. Porter. London: Continuum, 1996.

Clack, Brian R. *An Introduction to Wittgenstein's Philosophy of Religion.* Edinburgh: Edinburgh University Press, 1999.

Cochran, Clarke E. "Another Identity Crisis: Catholic Hospitals Face Hard Choices." *Commonweal*, February 25, 2000, 12.

Coffey, David M. "Quaestio Disputata Response to Neil Ormerod and Beyond." *Theological Studies* 68, no. 4 (2007): 900.

———. "The Theandric Nature of Christ." *Theological Studies* 60.3 (1999): 405.

Conley, John J. Joseph W. Koterski, eds. *Prophecy and Diplomacy—The Moral Doctrine of John Paul II: A Jesuit Symposium.* New York: Fordham University Press, 1999.

Copenhaver, Martin B. "Who Do You Say That I Am." *The Christian Century*, August 24, 1994, 779.

Cote, Richard G. *Re-Visioning Mission: The Catholic Church and Culture in Postmodern America.* Mahwah: Paulist Press, 1996.

Coupe, Laurence. *Myth.* London: Routledge, 1997.

Croken, Robert C. and Robert M. Doran, eds. *The Collected Works of Bernard Lonergan: Philosophical and Theological Papers 1965–1980*, vol. 17. Toronto: University of Toronto Press, 2004.

Cross, Laurence. "Escaping from a Polemical History: Until Hearts and Minds Are Changed." *The Ecumenical Review* 54.1 (2002): 172.

Culbertson, Diana. *The Poetics of Revelation: Recognition and the Narrative Tradition.* Macon: Mercer University Press, 1989.

Cupitt, Don. *Is Nothing Sacred? The Non-Realist Philosophy of Religion: Selected Essays.* New York: Fordham University Press, 2002.

———. *Life, Life.* Salem: Polebridge Press, 2003.

———. *Mysticism after Modernity.* Oxford: Blackwell Publishing, 1998.

———. *Sea of Faith: Christianity in Change.* Cambridge: Cambridge University Press, 1988.

Davis, Stephen T. *Risen Indeed: Making Sense of the Resurrection.* Grand Rapids: Eerdmans, 1993.

De Tavernier, Johan. "Love for the Enemy and Nonretribution: a Plea for a Contextual and Prudent Pacifism", in *Swords into Plowshares: Theological Reflections on Peace*, edited by Roger Burggraeve and Marc Vervenne. Leuven: Peeters, 1991.

Dellavalle, Nancy A. "Feminist Theologies", in *The Cambridge Companion to Karl Rahner*, edited by Declan Marmion and Mary E. Hines. Cambridge: Cambridge University Press, 2005.

Depoortere, Kristiaan. *A Different God: A Christian View of Suffering.* Leuven: Peeters, 1995.

Dietrich, Donald J. *God and Humanity in Auschwitz: Jewish-Christian Relations and Sanctioned Murder.* Edison: Transaction Publishers, 1995.

Selected Bibliography

Doherty, Jerry C. *A Celtic Model of Ministry: The Reawakening of Community Spirituality*. Collegeville: Liturgical Press, 2003.

Donovan, Mary Ann. "The Vocation of the Theologian." *Theological Studies* 65, no. 1 (2004): 3.

Doran, Robert M. *Theology and the Dialectics of History*. Toronto: University of Toronto Press, 1990.

Doyle, Dennis M. "Journet, Congar, and the Roots of Communion Ecclesiology." *Theological Studies* 58, no. 3 (1997): 461.

———. "Young Catholics & Their Faith: Is Being 'Spiritual' Enough?," *Commonweal*, September 8, 2006, 11.

———. *The Church Emerging from Vatican II: A Popular Approach to Contemporary Catholicism*. New London: Twenty-Third Publications, 1992.

Draulans, Veerle. "The Permanent Deacon as 'The Go-Between' Religious Leadership in Search of a Specific Identity," in *Practical Theology and the Interpretation of Crossing Boundaries: Essays in Honour of Professor M. P. J. van Knippenberg*, edited by Bert Roebben and Leo van der Tuin. Münster: Lit Verlag, 2003.

Dreyer, Elizabeth. *Manifestations of Grace*. Collegeville: Liturgical Press, 1990.

Dupré, Louis and James A. Wiseman, eds. *Light from Light*. Mahwah: Paulist Press, 2001.

Dupré, William. *Patters of Meaning: Reflections on Meaning and Truth in Cultural Reality, Religious Traditions and Theological Encounters*. Leuven: Peeters, 1994.

Edwards, Denis. *What Are They Saying about Salvation?*. Mahwah: Paulist Press, 1986.

Elwell, Walter A. and Philip W. Comfort. *Tyndale Bible Dictionary*. Carol Stream: Tyndale House Publishers, 2001.

Engelhardt, Hugo T. *The Foundations of Christian Bioethics*. London: Taylor and Francis, 2000.

Evans, C. Stephen. *Faith beyond Reason*. Edinburgh: Edinburgh University Press, 1998.

Evans, Gillian R. *The Church and the Churches: Toward an Ecumenical Ecclesiology*. Cambridge: Cambridge University Press, 1994.

Fackre, Gabriel. *Christology in Context: The Christian Story—A Pastoral Systematics*. Grand Rapids: Eerdmans, 2006.

———. *The Christian Story: A Pastoral Systematics*, vol. 2: Authority—Scripture in the Church for the World. Grand Rapids: Eerdmans, 1985.

Fahlbusch, Erwin and Geoffrey W. Bromiley, eds. *The Encyclopedia of Christianity*. Grand Rapids and Leiden: Eerdmans and Brill, 2008.

Falck, Colin. *Myth, Truth, and Literature: Towards a True Post-Modernism*. Cambridge: Cambrdige University Press, 1994.

Fatula, Mary A. *The Triune God of Christian Faith*. Collegeville: Liturgical Press, 1991.

Fennell, William O. *God's Intention for Man: Essays in Christian Anthropology*. Waterloo: Wilfried Laurier University Press, 1977.

Ferrara, Dennis Michael. "In Persona Christi: Towards a Second Naivete." *Theological Studies* 57, no. 1 (1996): 65.

Fichter, Joseph H. *Wives of Catholic Clergy*. Lanham: Rowman and Littlefield, 1992.

Fitzpatrick, P. J. *In Breaking of Bread: The Eucharist and Ritual*. Cambridge: Cambridge University Press, 1993.

Fuller, Reginald H. and Daniel Westberg. *Preaching the Lectionary: The Word of God for the Church Today*. Collegeville: Liturgical Press, 2006.

Galvin, John P. "From the Humanity of Christ to the Jesus of History: A Paradigm Shift in Catholic Christology." *Theological Studies* 55.2 (1994): 252.

Selected Bibliography

Geldhof, Joris. *Revelation, Reason, and Reality: Theological Encounters with Jaspers, Schelling, and Baader*. Leuven: Peeters, 2007.

Gibbs, Philip. *The Word in the Third World: Divine Revelation in the Theology of Jean-Marc Éla, Aloysius Pieris, and Gustavo Guttiérez*. Roma: Editrice Pontificia Università Gregoriana, 1996.

Godzieba, Anthony J., Lieven Boeve and Michele Saracino. "Resurrection-Interruption-Transformation: Incarnation as Hermeneutical Strategy A Symposium." *Theological Studies* 67, no. 4 (2006): 777.

Gowen, Donald E., ed. *The Westminster Theological Wordbook of the Bible*. Louisville: The Westminster John Knox Press, 2003.

Graham, Gordon. *Evil and Christian Ethics*. Cambridge: Cambridge University Press, 2001.

———. *The Re-enchantment of the World: Art versus Religion*. Oxford: Oxford University Press, 2007.

Greene, Colin J. D. *Christology in Cultural Perspective: Making Out the Horizons*. Grand Rapids: Eerdmans, 2004.

Griffin, David Ray. "Professing Theology in the State University," in *Theology and the University: Essays in Honor of John B. Cobb Jr.*, edited by David Ray Griffin and Joseph C. Hough. New York: The State University of New York Press, 1991.

Grigg, Richard. *Imaginary Christs: The Challenge of Christological Pluralism*. New York: The State University of New York Press, 2000.

Grillmeier, Allois and Theresia Hainthaler. *Christ in Christian Tradition*, vol. 2: From the Council of Chalcedon (451) to Gregory the Great (590–604), Part 2: The Church of Constantinople in the Sixth Century. Louisville: Westminster John Knox Press, 1975.

Groome, Thomas. "Shared Christian Praxis: A Possible Theory/Method of Religious Education", in *Critical Perspectives on Christian Education*, edited by Jeff Astley and Leslie J. Francis. Herefordshire: Gracewing Publishing, 1994.

Grootaers, Jan. "An Unfinished Agenda: The Question of Roman Catholic Membership of the World Council of Churches, 1968–1975." *The Ecumenical Review* 49.3 (1997): 305.

Groppe, Elizabeth Teresa. "The Contribution of Yves Congar's Theology of the Holy Spirit." *Theological Studies* 62.3 (2001): 451.

Guerriere, Daniel. *Phenomenology of the Truth Proper to Religion*. Albany: State University of New York Press, 1990.

Guthrie, Shirley C. *Christian Doctrine: Teachings of the Christian Church*. Louisville: Westminster John Knox Press, 1994.

Gwynne, Paul. *Special Divine Action: Key Issues in the Contemporary Debate*. Roma: Editrice Pontificia Università Gregoriana, 1996.

Haight, Roger. "The American Jesuit Theologian", in *Jesuit Postmodern: Scholarship, Vocation, and Identity in the 21st Century*, edited by Francis X. Clooney. Lanham: Lexington Books, 2006.

Haight, Roger. *An Alternative Vision: An Interpretation of Liberation Theology*. Mahwah: Paulist Press, 1985.

———. *Christian Community in History*. London: Continuum, 2004.

———. *The Future of Christology*. London: Continuum, 2005.

———. "Jesus and Salvation: An Essay in Interpretation." *Theological Studies* 55.2 (1994): 225.

Selected Bibliography

Hall, C. Michael. "Journeying on the Sea of Faith", in *Tourism, Religion, and Spiritual Journeys*, Dallen J. Timothy and Daniel H. Olsen. London: Routledge, 2006.

Harrington, Wilfrid J. *Revelation*. Collegeville: Liturgical Press, 1993.

———. *Seeking Spiritual Growth through the Bible*. Mahwah: Paulist Press, 2002.

Haught, John F. "Evolution and God's Humility: How Theology Can Embrace Darwin." *Commonweal*, January 28, 2000, 12.

———. *Responses to 101 Questions on God and Evolution*. Mahwah: Paulist Press, 2001.

Hayes, Michael A. and Liam Gearon, eds. *Contemporary Catholic Theology: A Reader*. London: Continuum, 1999.

Hays, Richard B. *First Corinthians*. Louisville: Westminster John Knox Press, 1997.

Hebblethwaite, Brian. *The Incarnation: Collected Essays in Christology*. Cambridge: Cambridge University Press, 1987.

Heelas, Paul. *Religion, Modernity, and Postmodernity*. Oxford: Blackwell, 1998.

Hennelly, Alfred T. *Theology for a Liberating Church: The New Praxis of Freedom*. Washington: Georgetown University Press, 1989.

Hermans, Chris A. M. *Participatory Learning: Religious Education in a Globalizing Society*. Leiden: Brill, 2003.

Herrmann, Eberhard. *Religion, Reality, and a Good Life: A Philosophical Approach to Religion*. Tübingen: Mohr-Siebeck, 2004.

Heyer, Kristin E. *Prophetic and Public: The Social Witness of U.S. Catholicism*. Washington: Georgetown University Press, 2006.

Hick, John *The Metaphor of God Incarnate*. Louisville: Westminster John Knox Press, 1993.

Hilkert, Mary Catherine. *Naming Grace: Preaching and the Sacramental Imagination*. London: Continuum, 1997.

———. "Revelation and Proclamation: Shifting Paradigms." *Journal of Ecumenical Studies* 29.1 (1992): 1.

Hilkert, Mary Katherine and Robert J. Schreiter, eds. *The Praxis of the Reign of God: An Introduction to the Theology of Edward Schillebeeckx*. New York: Fordham University Press, 2002.

Hill, Brenan R. *Exploring Catholic Theology: God, Jesus, Church, and Sacraments*. New London: Twenty Third Publications, 1995.

———. *Jesus, the Christ: Contemporary Perspectives*. New London: Twenty-Third Publications, 2004.

Himes, Kenneth R. and James Coriden. "The Indissolubility of Marriage: Reasons to Reconsider." *Theological Studies* 65.3 (2004): 453.

Hinze, Bradford E. "Reclaiming Rhetoric in the Christian Tradition." *Theological Studies* 57.3 (1996): 481.

Hodgson, Peter C. *Jesus, Word and Presence: An Essay in Christology*. Augsburg: Fortress Press, 1971.

Houlden, Leslie. *Jesus in History, Thought, and Culture: An Encyclopedia*. Oxford: ABC Clio, 2003.

Hyman, Gavin. *The Predicament of Postmodern Theology: Radical Orthodoxy or Nihilist Textualism?*, Louisville: Westminster John Knox Press, 2001.

Icenogle, Gareth W. *Biblical Foundations for Small Group Ministry*. Downers Grove, IL: InterVarsity Press, 1994.

Inge, John. *A Christian Theology of Place*. Aldershot: Ashgate, 2003.

Selected Bibliography

Insole, Christopher J. *The Realist Hope: A Critique of Anti-Realist Approaches in Contemporary Philosophical Theology.* Aldershot: Ashgate Publishing, 2006.

Iraola, Antton E. *True Confucians, Bold Christians: Korean Missionary Experience, A Model for the Third Millenium.* Amsterdam: Rodopi, 2007.

Irwin, Kevin W. "Liberation Theology." *Theological Studies* 55, no. 4 (1994): 675.

Johannesson, Karin. *God Pro Nobis: On Non-Metaphysical Realism and the Philosophy of Religion.* Leuven: Peeters, 2007.

Johnson, Elizabeth A. "The Word Was Made Flesh and Dwelt among Us: Jesus Research and Christian Faith", in *Jesus: A Colloquium in the Holy Land*, edited by James D. C. Dunn and Doris Donnelly. London: Continuum, 2001.

Jones, Gregory. *Embodying Forgiveness: A Theological Analysis.* Grand Rapids: Eerdmans, 1995.

Kaczor, Christopher, ed. *Proportionalism: For and Against.* Milwaukee: Marquette University Press, 2000.

———. "Thomas Aquinas on the Development of Doctrine." *Theological Studies* 62.2 (2001): 283.

Keenan, John P. "A Mahayana Theology of the Real Presence of Christ in the Eucharist." *Buddhist-Christian Studies* 24 (2004): 89.

Kemball-Cook, David. *Is God A Trinity?.* Lulu, 2006.

Kennedy, Philip. *A Modern Introduction to Theology: New Questions for Old Beliefs.* London: IB Tauris Publishers, 2006.

———. *Schillebeeckx.* Collegeville: Liturgical Press, 1993.

Kerr, Fergus. "The Reception of Wittgenstein's Philosophy by Theologians", in *Religion and Wittgenstein's Legacy*, edited by D. Z. Phillips and Mario von der Ruhr. Aldershot: Ashgate Publishing, 2005.

Knott, Kim. *The Location of Religion: A Spatial Analysis.* London: Equinox Publishing, 2005.

Komonchak, Joseph A. "The Church in Crisis: Pope Benedict's Theological Vision." *Commonweal*, June 3, 2005, 11.

Kotva, Joseph J. *The Christian Case for Virtue Ethics.* Washington: Georgetown University Press, 1996.

Krieg, Robert A. "Karl Adam, National Socialism and Christian Tradition." *Theological Studies* 60, no. 3 (1999): 432.

La Due, William J. *The Trinity Guide to Eschatology.* London: Continuum, 2006.

Lakeland, Paul. *The Liberation of the Laity: In Search of an Accountable Church.* London: Continuum, 2004.

Lamberigts, M., L. Boeve, T. Merrigan and D. Claes, eds. *Theology and the Quest for Truth.* Leuven: Peeters, 2007.

Lane, Dermot A. *The Experience of God: An Invitation to Do Theology.* Mahwah: Paulist Press, 1981.

Larbig, Torsten and Siegfried Wiedenhofer, eds. *Tradition and Tradition Theories: An International Discussion.* Münster: Lit Verlag, 2006.

Lawler, Michael J. and Thomas J. Shanahan. *Church: A Spirited Communion.* Collegeville: Liturgical Press, 1995.

Lawson, Paul D. *Old Wine in New Skins: Centering Prayer and Systems Theory.* New York: Lantern Books, 2000.

Lefebvre, Marcel. *Open Letter to Confused Catholics.* Herefordshire: Gracewing Publishing, 1986.

Selected Bibliography

Lennan, Richard. *Risking the Church: The Challenges of Catholic Faith*. Oxford: Oxford University Press, 2004.

Levering, Matthew W. *Sacrifice and Community: Jewish Offering and Christian Eucharist*. Oxford: Blackwell, 2005.

Levine, Michael P. *Pantheism: A Non-Theistic Concept of Deity*. Lodon: Routledge, 1994.

Lewis, Alan E. *Between Cross and Resurrection: A Theology of Holy Saturday*. Grand Rapids: Eerdmans, 2001.

Lewis, Gordon R. and Bruce A. Demarest, *Integrative Theology*. Grand Rapids: Zondervan, 1994.

Livingston, James C., Francis Schüssler Fiorenza. *Modern Christian Thought: The Enlightment and the Nineteenth Century*. Augsburg: Fortress Press, 2006.

Loewe, William P. "From the Humanity of Christ to the Historical Jesus." *Theological Studies* 61.2 (2000): 314.

———. *The College Student's Introduction to Christology*. Collegeville: Liturgical Press, 1996.

Loughlin, Gerard. "'To Live and Die upon a Dogma': Newman and Post/Modern Dogma", in *Newman and Faith*, edited by Ian Ker and Terrence Merrigan. Leuven: Peeters, 2004.

———. *Telling God's Story: Bible, Church, and Narrative Theology*. Cambridge: Cambridge University Press, 1996.

Lukken, Gerard. *Per Visibilia ad Invisibilia*, ed. Louis van Tongeren and Charles Caspers. Leuven: Peeters, 1994.

Macnab, Francis. *Don't Call Me Grumpy: What Older Men Really Want*. London: Pluto Press, 2006.

MacNamara, Vincent. "The Distinctiveness of Christian Morality", in *Christian Ethics: An Introduction*, edited by Bernard Hoose. London: Continuum, 2000.

Macquarrie, John. *Jesus Christ in Modern Thought*. London: SCM Press, 1991.

Markham, Ian S. *Truth and the Reality of God*. London: Continuum, 1998.

Marsh, James L. *Process, Praxis, and Transcendence*. Albany: State Uniersity of New York Press, 1999.

Martin, David. *On Secularization*. Aldershot: Ashgate Publishing, 2005.

Martin, Francis. *The Feminist Question in the Light of Christian Tradition*. Grand Rapids: Eerdmans, 1994.

Mbogu, Nicholas I. *Christology and Religious Pluralism: A Review of John Hick's Theocentric Model of Christology and the Emergence of African Inculturation Theologies*. Münster: Lit Verlag, 2007.

McBrien, Richard P. *Catholicism—New Study Edition: Completely Revised and Updated*. San Francisco: Harper, 1994.

McCready, Douglas. *He Came Down From Heaven: The Preexistence of Christ and Christian Faith*. Downers Grove: InterVarsity Press, 2005.

McDermott, Brian O. *Word Become Flesh: Dimensions of Christology*. Collegeville: Liturgical Press, 1993.

McEnhill, Peter and George Newlands. *Five Key Christian Thinkers*. London: Routledge, 2004.

McGonigle, Thomas C. and Phyllis Zagano. *The Dominican Tradition: Spirituality in History*. Collegeville: Liturgical Press, 2006.

McGrath, Alister E. *A Scientific Theology: Reality*. London: Continuum, 2006.

———. *Christian Theology: An Introduction*. Oxford: Blackwell, 2006.

Selected Bibliography

———. *The Christian Theology Reader*. Blackwell: Oxford, 2001.

———. *The Christian Theology Reader*. Oxford: Blackwell, 2006.

———. *The Science of God*. London: Continuum, 2004.

Mckenna, John H. "Eucharistic Presence: An Invitation to Dialogue." *Theological Studies* 60.2 (1999): 294.

McMahon, Christopher. *Jesus, Our Salvation*. Winona: St. Mary's Press, 2007.

McManus, Kathleen Anne. *Unbroken Communion: The Place and Meaning of Suffering in Edward Schillebeeckx*. Lanham: Rowman and Littlefield, 2003.

———. "Reconciling the Cross in the Theologies of Edward Schillebeeckx and Ivone Gebara." *Theological Studies* 66.3 (2005): 638.

———. "Suffering and Salvation: The Salvific Meaning of Suffering in the Later Theology of Edward Schillebeeckx." *Theological Studies* 69.1 (2008): 230.

———. "Suffering in the Theology of Edward Schillebeeckx." *Theological Studies* 60.3 (1999): 476.

McNeill, John J. *My Spiritual Journey: Both Feet Firmly Planted in Midair*. Louisville: Westminster John Knox Press, 1998.

Mertens, Herman E. *Not the Cross, but the Crucified: An Essay in Soteriology*. Leuven: Peeters, 1992.

Meyer, Marvin W. and Charles Hughes, eds. *Jesus Then and Now: Images of Jesus in History and Christology*. London: Continuum, 2001.

Michener, Ronald T. *Engaging Deconstructive Theology*. Aldershot: Ashgate Publishing, 2007.

Miller, Vincent J. *Consuming Religion: Christian Faith and Practice in a Consuming Culture*. London: Continuum, 2004.

Mitchell, Nathan. *Real Presence: The Work of Eucharist*. Chicago: Liturgy Training Publications, 2001.

Mize, Sandra Y. *Joining the Revolution in Theology: The College Theology Society, 1954–2004*. Lanham: Rowman and Littlefield, 2007.

Modras, Ronald. "In His Own Footsteps: Benedict XVI From Professor to Pontiff." *Commonweal*, April 21, 2006, 12.

Möller, Göran. *Ethics and the Life of Faith: A Christian Moral Perspective*. Leuven: Peeters, 1998.

Mongoven, Anne Marie. *The Prophetic Spirit of Catechesis: How We Share the Fire in Our Hearts*. Mahwah: Paulist Press, 2000.

Moniz, John. "Liberated Society." *Gandhian and Christian Vision Comparative Study*. Roma: EPUG, 1996.

Moore, Andrew. *Realism and Christian Faith: God, Grammar, and Meaning*. Cambridge: Cambridge University Press, 2003.

Morrill, Bruce T. *Anamnesis as Dangerous Memory: Political and Liturgical Theology in Dialogue*. Collegeville: Liturgical Press, 2000.

Moses, Gregory. "Faith and Reason: Naturalised and Relativised", in *Faith and Reason: Friends or Foes in the New Millenium?*, edited by Anthony Fisher and Hayden Ramsey. Hindmarsh: ATF Press, 2004.

Mueller, John J. *What Are They Saying about Theological Method?*. Mahwah: Paulist Press, 1984.

Mulcahy, Eamonn. *The Cause of Our Salvation: Soteriological Causality according to Some Modern British Theologians 1988–1998*. Roma: Editrice Pontificia Università Gregoriana, 2007.

Selected Bibliography

Murray, Paul D. *Reason, Truth and Theology in a Pragmatist Perspective*. Leuven: Peeters, 2004.

Nacke, Stefan, Hans-Bernd Köppen, Reinhard Mönninghoff, eds. *Am Puls der Zeit: Dimensionen einer Hochschulpastoral*. Münster: Lit Verlag, 2002.

Nasr, Seyyed Hossein. *The Need for a Sacred Science*. London: Routledge, 1995.

Newlands, George M. *Christ and Human Rights: The Transformative Engagement*. Aldershot: Ashgate, 2006.

———. "Christology," in *The Westminster Dictionary of Christian Theology*, edited by Alan Richardson and John Bowden. Louisville: Westminster John Knox Press, 1983.

Nichols, Aidan. *Catholic Thought since the Enlightenment: A Survey*. Herefordshire: Gracewing Publishing, 1998.

———. *The Panther and the Hind: A Theological History of Anglicanism*. London: Continuum, 1993.

Nyce, Dorothy Yoder. "Faithful and Pluralistic: Engagement among People of Living Faiths." *Cross Currents*, Summer 2003, 214.

O'Boyle, Aidan. *Towards a Contemporary Wisdom Christology: Some Catholic Christologies in German, English, and French*. Roma: Editrice Pontificia Università Gregoriana, 2003.

O'Collins, Gerald and Daniel Kendall. *Focus on Jesus: Essays in Christology and Soteriology*. Herefordshire: Gracewing Publishing, 1998.

O'Collins, Gerald. *Easter Faith: Believing in the Risen Jesus*. Mahwah: Paulist Press, 2004.

O'Grady John F. *Catholic Beliefs and Traditions: Ancient and Ever New*. Mahwah: Paulist Press, 2002.

O'Hanlon, Gerard F., *The Immutability of God in the Theology of Hans Urs von Balthasar*. Cambridge: Cambridge University Press, 2007.

O'Hare, Padraic, *The Enduring Covenant*. London: Continuum, 1997.

O'Meara, Thomas F. "Jean-Pierre Torrell's Research on Thomas Aquinas." *Theological Studies* 62.4 (2001): 787.

Omar, A. Rashied. "Overcoming Religiously Motivated Violence." *Cross Currents*, Spring 2005, 77.

Ormerod, Neil J. "'The Times They Are a 'Changin': A Response to O'Malley and Schloesser." *Theological Studies* 67.4 (2006): 834.

———. "A Dialectic Engagement with the Social Sciences in an Ecclesiological Context." *Theological Studies* 66.4 (2005): 815.

———. "Quarrels with the Method of Correlation." *Theological Studies* 57.4 (1996): 707.

———. "The Structure of a Systematic Ecclesiology." *Theological Studies* 63.1 (2002): 3.

Osborne, Kenan B. *Christian Sacraments in a Postmodern World: A Theology for the Third Millenium*. Mahwah: Paulist Press, 2000.

Pattison, George. *Thinking about God in an Age of Technology*. Oxford: Oxford University Press, 2005.

Pecklers, Keith F. *Worship: New Century Theology*. London: Continuum, 2003.

Pellegrino, Edmund D. and Alan I. Faden, eds. *Jewish and Catholic Bioethics: An Ecumenical Dialogue*. Washington: Georgetown University Press, 1999.

Perrin, David B. "Mysticism," in *The Blackwell Companion to Christian Spirituality*, edited by Arthur Holder. Oxford: Blackwell, 2005.

Perry, Michael J. *Love and Power: The Role of Religion and Morality in American Politics*. Oxford: Oxford University Press, 1991.

Pickard, Stephen K. *Liberating Evangelism*. London: Continuum, 1999.

Selected Bibliography

Pinto, Henrique. "The *More* Which Exceeds Us: Foucault, Roman-Catholicism and Inter-Faith Dialogue," in *Michel Foucault and Theology: The Politics of Religious Experience*, edited by James Bernauer and Jeremy Carette. Aldershot: Ashgate, 2004.

Placher, William C. *Narratives of a Vulnerable God: Christ, Theology, and Scripture*. Louisville: Westminster John Knox Press, 1994.

Pollefeyt, Didier. *Incredible Forgiveness: Christian Ethics between Fanaticism and Reconciliation*. Leuven: Peeters, 2004.

Portier, William L. *Tradition and Incarnation: Foundations of Christian Theology*. Mahwah: Paulist Press, 1994.

Prusak, Bernard P. "Bodily Resurrection in Catholic Perspectives." *Theological Studies* 61.1 (2000): 64.

———. *The Church Unfinished: Ecclesiology through the Centuries*. Mahwah: Paulist Press, 2004).

Radcliffe, Timothy. *What is the Point of Being a Christian?*. London: Continuum, 2005).

Ramm, Bernard L. *An Evangelical Christology: Ecumenic and Historic*. Vancouver: Regent College Publishing, 1993).

Ramshaw, Gail. "(ii) The Gender of God", in *Feminist Theology: A Reader*, edited by Ann Loades. Louisville: Westminster John Knox Press, 1990.

Rausch, Thomas P. *Reconciling Faith and Reason: Apologists, Evangelists, and Theologians in a Divided Church*. Collegeville: Liturgical Press, 2000.

———. *Who Is Jesus? An Introduction to Christology*. Collegeville: Liturgical Press, 2003.

Redford, John. *What is Catholicism? Hard Questions*. Huntington: Our Sunday Visitor Publishing, 1999.

Regan, David. *Experience the Mystery: Pastoral Possibilities for Christian Mystagogy*. Collegeville: Liturgical Press, 1995.

Rego, Aloysius. *Suffering and Salvation: The Salvific Meaning of Suffering in the Later Theology of Edward Schillebeeckx*. Leuven: Peeters, 2006.

Reno, R. R. "Theology after the Revolution." *First Things: A Monthly Journal of Religion and Public Life*, May 2007, 15.

Rich, Arthur. *Business and Economic Ethics*. Leuven: Peeters, 2004.

Rochford, Dennis. "The Theological Hermeneutics of Edward Schillebeeckx." *Theological Studies* 63.2 (2002): 251.

Rose, Lucy A. *Sharing the Word: Preaching in the Roundtable Church*. Louisville: Westminster John Knox Press, 1997).

Ross, Susan A. *Extravagant Affections: A Feminist Sacramental Theology*. London: Continuum, 2001.

Runzo, Joseph. *Ethics, Religion and the Good Society*. Louisville: Wesminster John Knox Press, 1992.

Rush, Ormond. *The Reception of Doctrine: An Appropriation of Hans Robert Jauss' Reception Aesthetics and Literary Hermeneutics*. Roma: Editrice Pontificia Università Gregoriana, 1997.

Russell, Letty M. *Church in the Round: Feminist Interpretation of the Church*. Louisville: Westminster John Knox Press, 1993.

Sardar, Ziauddin. *Postmodernism and the Other: The New Imperialism of Western Culture*. London: Pluto Press, 1998.

Satterlee, Craig A. *Ambrose of Milan's Method of Mystagogical Preaching*. Collegeville: Liturgical Press, 2002.

Sayés, José A. *El misterio Eucaristico*. Madrid: Editiones Palabra, 2005.

Selected Bibliography

Schaab, Gloria L. *Creative Suffering of the Triune God: An Evolutionary Theology*. Oxford: Oxford University Press, 2007.

Schloesser, Stephen. "Against Forgetting: Memory, History, Vatican II." *Theological Studies* 67.2 (2006): 275.

Schnackenburg, Rudolf. *Ephesians: A Commentary*. London: Continuum, 1991.

Schreiner, Thomas R. *Paul, Apostle of God's Glory in Christ*. Downers Grove, IL: InterVarsity Press, 2006.

Schreiter, Robert J. "Edward Schillebeeckx," in *The Modern Theologians*, edited by David Ford. Oxford: Blackwell, 1997.

———. *The Schillebeeckx Reader*. Edinburgh: T. & T. Clark, 1986.

Schubeck, Thomas L. "Ethics and Liberation Theology." *Theological Studies* 56.1 (1995): 107.

Schults, LeRon *Reforming the Doctrine of God: After the Philosophical Turn to Relationality*. Grand Rapids: Eerdmans, 2005.

Schwarz, Hans. *Theology in a Global Context*. Grand Rapids: Eerdmans, 2005.

Scirghi, Thomas J. *An Examination of the Problems of Inclusive Language in the Trinitarian Formula of Baptism*. Lewiston: Edwin Mellen Press, 2000.

Seidler, John. "Contested Accommodation: The Catholic Church as a Special Case of Social Change." *Social Forces* 64.4 (1986): 847–74.

Shannon, Trevor. "Jesus," in *Teaching Christianity: A World Religions Approach*, edited by Clive Erricker. Cambridge: Lutterworth Press, 1987.

Sharma, Arvind and Kathleen M. Dugan, eds. *A Dome of Many Colors*. London: Continuum, 1999.

Sherry, Patrick. "Modes of Representation and Likeness of God," in *Christ, Ethics and Tragedy: Essays in Honour of Donald MacKinnon*, edited by Kenneth Surin. Cambridge: Cambridge University Press, 1989.

Simon, Derek J. "Salvation and Liberation in the Practical-Critical Soteriology of Schillebeeckx." *Theological Studies* 63.3 (2002): 494.

Simuţ, Corneliu C. *A Critical Study of Hans Küng's Ecclesiology. From Traditionalism to Modernism*. New York: Palgrave Macmillan, 2008.

Simuţ, Ramona. "Reinterpreting Traditional Theology. An Interview with Edward Schillebeeckx," *Perichoresis* 5.2 (2007), 275–83.

Stapert, Calvin. *My Only Comfort: Death, Deliverance, and Discipleship in the Music of Bach*. Grand Rapids: Eerdmans, 2000.

Stewart, Elizabeth-Ann. *Jesus the Holy Fool*. Lanham: Rowman and Littlefield, 1999.

Stoker, Wessel. *Is the Quest for Meaning the Quest for God? The Religious Ascription of Meaning in Relation to the Secular Ascription of Meaning*. Amsterdam: Rodopi, 1996.

Surin, Kenneth. *The Turnings of Darkness in Light: Essays in Philosophical and Systematic Theology*. Cambridge: Cambridge University Press, 1989.

Swidler, Leonard J. *Yeshua: A Model for Moderns*. Lanham: Rowman and Littlefield, 1988.

Talar, C. J. T. "'The Synthesis of All Heresies'—100 Years On." *Theological Studies* 68, no. 3 (2007): 491.

Teevan, Donna. "Challenges to the Role of Theological Anthropology in Feminist Theologies." *Theological Studies* 64.3 (2003): 582.

Thabit Abdul-Masih, Marguerite. *Edward Schillebeeckx and Hans Frei: A Conversation on Method and Christology*. Waterloo: Wilfrid Laurier University Press, 2001.

Selected Bibliography

Thiselton, Anthony C. *The First Epistle to the Corinthians: A Commentary on the Greek Text*. Grand Rapids: Eerdmans, 2000.

———. *Thiselton on Hermeneutics: Collected Works with New Essays*. Grand Rapids: Eerdmans, 2006.

Thompson, Daniel P. "Schillebeeckx on the Development of Doctrine." *Theological Studies* 62.2 (2001): 303.

Thompson, Ross. *The Sacraments*. London: SCM Press, 2006.

Tilley, Terrence W. "Remembering the Historic Jesus—A New Research Program?." *Theological Studies* 68.1 (2007): 3.

Torevell, David. *Losing the Sacred: Ritual, Modernity, and Liturgical Reform*. London: Continuum, 2000.

Trigg, Roger. "Theological Realism and Antirealism," in *A Companion to Philosophy of Religion*, edited by Philip L. Quinn and Charles Taliaferro. Oxford: Blackwell, 1997.

———. *Understanding Social Science*. Oxford: Blackwell, 2001.

Tupper, E. Frank. "Theology, Christology, and Eschatology," in *Perspectives on Scripture and Tradition: Essays in Honour of Dale Moody*, edited by Robert L. Perkins. Macon: Mercer University Press, 1987.

———. *A Scandalous Providence*. Macon: Mercer University Press, 1995.

Utzinger, J. Michael. *Yet Saints Their Watch Are Keeping: Fundamentalists, Modernists, and the Development of Evangelical Ecclesiology, 1887–1937*. Macon: Mercer University Press, 2006.

Uzukwu, E. Elochukwu. *Worship as Body Language*. Collegeville: Liturgical Press, 1997.

Valkenberg, Pim. *Sharing Lights on the Way to God: Muslim-Christian Dialogue and Theology in the Context of Abrahamic Partnership*. Amsterdam: Rodopi, 2006.

van Beeck, Frans Jozef. *God Encountered: A Contemporary Catholic Systematic Theology*. Collegeville: Liturgical Press, 2002.

van den Brink, Gijsbert. *Almighty God: A Study of the Doctrine of Divine Omnipotence*. Leuven: Peeters, 1993.

van der Ven, Johannes A. *God Reinvented? A Theological Search in Texts and Tables*. Leiden: Brill, 1998.

van der Ven, Johannes A., Jaco S. Dreyer, and Hendrik J. C. Pieterse, *Is There a God of Human Rights? The Complex Relationship between Human Rights and Religion: A South African Case*. Leiden: Brill, 2004.

Vander Zee, Leonard J. *Christ, Baptism, and the Lord's Supper: Recovering the Sacraments for Evangelical Worship*. Downers Grove, IL: Intervarsity Press, 2004.

Vanhoozer, Kevin J. *Is There a Meaning in This Text?*, Grand Rapids: Zondervan, 1998.

———. *The Drama of Doctrine*. Louisville: Westminster John Knox Press, 2005.

———. *First Theology: God, Scripture, and Hermeneutics*. Downers Grove, IL: InterVarsity Press, 2002.

Vergote, Antoine. *Religion, Belief, and Unbelief: A Psychological Study*. Amsterdam: Rodopi, 1997.

Viladesau, Richard. *The Beauty of the Cross: The Passion of Christ in Theology and the Arts, from the Catacombs to the Eve of the Renaissance*. Oxford: Oxford University Press, 2006.

Viviano, Benedict T. *Trinity, Kingdom, Church: Essays in Biblical Theology*. Göttingen: Vandenhoek & Rupprecht, 2001.

Wainwright, Geoffrey. *Worship with One Accord: Where Liturgy and Ecumenism Embrace*. Oxford: Oxford University Press, 1997.

Selected Bibliography

Walls, Jerry L., ed. *The Oxford Handbook of Eschatology*. Oxford: Oxford University Press, 2007.

Wanamaker, Charles A. *The Epistles to the Thessalonians*. Grand Rapids: Eerdmans, 1990.

Wardi, Anissa J. "Inscriptions in the Dust: A Gathering of Old Men and Beloved as Ancestral Requiems." *African American Review* 36.1 (2002): 35.

Watson, Richard A. *The Breaking of Cartesian Metaphysics*. Indianapolis: Hackett Publishing, 1998.

Wedderburn, A. J. M. *Baptism and Resurrection*. Tübingen: Mohr-Siebeck, 1987.

Wells, George A. *Can We Trust the New Testament?*. Chicago: Open Court Publishing, 2003.

Whalen, Robert. "George Herbert's Sacramental Puritanism." *Renaissance Quarterly* 54.4 (2001): 1273.

Whalen, Teresa. *The Authentic Doctrine of the Eucharist*. Lanham: Rowman and Littlefield, 1993.

Wicks, Robert J. *Handbook of Spirituality for Ministers: Perspectives for the 21st Century*. Mahwah: Paulist Press, 2000.

Wiley, Tatha. *Thinking of Christ: Proclamation, Explanation, Meaning*. London: Continuum, 2003.

Williams, Rowan. *Wresting with Angels: Conversations in Modern Theology*. Grand Rapids: Eerdmans, 2007.

Williams, Stephen N. *Revelation and Reconciliation: A Window on Modernity*. Cambridge: Cambridge University Press, 1996.

Winter, Michael M. *The Atonement*. Collegeville: Liturgical Press, 1995.

Witczak, Michael G. "The Manifold Presence of Christ in the Liturgy." *Theological Studies* 59.4 (1998): 680.

Wood, Susan K. *Spiritual Exegesis and the Church in the Theology of Henri de Lubac*. London: Continuum, 1998.

Woodhead, Linda. "Theology: The Trouble It's In", in *New Directions in Philosophical Theology: Essays in Honour of Don Cupitt*, edited by Gavin Hyman. Aldershot: Ashgate Publishing, 2004.

Wright, Andrew. "Anglikanische Perspektiven II", in *Religion als Wahrnehmung: Konzepte und Praxis in unterschiedlichen Kulturen und Kirchen*, edited by Engelbert Groß. Münster: Lit Verlag, 2006.

Wright, Andrew. *Religion, Education and Post-Modernity*. London: Routledge, 2003.

Yaghjian, Lucretia B. "Flannery O'Connor's Use of Symbol, Roger Haight's Christology and the Religious Writer." *Theological Studies* 63.2 (2002): 268.

Yeo, Khiok-Khng. *Rhetorical Interaction in 1 Corinthians 8 and 10: A Formal Analysis with Preliminary Suggestions for a Chinese, Cross-Cultural Hermeneutic*. Leiden: Brill, 1995.

Yewangoe, Andreas A. *Theologia Crucis in Asia: Asian Christian Views on Suffering in the Face of Overwhelming Poverty and Multifaceted Religiosity in Asia*. Amsterdam: Rodopi, 1987.

Ziebertz, Hans-Georg, Friendrich Schweitzer, Hermann Häring and Don Browning, eds. *The Human Image of God*. Leiden: Brill, 2001.

Zuidberg, Gerard. *God the Pastor: The Spirituality of Roman Catholic Pastors in the Netherlands*. Leiden: Brill, 2000.

Index

Africa, 17
America, 17
Answers, x, 1–4, 9, 12, 144, 225
Anthropology, 6, 61, 64, 80, 110, 250, 258
Ascension, 96, 97, 109, 139, 148, 152, 181, 182, 210, 233
Asia, 17, 70, 99, 260
Atheism, 27, 35, 36, 156
Awareness, vii, ix, 12, 30, 57, 59, 61, 63, 65–73, 75–79, 81–83, 119, 137, 171, 201, 204–7, 231–32, 236, 238

Believer, 17–20, 28, 38, 42, 43, 46, 48, 50, 54, 94, 111, 113, 129, 134, 147, 151–53, 155, 156, 159, 164, 172, 183, 185, 199, 216
Belonging, vii, xvii, 139–41, 143, 145, 147, 149, 151–53, 155, 157, 161, 163–65, 237–40.
Bible, xiii, xiv, xv, 87, 107, 155, 164, 175–77, 185, 186, 224, 229, 233, 243, 248, 250–52, 254

Catholic, ix, xvi, xvii, 5, 25, 30, 32, 41, 45, 97, 99, 104, 111, 114, 115, 131, 172, 186, 211, 248–54, 256–60
Certainty, 21, 22, 34, 103
Christ, vii, x, xiii, xvii, 8, 17, 25, 30, 38, 39, 44, 51–53, 55, 59, 60, 64, 66, 71, 73, 75, 81, 83–85, 88, 89, 91–93, 95–101, 103–14, 119, 121, 124, 127, 129, 130, 133, 139, 140, 148–52, 154–60, 163–68, 170, 177–99, 201, 202, 204, 205, 208–15, 217, 231, 233–41, 243, 244, 247–54, 256–60
Christian, vii, ix, x, xvi, xvii, 1–7, 9, 11, 13–21, 23–28, 30, 31, 34, 42, 45, 49, 52, 54, 55, 57, 58, 60, 63–67, 69–71, 85, 87–93, 95, 96, 98–101, 104, 106, 110–15, 119, 123, 126, 128, 133–37, 139–41, 144–47, 149–51, 153–60, 164–66, 170, 172, 193, 195, 197, 200, 202, 204, 206–8, 212, 214, 215, 217–20, 223, 226, 230, 234, 237, 238, 242, 247–57, 259, 260
Christianity, xiv, 1, 2, 7, 10, 13, 19–22, 24–30, 43, 51, 52, 57, 60, 63, 64, 68, 73, 75, 80, 85, 90, 92, 97, 99, 100, 107, 108, 110–12, 121, 124, 126, 127, 129, 133, 140–42, 144, 146, 154–59, 166, 169, 188, 195, 197, 200, 211, 213, 215, 217, 218–23, 227, 228, 232–34, 236–38, 242, 246, 249, 250, 258
Christology, vii, ix, xvii, 11, 37, 40, 46, 70, 84–87, 89, 91, 93, 95, 97, 99, 101, 103, 105, 107, 109, 111, 120, 126, 140, 173, 176, 206, 210, 212, 233, 248, 250–52, 254–60
Church, vii, ix, xi, xiii, xvi, xvii, 2, 3, 5, 7, 10–14, 16–18, 32, 35, 39, 54–56, 58–61, 63, 65, 66, 69, 71, 72, 75, 76, 79–84, 87–90, 95, 99–115, 117, 118, 120–23, 125–30, 134, 136, 137, 139, 141, 143, 148, 149, 151–210, 212–19, 221–23, 226, 227, 230, 232, 233, 235, 238–44, 247–54, 257–60
Civilization, 63, 143, 146, 217, 221
Comfort, 18, 21, 22, 140, 155, 250, 258
Conscience, 10, 71
Contemporary, 1–3, 7–9, 21, 26, 29, 71, 86, 88, 89, 93, 97, 106, 107, 110, 115, 116, 140, 142–47, 150, 151, 153, 206, 211, 220, 222, 225, 227, 245, 247, 248, 250–53, 256, 259

Index

Creation, 57, 60, 62–69, 73–76, 79–83, 85, 108, 193, 204–6, 231, 244, 247
Criticism, ix, xi, xvi, 5, 10, 17, 27, 32, 66, 87, 180
Culture, 6, 12, 22, 23, 31, 66, 67, 87, 100, 146, 147, 221, 236, 242, 247, 249, 252, 255, 257

Death, xi, xiii, 5, 8, 20, 28, 30, 31, 36, 39, 51, 52, 67–72, 74, 79, 81, 82, 93–97, 100–108, 110, 111, 113–25, 127, 129, 135–39, 145–48, 149, 151, 155, 159, 178, 184, 185, 187–90, 194, 210, 211, 216, 228, 230, 231, 234–39, 258
Development, xvii, 2, 4, 9, 22, 33, 37, 40, 42, 68, 142, 145, 184, 226, 248, 253, 259
Dialogue, 24–26, 160, 216, 217, 248, 255, 256, 257, 259
Discoveries, 8, 148, 228, 237
Divinity, 106, 136, 234
Divorce, 19, 42
Doctrine, vii, xi, 2, 11, 12, 41, 48, 50, 53, 57, 60–63, 67, 70, 84, 86, 89, 91, 102, 106, 113, 115, 117, 119, 121, 123, 125, 127, 129, 131–33, 135, 137, 145, 147, 150, 152–54, 156, 157, 163, 180, 181, 193, 196, 218, 220, 226, 227, 234, 239, 240, 242, 245, 249, 251, 253, 257–60

Easter, 95, 119, 140, 256
Ecclesiology, vii, 139, 141, 143, 145, 147, 149, 151, 153, 155, 157, 159, 161, 163, 165, 169, 249, 250, 256–59
Empirical, 4, 10, 12, 13, 25, 44, 179, 188–90, 230
Enlightenment, xiv, 9, 10, 25, 256
Ethics, 19, 20, 45, 111, 112, 227, 242, 243, 248, 251, 253–58
Europe, 17, 106, 153
Existence, x, xiii–xv, 2, 7, 10, 11, 16, 20, 27, 30, 36, 39, 40, 43, 45–51, 53, 57, 58, 61, 62, 77, 78, 80, 82, 88, 90, 96–99, 104, 109, 119–21, 124, 129–33, 135, 136, 138–40, 146, 148, 155, 156, 158, 160, 166, 167, 169,173, 176, 181, 185, 186, 188, 198, 201, 206, 214, 221, 222, 224, 225, 229, 230, 232, 233, 235, 237, 239, 242, 244, 246, 248, 254
Existentialism, 42
Existentialist, xv, 43–45, 70, 166, 180
Expectations, xiv, xv, 2, 3, 45, 64, 88, 89, 91, 92, 97, 103, 107, 111, 126, 130, 134, 143, 145, 147, 164, 206

Faith, ix, x, 4, 6–12, 14–16, 18, 22, 26, 29, 32, 34, 36, 37, 50–54, 84, 89, 90–92, 100, 103, 104, 108, 109, 111, 114–20, 123, 127, 131, 132, 134, 140, 147, 149, 151–53, 156–61, 181, 182, 208, 221, 222, 225–27, 229, 230, 232, 234, 235, 237, 239, 240, 242, 244, 245, 249, 250, 252–57
Father, 18, 95, 104, 105, 108, 140, 148, 150, 152, 157, 186, 188, 190, 217
Feeling, 6, 7, 10, 45, 47, 58, 62, 63, 65, 111, 112, 143, 158, 159, 164, 221–24, 229, 239, 240
Future, xvi, xvii, 4, 5, 8, 9–14, 16, 17, 19, 21–23, 25, 27, 28, 29, 31–37, 40, 42, 44, 47, 50–55, 61–64, 69–71, 73, 75–78, 91, 103, 105, 109, 117, 124–26, 128–34, 140–48, 150–54, 159–67, 171–74, 176, 179, 184–86, 188, 204, 206, 207, 210–12, 215–19, 222, 225–28, 235, 237, 238, 244, 247, 251

God, vii, ix, x, xiii–xvii, 2–59, 61–86, 89–92, 94, 95, 97–106, 108–12, 114, 116–20, 122–36, 138–61, 163–68, 170–90, 194–96, 199, 201, 202, 204–8, 210–18, 220–60
Goodness, 45–48, 53, 80, 91, 103, 147, 199, 245
Greek, 25, 60, 63, 90, 106, 242, 259

Happiness, 122, 236, 237, 246
Health, 18
Hermeneutics, xv, 16, 20, 24, 45, 85, 93, 122, 134, 248, 257, 259
History, x, xi, xv, 3, 6, 11, 18, 24, 28, 29, 30, 32–35, 39, 40, 45, 52–54, 61–64, 68, 73, 75, 76, 80, 83, 84, 86, 89, 91, 94, 103, 104, 106, 108, 109, 120,

Index

History (cont.),
    121, 127, 129, 133, 140, 142, 145,
    147, 151, 153, 161, 163, 167, 169,
    171–75, 177–79, 181–86, 198, 202,
    203, 205–7, 210, 211, 215, 217, 221,
    226, 230, 236, 240, 242, 247–52,
    254–56, 258
Holiness, 218, 244
Holy, x, xi, 16, 18, 38, 87, 95, 99, 109, 139,
    140, 143, 149, 152, 159, 174, 183,
    187, 190, 200, 201, 209, 251, 253,
    254, 258
Homosexuality, 19, 43, 243
Hope, 8, 11, 28, 52, 54, 72, 73, 77, 78, 88, 89,
    103, 111, 117, 119–22, 124, 126, 129,
    131–33, 136, 143–54, 159, 161, 164,
    165, 168, 202, 208–10, 227, 241, 253
Humanity, x, xiv, xv, 4, 8, 9, 13, 23, 24, 29, 32,
    33, 35, 40, 44–50, 52–55, 57, 60–62,
    64, 66–81, 84, 85, 88, 91, 92, 97, 99,
    100, 103, 105, 107, 109–11, 113, 114,
    117, 119, 120, 121, 129–36, 138, 140,
    142–44, 147, 148, 150, 151, 153,
    159–64, 169–84, 186–91, 194, 195,
    197–203, 205–16, 218, 219, 221–24,
    226, 227, 230, 231, 233–36, 239,
    241–46, 249, 250, 254

Identity, 108, 178, 203, 224, 239, 240, 249–51
Incarnation, 70, 96–98, 109, 111, 128, 139,
    149, 175, 233, 251, 252, 257
Intellect, 8, 10, 18, 130
Intellectual, 7, 19, 140, 194, 243
Interpretation, x, xv, xvii, 2, 3, 12–14, 17,
    21, 35, 47, 48, 52, 57, 59, 61, 67, 89,
    90–94, 96, 114, 115, 118, 128, 129,
    131, 133, 138, 141, 147, 148, 152–54,
    172, 175, 180, 206, 214, 216, 220,
    236, 241, 248, 250, 251, 257

Jesus, vii, x, xi, xiii, xiv, xvi, xvii, 5, 6, 8, 14,
    25, 39, 52, 53, 55, 58, 59, 81, 82,
    84–130, 134–40, 143, 148–55, 157,
    159, 163–66, 168, 169, 175–79, 181,
    183–90, 194, 195, 201, 207, 210–14,
    216, 233–37, 247, 247, 250–59
Jews, 25, 90, 109, 110, 184

Justice, 9, 18, 51, 53–55, 63, 66, 71, 74, 99,
    117, 118, 123, 124, 156–58, 231, 241

Language, 37, 39, 42, 57, 60, 62, 64, 71–76,
    79, 88, 90, 107, 120, 128, 175, 177,
    186, 191, 196, 200, 204, 215, 221,
    224, 225, 233, 245, 249, 258, 259
Life, xiii, xiv, 3–9, 12, 15, 16, 18–23, 27, 28,
    30–32, 34–37, 40–55, 58, 68, 69,
    74, 76–79, 81–83, 91, 93–107, 110,
    111, 113–24, 126–41, 144, 145,
    148, 150–53, 155, 157, 160–62, 164,
    172–74, 176–78, 184, 186, 187–90,
    194, 197–201, 202, 208, 211, 212,
    214, 216, 217, 222, 223, 225–27,
    232–41, 243, 249, 252, 255, 257
Lifestyle, 20, 243
Logos, xiii, xiv, 52, 140, 148, 175, 211, 233
Lord, 38, 55, 66, 67, 105, 108, 160, 161, 179,
    186, 195, 199, 205, 259
Love, 9, 11, 20, 25, 49, 50, 54, 55, 63, 66, 68,
    73, 74, 77, 79, 80–83, 99–103, 105,
    109–12, 118, 132, 135, 137, 138, 148,
    149, 153, 156, 162, 168, 207–9, 212,
    217, 218, 231, 235, 241, 249, 256, 260

Majority, 3, 16, 23, 154, 218
Man, vii, xiii–xvii, 3–17, 19–23, 25–83,
    87–89, 97, 98, 100, 104, 108,
    110, 111, 115, 120, 124, 125, 133,
    139–50, 152–55, 158, 160–64,
    166–68, 169–79, 182–84, 186–91,
    194, 198–206, 208, 209, 211, 213,
    214, 216, 218–23, 225–27, 230–34,
    237–39, 241–43, 245–47, 250
Marriage, 10, 19, 42, 248, 252
Marxism, 24, 25
Meaning, 7–9, 18, 20–24, 27, 28, 31, 36, 42,
    44, 45, 47–50, 52, 58, 74, 77, 78,
    81–83, 87, 89–91, 101, 106, 110,
    115, 118, 120, 124, 126, 127, 133,
    134, 146, 153, 155, 160–62, 170, 178,
    179, 182, 193, 199, 211, 213, 216–19,
    221–28, 232–35, 237, 244–47, 249,
    250, 255, 257–60
Meaningfulness, 4, 36–40, 43, 44, 51, 52, 55,
    126, 209, 210, 228, 240
Mentality, 24

Index

Messiah, 105, 108, 177
Metaphysics, xv, 26, 27, 33, 40, 169, 172, 178, 206, 220, 221, 223–26, 228, 240, 241, 260
Middle Ages, 9, 25, 87
Minority, 17
Miracle, 15–17
Misery, 7, 8, 58, 59
Modernism, 4, 13, 229, 247, 250, 257, 258
Modernity, 8, 15, 16, 223–25, 233, 243, 245, 249, 252, 259, 260
Monologue, 24, 25, 261
Morality, 10, 18–20, 42, 43, 66, 152, 227, 231, 239, 243, 254, 256
Myth, 83, 101, 221, 222, 235, 245, 247, 249, 250

Nature, xv, 10, 26, 30, 44, 45, 51, 59, 66, 67, 70, 75, 80, 89, 98, 99, 101, 106, 108, 114, 122, 155, 174, 194, 206, 210, 229, 230, 233, 240, 244, 248, 249
New, x, 3, 5, 8–16, 20, 21, 23–25, 29–31, 34–36, 40, 41, 49–52, 56, 58, 80, 82, 87–90, 92, 94–95, 99, 105, 107–10, 118, 124, 126–30, 135–38, 140–45, 147, 148, 150–53, 159, 160, 163–65, 168, 170, 174–76, 178, 182–85, 187, 188, 190, 193, 195, 202, 205, 206, 213, 216, 221–23, 228, 230, 231, 233, 234, 237–40, 247–59
Non–believer, 48
Non–realism, iii, iv, vii, xvii, 220–25, 236, 239, 242, 245
Novelty, 2

Ontology, xv, 106, 136, 206
Opposition, 5, 67, 102, 196
Optimistic, 8, 9, 14, 28, 40, 47, 69, 80, 142, 203, 226
Orthodoxy, ix, 23, 106, 248, 252

Past, 3, 4, 7–14, 17, 22, 24, 29, 31–34, 40, 41, 77, 86–88, 126, 130, 142–47, 150, 152, 154, 160, 202, 213, 220, 225, 226, 232, 233, 238
Peace, 9, 54, 55, 112, 150, 205, 249
Pessimistic, 80
Philosophy, xv, 10, 60, 63, 69, 226, 231, 242, 249, 253, 259

Physics, 172, 173, 220
Pneumatological, 18, 38, 55, 94
Pneumatology, 94
Political, 24, 51, 59, 66, 69, 74, 101, 102, 113, 117, 118, 121, 130, 137, 149, 175, 183, 195, 207, 230, 234, 238, 249, 255
Politics, 14, 24, 74, 101, 148, 163, 207, 227, 256, 257
Poor, 58, 59, 90, 101, 102, 149, 234
Poverty, 18, 58, 59, 149, 260
Practice, 14, 20, 29, 47, 79, 118, 122, 135, 149, 178, 196, 203, 209, 245, 255
Prayer, 15, 16, 125, 215, 216, 217, 253
Preexistence, 96–98, 109, 233, 254
Preexistent, 52, 104, 175, 211
Proclamation, 3, 37, 39, 88, 89, 101, 102, 109, 110, 121, 252, 260
Progress, 2–5, 8, 12, 18, 22, 23, 35, 40, 41, 64, 65, 68, 70, 76, 78, 81, 83, 142–45, 225–27, 231, 232, 237, 243
Prosperity, 21
Protestant, 5, 25, 186

Radicalism, iii, iv, vii, xvii, 167, 215, 220, 222–25
Rationality, xiv, 1, 7, 9, 10, 11, 13–17, 20–24, 26–31, 41, 43, 102, 103, 130–33, 135, 166–68, 183, 206, 230, 233, 245
Reason, xiv, xv, xvii, 4, 6, 8, 13–15, 17, 20, 21, 30, 31, 40, 48, 49, 51, 54, 70, 96, 98, 101, 104, 105, 115, 116, 122, 130, 131, 133, 142, 149, 163, 166, 185, 202, 209, 210, 220, 221, 225, 226, 229, 239, 242, 250–52, 255, 257
Reassessment, 34, 128, 152, 156, 164, 220
Redemption, 51, 68, 114, 137, 154, 168, 182, 186, 190, 193, 195, 204, 205, 231, 244
Rediscovery, 231
Reflection, ix, 6, 7, 32, 37, 42, 111, 115, 116, 216, 225, 227, 248–50
Reformation, 9, 10, 25
Relevance, 8, 19, 38–41, 43, 55, 105, 130, 133, 154, 185, 210, 211, 213, 216, 218, 219, 224, 228, 230, 233, 235, 244
Religion, 3, 4, 6, 7, 11–14, 18, 23, 31–36, 44, 58, 63, 64, 85, 100, 103, 107, 141–46, 150, 156, 157, 163, 217, 217, 220–23, 227, 229, 234, 236–39, 241, 242, 245–49, 251–53, 255–60

264

Index

Resurrection, vii, xi, xiv, xvi, 11, 28, 53, 82, 83, 93–97, 103, 105, 109, 112–38, 140, 152, 155, 166, 188–90, 194, 198, 206, 210, 211, 233, 235–37, 248, 249, 251, 254, 257, 260

Revelation, xiii, xv, 3, 6, 26, 34, 38, 39, 51–53, 84, 86, 87, 89–92, 128, 147, 161, 170, 172, 220, 224, 248, 249, 251, 252, 260

Romans, 25, 114, 149

Science, 3–5, 7, 10, 12–14, 22, 25, 33, 34, 40, 41, 66, 67, 71, 74, 92, 142–45, 148, 150, 221, 222, 225, 227, 228, 230–32, 238, 239, 244, 255, 256, 259

Scripture, x, xiii, xiv, 38, 39, 58, 87, 91, 106, 107, 140–42, 148, 160, 161, 165, 172, 188, 233, 248, 250, 257, 259

Secularization, vii, xvii, 1, 3, 5, 7, 9–11, 13, 15, 17, 19, 21–29, 30, 35, 36, 52, 99, 141–43, 166–68, 193, 202–4, 206, 213, 215, 221, 225–27, 233, 243–45, 254

Sexuality, 19, 43, 243

Sickness, 18

Sin, x, xi, 5, 9, 14, 18, 19, 39, 47, 51, 52, 57, 67–81, 99, 101, 102, 109, 110, 114, 122, 123, 129, 137, 139, 140, 145, 148, 150, 152, 155, 156, 159, 160, 168, 175, 180, 186, 188, 195–97, 199, 210, 211, 230, 238, 244

Society, 1–5, 7–9, 12, 15, 16, 18, 20–24, 28–30, 32, 35, 49, 50, 52, 54, 55, 57, 58, 62–64, 67–70, 73, 74, 76, 82, 83, 99, 118, 123, 126, 137, 141–46, 160–62, 164, 166, 167, 184, 185, 209, 220–23, 225, 228, 230, 238, 245, 252, 255, 257

Sociology, 153, 226

Solidarity, 99, 102, 122, 168, 191, 193, 198, 207–9, 217, 241

Son of God, 104, 108, 177

Soteriology, 39, 248, 255, 256, 258

Spirit, xi, 18, 38, 74, 94–96, 99, 109, 127, 139, 140, 152, 159, 183, 187, 190, 195, 201, 204–7, 211, 212, 215, 222, 248, 251, 255

Spirituality, 31, 33, 151, 235, 243, 250, 254, 256, 260

Suffering, x, 3, 5, 8, 15, 19, 20, 23, 30, 34, 35, 39, 43, 46, 50, 53, 58, 60, 67–74, 78–82, 84, 89, 95, 98, 101–3, 105, 114, 115, 120, 122, 125, 130–32, 142, 149, 151, 158, 162, 175, 177, 183, 184, 194, 195, 198, 207, 212, 215, 216, 228, 230, 231, 234–36, 238, 239, 249, 255, 257, 258, 260

Supernatural, xiii, xiv, 1, 74, 75, 220–26, 228–39, 241, 242, 244–46

Symbol, 62, 73, 79, 105, 156, 176, 178, 185, 218, 221, 234, 242, 243, 247, 260

Symbolism, 245

Technology, 3–5, 14, 21, 22, 40, 41, 74, 142, 144, 226, 227, 231, 238, 256

Theism, 27, 35

Theistic (atheistic, anti-theistic), 27, 28, 35, 157, 245, 254

Theology, i, iii, iv, vii, x, xi, xiii–xvii, 1–28, 30–36, 38–44, 46–48, 50–54, 56–58, 60–64, 66–84, 86–90, 92–104, 106, 108–16, 118–24, 126, 128–34, 136, 138–42, 144–48, 150–52, 154–56, 158, 160, 162–66, 168, 170–82, 184, 186–88, 190–92, 194–96, 198–200, 202–4, 206, 208–18, 220, 222–26, 228, 230–42, 244, 246–60

Tradition, ix–xi, 6, 70, 77, 85, 87, 90, 106, 140, 152, 172, 207, 232, 248, 249, 251–54, 257, 259

Traditionalism, 4, 13, 35, 133, 221–23, 227, 258

Transcendence, xv, 15, 34, 40, 51, 89, 90, 108, 145–51, 163, 164, 172, 173, 178, 179, 194, 195, 211, 223, 248, 254

Transcendent, xv, 10, 12, 29, 30, 35–38, 40, 41, 43, 51, 77, 80, 84, 86, 89, 90, 96, 103, 105, 109, 119, 139, 140, 145, 147, 150, 160, 161, 166–68, 170, 173–76, 178, 181, 187, 194, 195, 201, 202, 204, 214, 228, 229, 240, 241

Transgression, 5

Trinity, xi, 38, 51, 61, 63, 68, 85, 89, 97, 121, 128, 152, 181, 182, 204, 248, 253, 259

Trust, 6, 10, 12, 15, 18, 19, 24, 44, 47–51, 53, 54, 63, 70, 106, 122, 124, 133, 145–47, 152, 210, 216, 228, 260

Index

Truth, 8, 19, 21, 25, 26, 58, 126, 147, 156–58, 160, 161, 203, 216, 222, 224, 232, 247, 248, 250, 251, 253–55

Unbeliever, 19, 156
Universality, 47, 48, 73, 100, 111, 112, 124, 158, 184, 204, 211, 224, 248

Validity, xv, 15, 17, 19, 21, 74, 101, 104, 105, 118, 135, 166, 180, 187, 193, 200, 204, 206, 214, 224, 233, 244
Value, xvii, 5, 7, 9, 20, 21, 24, 41, 46, 51, 54, 55, 60–66, 71–73, 75–77, 79–81, 83, 97, 98, 103, 113, 115, 130, 132, 133, 137, 145, 157, 158, 164, 167–85, 187, 188, 190–209, 211–23, 227, 231, 239, 241–46

Violence, 19, 26, 256

Wealth, 18, 75, 79
West, 5, 9, 17, 24, 34, 35, 69
Word of God, xv, 2, 3, 181, 182, 224, 250
World, vii, ix–xii, xiii, xiv, xvi, xvii, 1–13, 16–24, 29–31, 33–36, 40–49, 52–56, 61–68, 70, 75–81, 83, 85, 87–90, 100–103, 105, 107, 110–14, 116–27, 130–33, 135, 138–44, 146, 148, 150–83, 185–251, 256, 258